The Languages of Creativity

The Languages of Creativity

Models, Problem-Solving, Discourse

Studies in Science and Culture, Volume 2

Mark Amsler, Editor
Center for Science and Culture
University of Delaware

Newark: University of Delaware Press
London and Toronto: Associated University Presses

© 1986 by Associated University Presses, Inc.

Associated University Presses
440 Forsgate Drive
Cranbury, NJ 08512

Associated University Presses
25 Sicilian Avenue
London WC1A 2QH, England

Associated University Presses
2133 Royal Windsor Drive
Unit 1
Mississauga, Ontario
Canada L5J 1K5

The paper used in this publication meets the
requirements of the American National Standard for Permanence
of Paper for Printed Library Materials Z39.48-1984.

Library of Congress Cataloging-in-Publication Data
Main entry under title:

The Languages of creativity.

    (Studies in science and culture : vol. 2)
    Includes bibliographical references and index.
    1. Creative ability in science—Addresses,
essays, lectures.   2. Science—philosophy—Addresses,
essays, lectures.   I. Amsler, Mark, 1949–
II. Series: Studies in science and culture ; v. 2.
Q172.5C74L36   1986   501   85-40360
ISBN 0-87413-280-0 (alk. paper)

Printed in the United States of America

Contents

Preface

Creativity has long been displaced within both philosophical and scientific discourse as a psychological question not relevant to the context or the logic of justifying hypotheses. Creation is a mystery, an origination or invention *(creare)*, a bringing into being of that which before the moment of creation was not. It has often been excluded from the language of the philosophy of science.

But new questions often reorganize and redefine the concepts and prevailing terms that govern and shape a discourse. So with creativity. When the practice of science and scientific research is accepted as a topic for rhetorical analysis, when it is viewed as invention and generation, the concept of creativity becomes the focus of the description of concept formation and research programs. When the sociology of science and scientific research is included in the discourse of science, then creativity becomes a principal term for understanding how certain views of nature, human beings, and society are used as models or paradigms to help make sense of the world and our experience in it.

Creativity has traditionally been associated with artistic activity such as the creation of painting, poetry, and music. As such, the aesthetic dimension of creativity has been well developed in the West. The aesthetic dimension encompasses a complex of terms and values within which we comprehend and evaluate human productions as objects in themselves. For the most part, those productions have been described as imitations or aesthetic objects capable of inspiring psychological responses, pleasure, or pain. When the umbrella concept of creativity is extended to account for scientific activity as well, many assume that such a move implies that science is fiction, that everything is "rhetorical" and therefore not logical or rational. One finds, then, that even as the concept of creativity is inserted into the discourse of science and scientific research, it continues to be associated with the mysterious bringing into being of that

7

which before did not exist. Therefore, creativity continues to be suspect.

Part of the problem with creativity in the philosophy of science is that traditionally the concept has been bound up with the transcendent, with God: *In principio creavit Deus caelum et terram.* Within the metaphysical scheme, all human creations are imitations and images (*recreations*) of the original creative act of God, though not themselves coequal with that original creation. In this view, human creations are representations of the world, imitations of the world that God created or presented. A chain of creations is generated in which the created world becomes the model for what human beings—*imagines Dei*—create as they reproduce the divine act of creation. The sacred mystery of creation becomes a way to master nature and the world.

Though less theological and less transcendental, most modern accounts of creativity implicitly reproduce or repeat this pattern. Hans Reichenbach has distinguished the context of discovery from the context of justification. The former belongs to the mysterious bringing into being of that a priori existent which was not known or recognized by human consciousness. The context of justification consists in finding reasons and proof for why what was found in nature of the world was not created new but was really there all the time in the world, waiting to be named and given being in the human world of cognition. In this view, human beings do not create; they discover and justify their perceptions and intuitions. They master nature at a distance. Classical physics as described by Newton and continued thereafter was modeled on the transcendental scheme of the search for the father as the origin without origin. Classical physics attempts to attain what was represented and recreated, but not created itself.

Newton's notion of the law of the father approaches Kant's notion of the law in the *Critique of Judgment.* For Kant, all our experience is subject to the ordering of schemata that, as concepts formulated primarily in language, supplement our sensations and enable us to recognize sensations as meaningful experiences. However, Kant withdrew from claiming that all experience is necessarily rule-governed. Rather, he set aside the creative act as something that was genuinely not rule-governed insofar as its final outcome is concerned. Creativity is ultimately mysterious. In the *Critique of Judgment* Kant claims that the rules of art, as opposed to those of science, are not always already available but are in part given to art by the true genius. Kant steers a slippery course through the Sylla and Charybdis of artistic creation and scientific necessity, a navigation whose success depends on distinguishing clearly between artistic creations and scientific discoveries. But Kant further complicates and smudges his own scheme when he argues that strategies, as rules that govern human thought and action, combine problems of perception (as factual, empirical investigation) with those of judgment (as transcendental-logical investigation). The concepts determine in part what counts as evidence or facts, while those very pieces of evidence and facts are used to support or change the concepts that control our perception of them. The distinction between empiricism and transcendental logic, like that between subject and object, is at once fundamental to most Western theories of creativity as well as a questionable distinction when framed in the dialectic between subject and object, understanding and discovery elaborated in Kant, phenomenology, hermeneutics, and, most recently, deconstruction.

We arrive now at a moment previously unprepared for, at least consciously. Creativity in the West has been modeled largely on the transcendental scheme of the divinity who presents and the human beings who represent, the divinity who creates and the human beings who recreate. But there is a contrary move. God wills, and human beings revolt and so create. Creativity is either submission or transgression, as in Kant's dialectic between rule-governed and unruly activities. Similarly, this collection of essays on the topic of creativity in the sciences and the arts is inevitably transgressive, crossing recognized borders, appropriating disciplines and languages. Many of the essays here simply do not stay put, but find a place in the discourse of literary theory as much as in the philosophy of science. But all the essays are submissive, too. They all play the game of academic writing precisely according to the rules, with appropriate vocabulary and syntax, accompanying documentation and evidence, and acceptable modes of argument. In this sense, all the essays presented here are formally familiar and acceptable within the community created by academic discourse. Nonetheless, many of the essays violate the rules for categorizing the varieties of language and discourse within academic writing. Formally, the essays are "proper" academic writing; conceptually, they merge, appropriate, graft, and translate discourses often marked as outside the borders of subdisciplines such as aesthetics, philosophy of science, or literary theory. Likewise, this introduction and the editorial apparatus frame the essays within a particular scheme to which each essay may not wholly submit. The essays in this collection often create their own discourses even as they are constructed according to the conventional rules for generating academic writing. They fit, yet they do not fit. But they all fit in this volume and create without always knowing how or intending to do so another language of creativity, familiar and "passing strange."

Mark Amsler

The Languages of Creativity

The Two Cultures Today: A Third Look

MAURICE A. FINOCCHIARO

University of Nevada

The problem of the two cultures goes back at least to Plato. In the *Phaedo* he portrays the last dialogue Socrates had with his friends while he was awaiting execution in prison. Amid such lofty topics as the immortality of the soul, the finality of death, and the existence of the afterlife, the discussion includes a brief autobiography. Socrates says that in his youth he was interested in scientific questions about the causes of natural phenomena, but then he grew up and became concerned with moral questions about the meaning of human life, the improvement of human character, and the pursuit of wisdom.[1] Now, I regard Socrates as one of the greatest moralists who ever lived and a great philosopher as well; indeed, I would go so far as to say that the specific significance of this philosophy lies in his moral theory and practice. This means that I would want to judge the case of Socrates bringing intellectual activity from the heaven of natural science down to the earth of moral inquiry as an appropriate one for his time and place, and an instructive one for posterity.

However, I am in no mood to put into practice Alfred North Whitehead's aphorism that Western philosophy is a series of footnotes to Plato, for I do not share Whitehead's constricted view of Western philosophy or his cult of Plato. Instead my Platonic footnote should be taken as an expression of my commitment to the historical method of investigation, and so I immediately pass on to a second historical footnote.

The problem of the two cultures reappeared about two thousand years after the so-called father of Western philosophy, namely with the so-called father of modern science, Galileo Galilei. The terminology was different then, and the contrasting terms were *philosophy* and *mathematics*. The cultural

13

revolution was also different, indeed the reverse of the Socratic one, since the required change was to give up what was called "philosophy" in favor of what was called "mathematics." Nevertheless, the underlying problem of the apparent tension between these two cultural forms, and whether this appearance corresponds to reality, was essentially the same. The classic illustration of this occurred in Galileo's middle age, after he had served for twenty years as professor of mathematics at the University of Padua, during which period he had done most of his research on the motion of bodies and the foundations of physics. At the end of this period he built the first scientifically useful telescope and thereby made a number of astronomical discoveries, which together with his physics of motion convinced him of the truth of the new Copernican cosmology. These discoveries led him to seek a new job, equivalent to being scientific advisor to the grand duke of Tuscany in Florence. In his petition for the position, however, Galileo was rather fussy about his title. He asked for, and eventually obtained, the title of "philosopher" besides that of "mathematician," on the grounds that, as he put it, he had spent more years studying philosophy than he had spent months studying mathematics.[2] In twentieth-century terminology, Galileo's remark means that at this time one would be a more serious lover of wisdom by studying physics and cosmology, as he had done, than by studying what passed for philosophy in the culture.

The examples of Socrates and Galileo, besides being intrinsically interesting and besides exhibiting my own version of the historical method, provide a rhetorical justification for the number three mentioned in my title. For, jumping three-hundred years after Galileo and coming back to the twentieth century, one could easily agree with the great Spanish philosopher José Ortega y Gasset's opinion that the cultural problems of this age are comparable in depth to those of the age of Galileo.[3] Thus, in one sense, the third look at the question of the two cultures is the one that the twentieth century needs to take to come to grips with it, cognizant of contributions by Socrates and Galileo. In another sense, the third look is also the one that I shall be developing myself within a less grand triad of positions. This more modest undertaking begins with C. P. Snow, who after all introduced the terminology I am using to formulate the problem; it will then discuss the views of sociologist Theodore Roszak, which acquired great notoriety about ten years ago; and it will end with an analysis of the Report of the Humanities Commission (1980).

In 1959 C. P. Snow delivered at Cambridge University a lecture entitled "The Two Cultures and the Scientific Revolution,"[4] which soon became both famous and infamous. It gave rise to what some critics described as the "Great Debate of Our Age"[5] and elicited abusive criticism, the like of which is seldom found in literature.[6] It should be kept in mind that Snow was himself both a scientist who had done a little original research and had held important positions in British scientific administration, and also a notable writer of numerous novels. The two cultures to which he was referring were the attitudes and thought and behavior patterns of two groups: on the one hand, scientists such as mathematicians, physicists, biologists, and chemists, and on the other hand, what he called "literary intellectuals."

He began by calling attention to the mutual ignorance, incomprehension, and lack of communication between the scientific and the literary segments of our culture. For example, he asked rhetorically, how many scientists could comment intelligently on one of Shakespeare's plays, and how many literary intellectuals could state and explain the Second Law of Thermodynamics? This cultural gap appeared to him to be extremely dangerous and problematic because of its connection with another gap, the socio-economic one between industrialized and underdeveloped countries. He was morally wounded by the fact that most of the world was still living in conditions like those of preindustrial Europe, where people lived a nasty, brutish, and short life, filled with hunger and disease, with infant mortality more than 50 percent and a median age of death lower than the median age of marriage. And he was politically worried that if Western countries did not eliminate this gap between rich and poor, then communist countries would, with the consequence that the West would decay into historical insignificance. Snow went on to argue that the only hope he saw of solving this problem of world hunger and disease was what he called the "scientific revolution," by which he meant the large-scale and systematic application of science and technology to industry for the improvement of economic and material conditions. The immediate task, as he saw it, was for us to rethink our education, and so he ended with a plea for educational reform designed to close the cultural gap by making scientists more sensitive to human suffering through the study of literature and literary intellectuals more willing to appreciate the value of the material benefits derivable from the scientific revolution.

So far his analysis would seem admirably judicious, and it would have aroused little controversy, if any. However, in the course of his argument he had criticized literary intellectuals for their pessimism and conservatism, for never having come to grips with the old industrial revolution, for being, as he put it, "natural Luddites." In view of this criticism, his call for closing the gap between the two cultures must have appeared as a suggestion that it should be done at the expense of the literary one. It was probably this criticism and this implication, which need to be accepted, that generated the heat in the controversy that followed.

I have no intention of discussing the details of this controversy. What is important to note is that, as Snow himself admitted a few years later,[7] his problem and his views had been "in the air" for some time, which explains the attention they received and the amount of discussion they generated. In fact, I can testify that it was at about that time that I, without having heard or read him, began to *live* the problem he had formulated. My life then was that of an undergraduate at the Massachusetts Institute of Technology, where I had gone to study what I called theoretical physics. However, I soon discovered in my freshman year that the professional pursuit of this subject would have prevented me from paying proper attention not only to such questions as the meaning of life in general, but even to the question of the nature of scientific inquiry itself. So I found myself gravitating toward the M.I.T. Humanities Department, taking courses in philosophy, and eventually majoring in humanities and science, with concentrations in philosophy and physics. My concern with the question continued in graduate school at the University of California at Berkeley, where *my* problem took the following form. Having decided to specialize in philosophy of science, I now had to be on guard against the scientism that prevailed in the field. My explorations of humanistic and scientistic approaches to understanding science resulted in a commitment to the historical approach in philosophy of science, on the conviction that the historical method is the essence of the humanities.[8] In short, the form that the problem of the two cultures took within my own life was that of the relationship between the sciences and the humanities, and my solution was to take scientific inquiry as the object of my studies, but to follow a humanistic approach in so doing.

However, if there was a similarity between my problem and the social one, there was none between my solution and society's. Instead, Snow's scientific revolution was sweeping this country, and more generally the West, so much so that by the end of the decade its excesses generated a counterrevolution. The problem of the two cultures was still with us, with the difference that now their roles had reversed: whereas ten years earlier science had been perceived as the panacea, now it was felt to be the source of new widely prevalent ills and miseries. The best example of such antiscience views is perhaps the works of sociologist Theodore Roszak.

The titles and subtitles of Roszak's books bear witness to the new mood. In 1969 Roszak published his first book, entitled *The Making of a Counter Culture* and subtitled "Reflections on the Technocratic Society and Its Youthful Opposition."[9] And in 1972 he published a study called "Politics and Transcendence in Post-industrial Society," announcing that he could see *Where the Wasteland Ends.*[10] For Roszak the manifest evils of the age are such things as the artificial environment of urban-industrial life, the technocratic character of politics, the narrowness and alienation of human consciousness, the impending ecological catastrophe, and the pollution within and about us. He argues that science is to blame for these evils in the sense that they are the direct result of the hegemony of the scientific attitude—that is to say, of a way of thinking that is impersonal, methodic, objective, reductionistic, and cumulatively progressive. It should be noted that Roszak is making a very strong claim here since he is saying that the root cause of the wasteland is not merely the misapplication of neutural scientific knowledge by evil persons, but rather the scientific way of thinking as such. It is difficult to find a single positive term under which to subsume Roszak's way to salvation. What he favors are perhaps suggestive enough: poetry, Romanticism, art, imagination, myth, ritual, visionary power, subjectivity, transcendent symbols, mysticism (in short, the garbage heap of the positivists). His point is that we need to learn or relearn how to appreciate these areas and to develop our mental powers appropriately.

Perhaps the key concepts are poetry and imagination. So his central message is that we need to replace the dominant culture centered on scientific reason with the lost or forgotten one centered upon the poetical imagination.

The seductive plausibility of Roszak's argument can best be seen with the example of animism. It is certainly true that it is an essential part of scientific objectivity to regard natural phenomena as inanimate objects, and it is easy to see that if we were to abandon this view and respect the world of nature in the same way that we respect human beings, then the ecological and pollution problems would be prevented or alleviated. However, in my opinion, the difficulty is that physical objects are in fact inanimate; thus the "sacramental view of nature" that Roszak advocates is at best a useful lie. Moreover, I would say that the real problem was one of excess: Snow's scientific revolution had been carried too far, or to be more exact too far in some ways and in some places and not far enough in other ways and in other places. Why replace this excess in one cultural direction with another in the opposite direction?

But among the many virtues of America, judiciousness is not one of them. And so it was that in the seventies Roszak's counterrevolution swept the country, as Snow's scientific revolution had done in the sixties. Since the term *counterrevolution* may be unnecessarily prejudicial, a more suitable phrase is *humanistic revolution*, which, in fact, connects better with my next point.

Where are we today in the eighties? I am sorry to report that there seems to be a ten-year cultural cycle, at least in the United States, for there are now clear signs of an antihumanities movement. Two pieces of evidence will perhaps suffice. First, there is President Reagan's budget. The total allocation for the National Endowment for the Humanities was cut by about one-half,[11] while that for the National Science Foundation was one of the few items left essentially unchanged;[12] moreover, the amount specifically itemized for physics, mathematics, and engineering was increased by 10 to 20 percent,[13] while the amount for the social sciences was cut by about three-fourths.[14] I merely observe this fact since such cuts and such discrimination may be perfectly justified. In fact, I do know one justifiable discrimination in particular, namely that there is today an acute shortage of engineers but an oversupply of humanists and social scientists. Nevertheless, my observation remains that an antihumanities movement is gathering momentum.

In fact, and this is my second piece of evidence, such a movement may have even found its theoretical spokesperson, though I hesitate to make categorical claims on account of the fluidity and immediacy of the situation. The self-appointed head of the antihumanities forces is a Washington editor of *Harper's* magazine named Michael Macdonald Mooney. He is the author of a book entitled *The Ministry of Culture*[15] and of a homonymous previewing article in the August 1980 issue of the magazine. The article is a vicious, pompous, and insubstantial attack on the National Endowment for the Humanities, the National Endowment for the Arts, and the Federal Council on the Arts and the Humanities.[16] The latter he dubs the Ministry of Culture. I do not think his views merit any further summary, but one of his misconceptions deserves attention. He has attempted to show that the operative meaning of the term *humanities* is that of the word *humanism* in the special sense of the "religion of humanity." In his zeal, to support his point, Mooney manages to misquote the *Oxford English Dictionary*, which has no entry for the word *humanities*. It does not seem to matter to him that the 1965 federal law creating the National Endowment for the Humanities defines it as "language, literature, history, philosophy, and so forth." Nor does he take seriously the agency's attempt to give an explanatory definition, according to which the humanities are "civilization's study of itself."[17] Mooney merely pokes fun at both of these definitions.

There is one other definition of *humanities*, which, if the problem were not so important, one could perhaps dismiss as a mere curiosity. The source is nothing less than the unabridged edition of *Webster's Third New International Dictionary*, whose latest edition of 1976 defines the humanities as "the branches of learning regarded as having primarily a cultural character and usually including languages, literature, mathematics, and philosophy." Yes, mathematics is explicitly named. Because of this inclusion, and because of the reference to the "cultural character" of these branches of learning, it would be literally impossible to exclude the second one of the two cultures we have been examining. That is to say, the definition is too broad and includes all disciplines. One wonders how the Webster's unabridged dictionary got its reputation.

Fortunately, there is at least one ray of hope in this whole situation. That is the report of the Rockefeller Commission on the Humanities, which, although not strictly concerned with the problem of the two cultures, contains views whose criticism and elaboration will allow me to develop my own third look. The report was published by the University of California Press under the title *The Humanities in American Life*.[18] The commission was chaired by Richard W. Lyman, former president of Stanford University and current president of the Rockefeller Foundation, and it consisted of thirty-one other members, including scholars, academic administrators, business leaders, and representatives of foundations, media, and the arts. The report advertises itself as a rethinking of the place of the humanities in America's culture and a national survey for the eighties. It is addressed to educators, students, state and federal government politicians and bureaucrats, museums, libraries, the media, foundations, and the general public. Generally speaking, I would say that the strength of the report lies in the fact that its recommendations are numerous, often concrete, and generally sound; however, the rationale it offers to support its recommendations is weak, and the weakness is due partly to inadequacy in the rethinking done in the report, partly to a kind of humanistic insularity, and partly to the unclarity of its motivating problem.

Its most important recommendations are, I believe, those that concern critical thinking, interdisciplinary integration, and the evaluation of science and technology. Concerning the last, the report advises that, at the college level, all efforts to give fresh meaning to a liberal education should include studies of questions of value underlying science and technology and should recognize the importance of the humanities in dealing with them.[19]

I completely agree with this recommendation about the evaluation of science. However, one will search in vain for a coherent justification in the humanities report.[20] What I would argue is the following. First, to show why a liberal education must include such questions of value, it is enough merely to give some examples: two value-questions underlying science are whether the scientific theory of evolution invalidates the biblical story of creation, and whether there is any reason for thinking that Steven Goldberg's theory of the inevitability of patriarchy is unscientific;[21] and two questions of value underlying technology are what are the human and social consequences of the ongoing computerization of the world, and what are the prospects for solving the energy crisis. Next, to show why the humanities are crucial I would say that everybody would agree that an essential ingredient of any definition of the humanities is that they deal with questions of value. But this is only half of the story. The tricky part is to identify the specific disciplines. Although some might think first of moral philosophy, literary criticism, and history, I see no reason to exclude the psychology of personality, political theory, applied sociology, cultural anthropology, comparative economics, and pedagogics. Values are studied as much in the latter group of disciplines as in the former. My conclusion is that to uphold the humanities report's recommendation about the evaluation of science and technology, one must expand the concept of the humanities to include what are commonly called the social sciences.

This conclusion can also be supported by reference to NEH's own self-image, referred to above as the explanatory definition that the humanities are "civilization's study of itself." Clearly the so-called social sciences study various aspects of civilization. What would be excluded here would be the natural sciences themselves, since their object of study is nature. In short, the evaluation of science cannot be done within science, though it presupposes science in the sense of some acquaintance with the scientific topics that gave rise to the value-question; that is, scientists study such things as numbers, atoms, molecules, and organisms, whereas the study and evaluation of what scientists do is one of the tasks of those disciplines that study human affairs.

A third argument in support of my conclusion to expand the concept of the humanities would be one designed to persuade social scientists themselves. I suspect that many of them might either politely decline the offer to be counted as humanists or regard it as an insult. They would say that they are scientists and that value-judgments are no part of scientific objectivity; thus, the above-mentioned branches of the social sciences might very well study values, so the argument goes, but the description and explanation of values are different from the evaluation of values. To answer such concerns, one would have to show that certain kinds of value-judgments, while not examining human values as such, do have an essential role in the natural sciences themselves: there are logical value-judgments involved in the evaluation of evidence vis-à-vis conclusions and data vis-à-vis theory; and there are methodological value-

judgments involved in choosing between two or more competing theories, by considering such factors as simplicity,
explanatory power, predictive ability, precision, depth, com-
prehensiveness, and so on.[22] So I would say to a social scientist
that, if he is worried about being scientific, he can be more
scientific by giving up the scientism of absolute value-
neutrality and engaging in whatever evaluation the situation
requires.[23] Another consideration I would add is that it is about
time for the social sciences to rethink their status, now that
they are being expelled from the National Science Foundation,
or, to be more exact, quartered rather than expelled,[24] though I
do not know which is better.

The report's recommendation about interdisciplinary integration is more general than the previous one, in that it is
meant to apply to the curriculum of secondary schools as well
as colleges. It states that the curriculum should include integrative courses that connect the humanities with each other and
with other fields.[25] Here the report makes a crucial clarification
when it distinguishes between the kind of integrative courses it
is talking about and the usual so-called interdisciplinary ones.
What it says is so clear and incisive that I can perhaps be for-
given the following extended quotation:

> . . . courses combining several fields do not automatically evoke
> superior faculty wisdom or student comprehension. Indeed the
> terms *interdisciplinary* and *team-taught* have acquired a mystique
> that may be misleading; they can disguise shoddy, ill-conceived
> courses that merely dilute a variety of subjects rather than unite
> them in any coherent or imaginative synthesis. Humanists are of-
> ten reluctant to undertake a genuine exploration of cross-
> disciplinary problems and their social and ethical implications. In
> planning interdisciplinary courses, faculty often skirt the craggy
> terrain of intellectual and pedagogic assumptions and stay in the
> bureaucratic foothills of interdepartmental coordination. Such
> courses, if poorly conceived, may mislead students into believing
> that a superficial collection of facts about a variety of subjects is
> evidence of a depth of knowledge. On the other hand, there are
> courses in single disciplines where a genuine synthesis of various
> kinds of knowledge is nearly achieved by a teacher who has
> thought deeply about the relationships among disciplines.[26]

Having clarified this point, I need to note another, namely
that the report does not in fact say that the humanities have a

special prerogative for such integrative courses. Even using expanded conception that includes the social sciences freed from scientism, if the integration we seek involves the natural sciences, then I see no way of arguing that humanists are as a rule better equipped for such courses than scientists.

Of course, it would be easy and it is tempting for me as a philosopher to argue that philosophy is in fact the one discipline whose specialty is precisely such integrative courses. The argument could be made on both historical and theoretical grounds. In fact the history of philosophy can be easily seen as a series of great cultural syntheses; and theoretically one could say that the theory of knowledge is one of the main branches of philosophy, and hence the integration of knowledge is merely one of its subtopics. But such philosophical imperialism is no part of my intention here, and I am realistic enough to know not only that other philosophers have other conceptions of philosophy, but also that even integration-minded philosophers have no monopoly on integrative courses. For example, I think that a well-developed course in intellectual history could perform such a function; that the sociology of knowledge offers tremendous possibilities; that classically oriented rhetoric, now usually assigned to communication studies departments, could serve as a way of integrating the humanities and social sciences, if not the natural sciences; that the discipline of pedagogics has an intrinsically integrative dimension; that the special sciences from astronomy to zoology can be appreciated in their interdisciplinary and humanistic dimension when they study and teach their own history.

For example, consider a course on scientific method that begins with the nominal definition that it is the method, if any, used by great scientists to make their discoveries (then one proceeds to study classic examples such as Galileo, Newton, and Huygens); distinguishes between the surface and the deep-structure methodological features of their procedures; explores the possibility that, though the surface features do not apply to the humanities and social sciences, the deep-structure does; and then self-consciously reflects to what extent the approach to scientific methodology exemplified in the course is or is not in conformity with the surface and/or deep features of scientific method.[27] Such a course, I dare say, would be integrating the humanities with each other and with the natural sciences, as the humanities report asks. Or consider another course that would discuss the following questions: is it correct to define wages, as most economists do, in terms of the marginal productivity of labor; are sociologists correct in assuming the functionalist principle that equilibrium is the normal state of society; is it correct to assume, as most history books do, that the causes and consequences of historical actions can be discussed independently of the material forces that are the motor of socio-historical developments; is the task of philosophy to interpret or to change the world; and what is the political theory that controls the behavior of communist countries and rules the lives of its inhabitants? A course consisting of the scholarly and critical study of Marxism can touch upon all these questions and can interrelate the several mentioned disciplines indirectly by way of contrast. Or, finally, consider an introductory philosophy course where philosophy is presented not as a specialized subject studied for its own sake, but as a way of thinking that can be applied, and has been applied throughout the ages, to the most diverse topics and problems. Selected classical philosophers would then be studied partly for the nonphilosophical, but rather moral, religious, scientific, social, or political problems they faced, and partly as examples of such philosophic procedures as rationality, judiciousness, universal relevance, criticism, and practical orientation. Finally, these procedures could then be applied to a new and important subject matter, as, for example, the systematic interpretation and criticism of classic texts and books, such as those already read. And this brings me to the humanities report's third recommendation.

The report's single most important and sweeping recommendation deals with critical thinking and is addressed to educators at all levels. They are advised to recognize critical thinking as one of the most basic cognitive skills and to emphasize the value of the humanities for its development.[28] In elaborating the rationale for this recommendation, the report does make one crucially important point, namely that there is a very intimate connection between writing and critical thinking. I would add that there is an equally close relationship between reading and critical thinking.[29] Reading comprehension is perhaps the most basic kind of critical thinking, while writing out one's opinions and the reasons for them is perhaps the second most elementary type of critical thinking.

But what is critical thinking in general? The report does not say. Let me elaborate by saying that critical thinking is a type of thinking aimed at the criticism of someone or something; here criticism would mean fault-finding—or perhaps more generally evaluation—that is the determination of either fault or worth. At least in the present context this definition would be inadequate since it would make critical thinking indistinguishable from evaluation or the study of questions of value, which has already been treated separately. I believe that by critical thinking the report means reasoning, which is a type of thinking where thoughts are interrelated in such a way that some act as reasons for others and some are drawn as conclusions from others. In short, critical thinking is the giving of reasons or the drawing of conclusions. When understood in this manner, it is easy to see why the report recommends critical thinking for all levels of education. The progression from one level of education to another may be easily conceived as the mastery of successively more sophisticated and complex kinds of reasoning.

However, the other part of this recommendation, the value of the humanities for the development of critical thinking, is problematic. Although there is no question in my mind that the humanities do develop the skill of reasoning, so do the sciences, especially mathematics and physics. In fact, I would say that reasoning is the great unifying thread underlying the sciences and the humanities. It is also the crucial distinguishing characteristic between all such disciplines on the one hand, and poetry, fiction, imaginative literature, and any kind of art form on the other. This brings me to my last thesis.

My slogan here would be diversity within unity. The natural sciences and the humanistic disciplines (including the social sciences) are distinct from the point of view of subject matter, which is, respectively, natural phenomena and human affairs. Other grounds for distinctions would be in terms of methodological surface procedures typically proper and effective in one domain but not the other, for example mathematization and experimentation, evaluation and historical method. Underlying such differences one can detect a unity definable in terms of a concept like reasoning. This unity is important not only because it solves, or promises to solve, the problem of the two cultures I have been examining, but also because it recognizes another cultural split that should not be hidden, namely that between ratiocinative disciplines and art forms. I will end with an elaboration of this new problem of the two cultures, but before doing so let me make a reference in order both to qualify this alleged novelty and to add some authority to my view of diversity within unity. This view is simply my own version of the theory put forth in Benedetto Croce's *Aesthetic* of 1902.[30] I have, however, poured a bit of new wine into that old bottle. In fact, to mention just one example, the articulation of the distinction between surface and deep-structure features of disciplines and of the argument that reasoning is the fundamental deep-structure feature of natural science cost me about five years' work and yielded a book that was published in 1980.[31]

At one level this point can be appreciated easily enough. Whenever a physicist or biologist makes a claim, entertains an idea, or writes down a sentence, it always makes sense to ask him the reason why he does that. In other words, all scientific beliefs must be supported by evidence and arguments. This is not to say that such arguments have to be conclusive or irrefutable, but rather that the scientist must show by what process of reasoning one may arrive at these conclusions. The same applies to social scientists, to philosophers, to historians. It even applies to literary or art critics, though not to novelists, poets, playwrights, and painters. This is the instructive contrast.

In fact, consider the utter absurdity of asking Shakespeare to enumerate his reasons for having Macduff say about Macbeth, "He has no children," when he learned of the murder of his wife and son caused by Macbeth.[32] Clearly, Shakespeare just made it up; obviously it is enough that he felt like putting those words in Macduff's mouth. Shakespeare was engaged in an act of imagination, not one of reasoning. Now suppose a literary critic writes that Macduff's utterance is an expression of his rage for being unable to do Macbeth equal harm by killing his son;[33] here it would be perfectly legitimate to ask the critic why he thinks so, and his reason, whether ultimately valid or not, would be highly informative. If the critic were to say that his assertion is merely what he feels, then he would be creating a piece of fiction occasioned by Shakespeare's fiction, and one could answer with justice that one piece of fiction is enough.

Even where it looks as if the artist is reasoning, he is not, but rather he is portraying reasoning. If the portrayal of reasoning were itself reasoning, then the portrayal would acquire the same quality as the reasoning being portrayed; that is, the portrayal of reasoning would be effective when the reasoning was valid and ineffective when the reasoning was invalid. That there is in fact no such coincidence can be illustrated by the passage in Strindberg's *Dream Play* where the schoolmaster asks the officer what twice two is and the latter replies: "Twice two—is two, and this I will demonstrate by analogy, the highest form of proof. Listen! Once one is one, therefore twice two is two. For that which applies to the one must also apply to the other."[34] This piece of illogic happens to have great aesthetic value.

To conclude, I believe that this type of argument shows that the interpretation and criticism of imaginative literature is an instance of reasoning. Its objects, namely images, are different from those of other disciplines, but its mental activity is essentially the same. These considerations also show that what is going on in the creation of imaginative literature is a different mental activity. I can also join Croce in holding that a diversity within unity, similar but not identical to the one that interrelates the humanistic and the scientific cultures, also interrelates these ratiocinative disciplines and the art forms. We have just seen what this latter diversity is. Their unity would be that they are both ways to understand reality.[35] But this is a difficult idea that I cannot elaborate in this context.

NOTES

1. Plato, *Phaedo* 97A-99E.

2. Galileo Galilei, *Opere*, ed. A. Favaro, 20 vols. (Florence: Barbera, 1890–1909), 10:353. Cf. *Discoveries and Opinions of Galileo*, ed. and trans. S. Drake (Garden City, N.Y.: Doubleday, 1957), 64. Galileo's methodological and philosophical remarks are notoriously liable to interpreting them to suit oneself. I have attempted both to explain and correct this situation in my *Galileo and the Art of Reasoning: Rhetorical Foundations of Logic and Scientific Method* (Boston: D. Reidel, 1980), esp. chaps. 5 and 6.

3. José Ortega y Gasset, *Man and Crisis*, trans. M. Adams (New York: Norton, 1958), 10–11. The original Spanish title of this book is *En Torno a Galileo*.

4. C. P. Snow, *The Two Cultures and a Second Look* (Cambridge: At the University Press, 1964), 1–51.

5. Cf. David Shusterman, *C. P. Snow* (Boston: Twayne Publishers, 1975), 25.

6. Ibid., 26.

7. Snow, *Two Cultures*, 55.

8. For some relevant discussions, see my *History of Science as Explanation* (Detroit, Mich.: Wayne State University Press, 1973).

9. Theodore Roszak, *The Making of a Counter Culture* (Garden City, N.Y.: Doubleday, 1969).

10. Theodore Roszak, *Where the Wasteland Ends* (Garden City, N.Y.: Doubleday, 1972).

11. From $106.5 million in fiscal 1981 to $59 million in 1982, or a 45 percent reduction, to be more exact. Cf. *The Chronicle of Higher Education*, 23 March 1981, 12.

12. A 6 percent reduction, from $1.096 billion to $1.034 billion, to be more exact. Cf. *The Chronicle of Higher Education,* 16 March 1981, 11.

13. Ibid., 11.

14. Or to be more exact, from $33.6 million to $10.1 million within the NSF (ibid., 14), and from about $1 billion to $200 million for all federally sponsored social research (*Chronicle,* 6 April 1981, 11).

15. Michael Macdonald Mooney, *The Ministry of Culture: Politics in Art* (New York: Simon and Schuster, 1980).

16. Michael Macdonald Mooney, "The Ministry of Culture," *Harper's,* August 1980, 23–32.

17. Moony, "Ministry," 24.

18. *The Humanities in American Life,* Report of the Commission on the Humanities (Berkeley: University of California Press, 1980).

19. Ibid., 21–22, 22–23, 69–71.

20. I found the report somewhat confusing as a result of remarks like the following: "at their most vivid, the (humanities) are like the arts as well as the sciences. The humanities are that form of knowledge in which the known is revealed. All knowledge becomes humanistic when this effect takes place" (p. 2); "science and technology have been a domain of the humanities in Western culture since its Greek origins" (pp. 13–14); and "a more than passing acquaintance with the natural and social sciences is inseparable from the critical and interpretive capacities developed through the humanities" (p. 70).

21. Steven Goldberg, *The Inevitability of Patriarchy* (New York: William Morrow, 1973).

22. For some recent discussions see my *Galileo and the Art of Reasoning,* especially chaps. 6 and 17; my "The Concept of Judgement and Huygens' Theory of Gravity," *Epistemologia,* in press; Harold I. Brown, *Perception, Theory and Commitment* (Chicago: University of Chicago Press, 1979), 145–51; Marx Wartofsky, "Scientific Judgment: Creativity and Discovery in Scientific Thought," in *Scientific Discovery: Case Studies,* ed. Thomas Nickles (Boston: D. Reidel, 1980), 1–20; Thomas S. Kuhn, *The Essential Tension* (Chicago: University of Chicago Press, 1977), 320–39; and Joseph Weizenbaum, *Computer Power and Human Reason: From Judgment to Calculation* (San Francisco: Freeman, 1976), esp. 14–16.

23. Note that what I am rejecting is "absolute" value-neutrality, by which I mean the theory and the attempted practice of never engaging in value-judgments. This is *not* to say that one should, for example, confuse evaluation with description and with explanation, or that one ought to adopt a wishful thinking type of approach, according to which ideas are regarded as true when it would be nice for them to be true and false when it would be bad for them to be correct.

24. Cf. the figures in notes 11 to 14 above, and the text pertaining to them.

25. *The Humanities in American Life,* 6, 21, 46, 71, and 73ff.

26. Ibid., 76. Needless to say, there is no reason to interpret the report as claiming that team-taught interdisciplinary courses of the traditional kind have *no* place at all in the curriculum. The point is rather that they must be distinguished from integrative courses and handled with great care.

27. Such questions are dealt with in my *Galileo and the Art of Reasoning.*

28. *The Humanities in American Life,* 22, 36, and 44.

29. A discussion of this thesis may be found in Michael Scriven, *Reasoning* (New York: MacGraw-Hill Book Co., 1976), esp. chap. 1.

30. Benedetto Croce, *Estetica,* 11th ed. (Bari: Laterza, 1965). English translation:

Aesthetic as Science of Expression and General Linguistic, trans. D. Ainslie (1909; reprint, New York: Farrar, Straus and Giroux, 1972).

31. My *Galileo and the Art of Reasoning.*

32. William Shakespeare, *Macbeth,* 4.3.216.

33. Cf. Benedetto Croce, *Ariosto, Shakespeare and Corneille,* trans. D. Ainslie (1920; reprint, New York: Russell & Russell, 1966), 310–12.

34. August Strindberg, *Plays,* trans. E. Sprigge (Chicago: Aldine, 1955), 561–62.

35. This would stem from Croce's thesis that art and poetry are forms of cognition.

Science and the Interpersonal

JOSEPH AGASSI

Boston University

The major shift in recent years in the literatures about science is from the view of science as the knowledge possessed by an individual or a collection of individuals to the view of science as a social institution and as an aspect of modern society, with scientists as a social class, with science policy as a major political item on the permanent agenda of every modern state, and so on. It seems clear that when science is viewed as a social phenomenon, social philosophy is in evidence, and the view of science as a social phenomenon is judged differently from the different vantage points of different social philosophies. In particular, the social philosophy that deems society a mere collection of individuals—reductionist individualism or psychologism—will make the least of the recent shift, whereas the social philosophy that deems people mere members of society—reductionist sociologism or organicism or holism—will make the most of it. Thus, holders of the former views will discuss mainly individuals and their separate contributions to science, whereas the latter will observe science on a large scale and declare no individual scientist indispensable. Without elaborating on this it may be noted that interpersonal interaction is played down by both of these extremes. It is made the most of by the various interactionist schools; but one need not be a member of any of these schools to appreciate interpersonal interaction. Indeed, it was stressed by Karl Popper—not an interactionist—in 1935. How does the recognition of the presence and importance of scientific interaction alter our view of science?

A Scientific Ideal

Philosophers have been investigating for centuries the question, What is science? Indeed, ever since science became a familiar aspect of society, there was fascination with the question, What is it? Yet the answer was there still earlier. Long before science existed as a traditional social entity, as an accepted social institution, there was the institutionalized ideal of science, and science was traditionally and generally identified with that ideal, and as a matter of course. Hence, the question, what is science, was not what really troubled those who pondered on it. Perhaps that question may stand for another one: does the science as we know it fulfill our ideal of it? Does it, that is to say, abide by that ideal? Or does it, at least, approach that ideal? Alternatively, we may be asking, what ideal does institutionalized science endorse and/or implement, and are the two, the endorsed and the followed, the same? The question, what is the ideal of science, fits very well with a general sociological approach, invented by one of the founding fathers of modern sociology, Max Weber; it is known as ideal-type theory. Also, it is not new to Weberian sociology to distinguish between the idea that one openly endorses and the idea that one tries to implement. Roughly, Weberian ideal-type sociology says that a society or a subsociety or a culture or a subculture is best characterized by both the ideals it openly endorses (and the expression of that endorsement in daily life) and the ideals it tries to implement.

There is a serious difficulty lurking here. If we take the ideal type of early Protestant—the most famous one, since it was the object of Weber's best-known studies (and indeed the paradigm of all specific ideal-type theories)—then one need not separate the openly endorsed idea and the one that is lived by. And then the true believer is easily distinguished from the mere conformist. It is the true believer who provides and sustains the openly endorsed and practically implemented ideal, regardless of his or her scarcity, since the conformist emulates the true believer. Or, the opposite may be the case: Protestantism had a declared ideal that was radically different from the one it attempted to implement; the value of Protestantism is in its full and strict idea of conformity, in its success in imposing conformity; and the declared ideal was just the idea justifying conformity and may well be merely cosmetic, endorsed literally only by the naive dim-witted true believer.

The choice between the two options was often made on an ideological basis. Emile Durkheim, another founding father of modern sociology, took all religion and ideology to be social cement and its endorsement to be mere post-hoc justification of social cohesion. That is to say, any ideology or religion, whatever it seems to assert, in reality asserts only the value of social cohesion. When Americans say they are one nation under God, then, they do not speak of God but affirm the Durkheimian thesis that national unity is very important and that it is served by declaring belief in God. Hence, the person who is willing to compromise ideals for the sake of social cohesion is right and the one who clings to the letter of the ideal and causes social schism is wrong.

Durkheim's idea was fully endorsed by Bronislaw Malinowski, one of the founding fathers of empirical (field work) social anthropology and the most influential social anthropologist to date. Loath to ascribe to primitive people the silly superstitions that they expressed when asked to present their views on the diverse matters, Malinowski applied to their views a type of Durkheimian analysis. The question of whether Durkheim and Malinowski could regard science in the same light was left open by the two anthropologists. It must be left open, and for obvious reasons: a positive answer makes their own views no more than a kind of religious or a magical ideology, a mere post-hoc justification of their own activity that makes sense only as a social cement within the social setting in which they lived; whereas a negative answer makes science the only true ideology, and thus, by a clear implication, it makes all nonscientific ideology inferior to ours—quite the contrary to their intentions.[1] But Durkheim and Malinowski wanted it both ways: they did not wish to dismiss magical and religious views as "wrong" yet they wished their own views to be taken as scientific—in other words, as more than mere social cement. They thought that what they said was true in an objective sense in which magical views are not.

No matter how, if at all, Durkheim and Malinowski could accomplish this goal and have it both ways, the very wish to have it both ways indicated their awareness of the difference between a true believer and a mere conformist, since they regarded religious people as conforming to their doctrine for the sake of mere social cohesion, yet the scientist was a true believer in science.[2] Moreover, if ever a society existed whose ideology would coincide with the Durkheim-Malinowski theory, then that society would be the only one with an absolutely true ideology, the only one where the conformist and the believer would be one. Hence, for every other ideal type, there can be and there often are individuals who are true believers and those who are mere conformists. Nor is it hard to find out who is who. This brings me back to the initial question: is the true believer or the mere conformist the true ideal type? Since there are conformists in matters scientific as well—as the following story easily illustrates—the question also obtains for the case of the faith in the ideal of science: is the true practitioner of science the one who contributes to the cohesion of the scientific community or the one who strives for its ideals when even this causes strife and schisms?

Perhaps one could handle this question by first studying the original question of this essay: what is the ideal of science? It is hard to say, and even a very superficial empirical investigation may easily reveal that scientists may profess diverse ideals and conform to different and more diverse ones. Perhaps the Weberian ideal-type theory is simply not good enough for the investigation of science.[3]

Nevertheless, I wish to present what I consider the scientific ideal; I present it neither as an ideal theory nor as one endorsed by most scientists. Hence it is anti-Weberian in most respects. It is best presented by an illustration, a short story or parable of sorts.

The story begins with a group of bona fide scientists—let us isolate them as much as possible, say a group of astronomers working in an astronomical observatory on a remote high mountain. Of course, not all people in the observatory are astronomers; the observatory is part of a station, and on the station are a few members of the nonscientific crew—maintenance workers, transporters, caterers of food, and other providers of services. Yet the two sets are a world apart: the maintenance crew seldom mingles with the astronomers. The astronomers are, first and foremost, very busy, since they spend only a part of the year in the observatory according to a fixed schedule, and must make the best of their short stay, especially since they are very ambitious and hard-working by disposition. Note I am describing here an all-male or almost all-male preserve, which enhances the distance between the two sets. The scientists are usually sexually abstinent for the duration, whereas the permanent crew is left to its own arrangements, which vary from abstinence to living with a family (especially if the couple are both members of the maintenance crew). Even the abstinence of the abstinent crew members dif-

fers from that of the scientist. The sexual abstinence of the
scientists is free of ideology, but only apparently so. It seems
free of ideology since it is imposed only for the duration, since
most of them are family men and since, though avowed sexists,
most of them are sexually quite liberated. Yet the ideology that
brings about abstinence in the circumstances is a high morality
that precludes sexual adventurism and fosters a dedication to
work—the Protestant ethics as described by Max Weber and
applied to the community of science by Robert K. Merton. This
is not to deny Lewis Feuer's critique of Merton, based on the
claim that the official ideology of the scientific revolution and of
the Enlightenment was hedonistic and utilitarian. Rather, I observe that hedonists often practice ascetic morality of one sort
or another and that the work ethic of the modern middle class
permeates the community of science, much to its detriment
and to the detriment of even the scientific output (maximum
input seldom equals optimum output). In any case, Claude
Levi-Strauss has opened our eyes to the possibility that scientists follow at times Merton more than Feuer and at times the
other way around. This, I think, is the truth. Hence, when the
scientists do get together, they talk shop, mainly astronomy,
but also scientific gossip. The maintenace crew is less educated,
hardly interested in science, and talks a lot about sex. The two
teams are, finally, hardly on friendly terms, though relations
are always cordial as a matter of course. They must be if a small
community is to keep efficiently busy.

Suppose one day there is a gathering. There is always a
gathering when shifts change, when a large transport appears,
or when some unusual find is heralded. For some reason practically all the astronomers are gathered one morning in the
cafeteria and the conversation is rather animated. Somehow or
other, one member of the maintenance crew has become involved as well. He is an odd ball, rather elderly and usually
reticent. Yet now it seems that he is fairly familiar with astronomy and even has a somewhat clear idea of what the scientists are doing: he even follows details of their specific
shoptalk.

The conversations across the large cafeteria soon die out; it
turns out that they all find it rather unusual and want to listen
to the odd ball. As reticent people often do, he cannot resist the
temptation of the spotlight once it rests on his own shoulders.
Before anyone realizes what is going on, he is addressing the

august scientific crowd that just happened to be there, still munching on a last bit of breakfast or sipping the second or third cup of coffee after a long, tiring work night. His speech is a clear expression of heresy, and not a new one, either. For the sake of simplicity, let us suppose he says, "You all think the sun rises in the east and sets in the west, but I have reason to think otherwise."

The reactions to the little speech, once it is over, are varied but quite normal. They range from the very polite through the noncommittal to the rudely dismissive. What all members of the august audience share is the utter loss of all interest. Nor can one blame these people: they are experts; he is an animated amateur. Clearly, were he better trained, he would have started not by declaring his convictions, much less by dismissing their convictions to the contrary. Rather, he could easily find one of them who would tell him why they preferred their opinion to his.

Nevertheless, a second unusual event follows the first: one astronomer protests. "Let us hear his reasons," he pleads with his peers, "let us have him explain himself. Perhaps he has something interesting to say after all."

The rest of the story is sheer embarrassment. Most people who say they have reasons do indeed have reasons, but usually very poor ones. Holders of unorthodox views especially have little chance to offer good reasons in their favor. The holders of orthodox views hear them defended repeatedly on each street corner; and these views are orthodox perhaps because many reasons regularly adduced in their favor are popular and even good. Holders of unorthodox views do not have this advantage. Moreover, the holder of unorthodox views has two additional tasks to perform which are far from easy. He has first to discover good arguments in defense of his views and then to learn to articulate them well.

Now back to the elderly reticent maintenance man who has turned out to be an animated amateur astronomer with some unorthodox ideas. He is offered a chance to give his reasons, and with all good will one can only conclude that he had neither good reasons nor the gift of articulation. Oh, there are a few people in his audience who, from discomfiture and out of good will, try to help him articulate his reasons. Yet the more they try the more the poverty of his ideas and his reasoning becomes apparent. Finally, an uncomfortable silence prevails;

the embarrassment turns into hostility—a very mild one, no doubt, but quite unmistaken, and one directed at the odd astronomer who had proposed that the elderly amateur be offered a chance to explain himself. As for the odd astronomer himself, he sits in his corner, his eyes fixed on an empty plate before him, his hand fiddling with a fork, seemingly gathering some crumbs left on the plate; from time to time he shrugs a shoulder as if to deflect the glances his peers dart at him now and then. End of story.

As far as I am concerned, in the whole learned scientific crew gathered that morning in the large cafeteria in the isolated observatory on a distant mountain, there is only one true scientist. And while he sits there, in profound discomfort, absorbing public censure, he might lose this fine quality, his partaking in the scientific ethos. I do not quite know what meaning to attach to his shrugging of a shoulder; he may be overcoming the censure of his peers, learning to live in an even greater isolation, yet keeping the spark of human curiosity. Or he may be succumbing to pressure and saying to himself, They are quite right; we do not have the time necessary to listen to every passing amateur and to every passing dissenter. I hope he is not saying that; I wish to encourage him and tell him how much I hope he remains a scientist to the last. Scientists, after all, are so rare that losing even one of them is a very great loss to the scientific ethos as a whole.

The Scientific Attitude

The above piece of fiction can be presented to natural scientists, if they have the patience for a piece of fiction, and to philosophers of science. As an empirical fact let me report that it is found intriguing and rather entertaining, and the listeners usually sympathize with the hero yet tend to endorse the attitude of his disapproving peers. The question is, What does it all signify?

In order to see this we may wish to take a step or two back. Matters of this sort are not very easy to view comprehensively. One may take a broad commonsensical view of things, or one may take a viewpoint that is more philosophical, more explicitly and consciously anchored in some principle, in some accepted philosophy of science.

The commonsense view of the matter is very commonsensical and as follows: although cranks have an unreasonable demand for our attention, yet at a rare moment they may have some interesting ideas and observations. Paul Feyerabend is a philosopher who has won much acclaim because he has noticed that every crank may have something worthwhile to offer, that unless we study his contribution we cannot be sure he is worthless and should be dismissed, that therefore everyone has an equal right for our attention. The absurdity of this position is manifest to everyone who knows that there is enough literature on parapsychology or on astrology or on flying saucers to engage anyone for unlimited time. Of course, the commonsense view of the matter thus invites one to glance at the literature one judges worthless and keep an open mind about it. But common sense offers no criterion about what level of investment of effort in that direction is wise. We cannot expect common sense to offer a comprehensive view: for this, some analysis is needed, which may lead to a criterion that may be of help. For this criterion one may go to the philosophy of science.

The classical philosophy of science was very much bound up with a certain attitude advocated by the fathers of modern philosophy of science, chiefly Sir Francis Bacon and René Descartes, in the first half of the seventeenth century, and fostered by the Royal Society of London in the second half of that century. It was this society that prescribed the scientific bon ton. The attitude they prescribed, however, was entirely individual, not at all interpersonal, as in the above story. It was openminded eagerness; it was doubt about current knowledge and hope about future knowledge. There was a political aspect to this, no doubt, an egalitarianism as far as one's ability to learn was concerned, and a nonsectarianism in one's intellectual affairs and in one's chosen membership in a learned society. Tolerance was thus a derivative of nonsectarianism, on the understanding that everyone has the right to one's opinion and no one has the duty to listen. Yet the willingness to learn does, of course, prescribe listening, and (for many technical reasons) listening must be selective. What was the selection rule?

It is quite reasonable to assume that no discussion of individual selection rules ever took place: the whole matter arose first in empirical psychology late in the nineteenth century and achieved a modicum of prominence in the early twentieth century. But there was the question of selection in the public domain. It won little attention, since the public servants, editors, committees arranging public lectures, and the like were supposed to cater to a multiplicity of individual tastes. On the assumption that a public is a multiplicity of individuals, this is an obvious conclusion.

All this was taken for granted, then, and served as no more than the appropriate background material for discussions of science and scientific character: was this theory or that theory worthy of the honorific status of science? The scientific attitude was not ignored when theories were discussed; it was taken for granted. Indeed, the mixture of a broad-minded skepticism and a profound quest for knowledge that supposedly characterizes the scientific attitude is prcisely what made so typical such questions as which extant theory is scientific and why? For these were the theories to select as worthy objects of attention.

From time to time science writers stressed the tension or the polarization between the skepticism and the optimism built into the scientific attitude, and this may be taken as evidence that the scientific attitude served as background. But such evidence is hardly necessary since the scientific attitude—and the resulting tense polarization—is precisely what makes the prevalent discussion of the demarcation of scientific theory so important.

The picture changed when the demarcation of the scientific attitude began to intervene with the demarcation of scientific theory. This happened when Henri Poincaré early in the twentieth century expressed an unorthodox view about science. He said that scientific theory stands in regular need of minor corrections and adjustments. He added that a theory remains scientific if and only if its correction is effected openly and not surreptitiously. Here a new factor was added, it may be claimed, to the scientific attitude, namely openness or honesty. Yet one may cogently reject this claim and argue that this factor, the demand for openness or honesty, is traditionally a part of the scientific attitude and thus no innovation in the least. This argument is true, yet an innovation took place all the same. The innovation was in the claim that the status of a theory depends on our attitude: the scientific status of a theory depends on our readiness to admit openly and honestly some of its shortcomings and to present our contributions as modifications of that theory. Yet this point of Poincaré's ideas was not widely noticed because of the popular success of a more backward-looking yet very revolutionary-seeming popular philosophy of science.

It is hard to pinpoint the place of the scientific attitude in the philosophy of the leading twentieth-century school of philosophy of science, the logical positivists or the logical empiricists or the Vienna Circle and its derivative, or in the philosophy of any other of the schools stemming from the early work of Ludwig Wittgenstein, his *Tractatus Logico-Philosophicus* of 1922. This book does exhibit an attitude, indeed a total commitment to utter clarity and to the certainty that it should bring in its wake. If skepticism and hope were still there, then they were directed not at scientific theories at all but at clarity; a philosopher had to doubt that philosophy has attained clarity and to abandon all hope that clarity might ever be attained in philosophy so that it will come and settle all philosophic matters. This sounds as if positivism ignores philosophy and looks at science optimistically. It was true that classical positivism, from Bacon to Ernst Mach, had this very quality; it was, indeed, science-oriented and thus optimistic. Yet this is no longer true of the works of Wittgenstein and his diverse followers. Their positivism addressed the internal affairs of philosophy; it had no proposal for science, nor much interest in its detailed workings. Yet the shift was performed in the name of the continuity of the traditional positivistic hostility to all philosophy and its endorsement of clarity as the heart of scientific rationality and as utter impersonality.

This is why, when Karl Popper's *Logik der Forschung* of 1934, or its expanded translation, *The Logic of Scientific Discovery* of 1959, caught readers' attention, they found hardest to comprehend his coupling—his explicit and quite systematic coupling—of attitudes and theories. He demarcated scientific theories, not attitudes, yet he added a condition relating to attitudes. Theories are scientific, he said, if and only if they are empirically refutable; this, however, is conditioned on our willingness to subject theories to empirical tests and our readiness to jettison them once they are empirically refuted. It is a fact within living memory that people found this very puzzling. If, on the one hand, theories are to be taken as abstract entities, then their status should not involve attitudes; if, on the other hand, theories are crystallizations of people's attitudes, of people's views and values, then there is no need to add attitudes to the judgment of their status. Of course, they may all be false; nor does it matter any longer. Today, only a couple of decades later, attitudes are very fashionable, perhaps because sociologists have made them respectable, perhaps because science as a social phenomenon has become the vogue in many circles.

Parenthetically, I have observed that it was easier to conceive of Poincaré's philosophy of science as attitudinal than Popper's, since Popper is a realist who has to explain how our attitudes matter to Mother Nature, whereas Poincaré was a conventionalist.

Popper's theory of science prescribes, it seems, the upholding of the best available views and the best available information, while trying to sincerely test them—and thus to overthrow them. The attitude just described seems more intolerably polarized than the classical attitude of doubt plus hope, since it is that of hope plus doubt—hope that current successful theory is true, not just hope about the unspecified future; yet also doubt about it, not doubt about one theory and hope about another, but hope and doubt about one and the same theory. In the classical model doubt is resolved and turned into knowledge; in Popper's 1934 model obligatory endorsement is dissolved into rejection, even obligatory endorsement of a given theory as true coupled with the obligatory attempt to undermine it as false.

What has happened? How did the cold clarity and comforting impersonality of science become such a neurotic nightmare? The answer is in the very rejection of the impersonality of science and its replacement by the conventionalist concept of interpersonality. This way, putting Popper's theory in terms of interpersonal attitudes seems a very adequate improvement; some people do endorse some views, others do endorse other views, and the different parties may attempt to engage in a critical debate. When they do, says Popper in his *Conjectures and Refutations* of 1963, then science flourishes.

This completed shift from the impersonal to the interpersonal forcefully raises the question of the selection of people to engage with, of occasions for engagements, and so on: Whom should I take for a partner for a critical debate? What should be the agenda for our debate? And this question is raised both individually and publicly. Moreover, there is no need to assume that the public choice is no more than a multiple individual choice: the public selects editors who use their own judgment as to what the public should debate. (Hence both classical social philosophies—reductionist individualist psychologism and collectivist holism—are in error.)

More important, the interpersonal attitude is much richer and more significant for science than anything presented thus far by most writers about science. We may notice this while considering the attitudes preceding or heralding the scientific attitude. This consideration turns out to have quite a rich background.

The discussion of prescience has been very popular ever since the advent of science. Historians of science were always quick to observe that prescientific technology, as well as folk wisdom, and even popular mythology and superstition, contains much that agrees with the best scientific knowledge currently available. All this was rudely set aside by Sir James Frazer, who at the turn of the century branded magic as pseudoscience and deemed religion intellectually inferior to magic, though he viewed as proper the stages of intellectual development of any culture from magic though religion to science. This idea was extremely influential—especially in antireligion positivistic-rationalistic circles—yet it did not put an end to the view that prescientific knowledge exists; nor was it meant to. Perhaps in opposition to Frazer, perhaps not, quite a few writers declared science to have emerged out of magic. One may mention obscure post-Frazerian writers like Robert Eisler, or ones very fashionable today, like D. P. Walker and Frances Yates. Sir Karl Popper, too, has contributed to this trend. Rather than relate prescientific magic and scientific technology, as most writers on the topic do, or magic and science, as Eisler, Walker, and Yates do, he spoke of myth and scientific theory. He advocates the view that science was distilled out of myth. The conflict of opinion is not resolved, and it is possible to see in Claude Levi-Strauss the latter-day Frazerian, since he agrees with Frazer and not with Popper when he distinguishes sharply between scientific theory proper and mythology, which he labels "the science of the concrete." Similarly Ernest Gellner, whose views generally accord with Popper's on scientific method, yet who sharply dissents from Popper on science and myth, declares there is a "great divide" between myth, magic, superstition and so on, and the "disenchantment" of the world that, he says, the scientific attitude has effected (the term is Max Weber's).

The Scientific Tradition

An older contemporary of Karl Popper, the philosopher Michael Polanyi, whose fame is now posthumously and correctly on the rise, especially since his views are popularized by Thomas S. Kuhn, presents a totally different view of science. Science is, doubtless, a body of theories endorsed by the scientific community. Yet we cannot demarcate these theories in any other way, he taught, than by the claim that they are endorsed by the scientific community. Nor, he added, can the scientific community be characterized abstractly, but it has to be observed as a living tradition. To become a scientist, one must apprentice oneself to a scientist, live in the master's workshop, and imbibe the master's attitudes, techniques, and knowledge. Were science characterizable in any given literature, then it would be possible to acquire it by mastering that literature. Yet to be a scientist one must apprentice oneself to the scientific tradition.

The view of Polanyi is social or sociological, and it is the view of science as an autonomous guild and a community (in Ferdinand Toennies's sense). Two interesting questions regarding Polanyi's theory are worth asking. First, what are the antecedents of science? Clearly, guilds, guild mentality, and so on preceded science. So did, in particular, guilds with high expertise, whether of the arts or of nonscientific learning, or even clerical guilds or orders or church hierarchies. What, then, made the transition from the prescientific communities to guilds to the scientific community? Second, what are the interpersonal relations in a guild in general and in the scientific community in particular? There is no answer in Polanyi's theory, except to say that the master-apprentice relation is that of an overall authoritative transmission of expertise and that somehow the community of science includes the leaders and the led.

Not surprisingly, Polanyi's views find no easy, comfortable place within the community of positivist-rationalist philosophers of science. Many of them try to ignore him. One of the well-known and leading philosophers of science, Adolf

Grünbaum, has declared him an irrationalist and thus an enemy of science and scientific philosophy. Yet Polanyi is hard to dismiss. Why?

It is hard to say. Polanyi seems to say very little, and intentionally so: he says that science is a living tradition which cannot be forced into a simple schema, so that, not surprisingly, he has no simple schema for characterizing science, and he rejects all existing ones. Yet somehow he seems to accommodate many important factors ignored by other philosophers of science. His stress on the interpersonal aspect of science (in one conspicuous place he uses the term "I-thou relations," thereby alluding to Martin Buber) has particularly made him opaque to some traditional, positivistic philosophers of science who cling to science as impersonal, yet it has also endeared him to all those who are concerned with the social and political components of science.

What Polanyi does say, and he seems to be quite clearly right on this point, is that one cannot have it both ways. Science is traditionally viewed by philosophers as impersonal and abstract and utterly clear and certain and utterly this or that. And this may be very satisfying to all those who do not care too much about the social and political aspects of science. But science does have these aspects. Neglecting them was permissible in times when science was the concern of no one but the individuals devoted to science. For science was then left to the scientific community to handle in its own ways, which are governed by tradition and, to Polanyi's mind, quite adequately. But since the world of politics got wise to the social and political importance of science, politicians have attempted to take care of these social and political components—with the intent to serve interests alien to science and to the scientific community. In self-defense, then, the scientific community must undergo a transformation and become aware of its social and political traditional autonomy, and, Polanyi declares, this autonomy must be protected from intruders. To that end the scientific community has to relinquish its traditional view of science as impersonal and notice its highly interpersonal tradition.

Thus, Polanyi did attempt to effect a change; indeed he attempted a revolution within the community of science. Yet it is no more than the revolution implicit in every counterrevolution: that of making the tradition self-aware and fortifying it.

For example, I raised a question in this essay about the

agenda of any interpersonal scientific discourse. I observed that common sense takes care of this question piecemeal and with no hard-and-fast criterion. I sought a philosophic criterion and offered two: Poincaré's and Popper's. (The classical philosophies of science, excluding the interpersonal in favor of the impersonal, leave no room for the question and so do not answer it, of course.) Polanyi has argued that both these criteria can, and at times do, clash with scientific common sense. And then, in Polanyi's view, common sense should win against the criteria it clashes with. Not that common sense is always right. Polanyi himself was once in the right yet rejected by common sense. When common sense caught up with him, he did not say I told you so. He said instead, This is as it should be.[4]

Nevertheless, Polanyi is wrong on the very aspect on which his contribution is so valuable, namely, on the social and political components of science. First of all, the tradition of science is open and democratic, whereas he saw it as an elitist workshop system open only to young, dedicated apprentices. Elitism brings about power and power corrupts.[5] Second, social science attempts to offer theories about the common sense of diverse social sets and subcultures, and Popper's pluralist theory of science is a good shot in that direction—especially his theory of the interpersonal relations in science as friendly/hostile. The defense of the common sense of science cannot make it beyond scientific efforts to have theories about it.

Yet there are different kinds of interpersonal relations among scientists, and indeed a great variety of them, some more becoming to science, some less appropriate. It is not possible, therefore, to decide by sheer observation which interpersonal relations among scientists are more scientific, which are less, and so we need a social scientific study of all these matters.

Science as Curiosity Institutionalized

Let us agree for a moment that there are interpersonal relations that are becoming to science, such as those described in the fable narrated early in this essay. We may find all the components of the attitudes described in prescientific society—toleration and patience and nondefensiveness and a disinterested readiness to consider ideas that at first look rather absurd. Certainly these attitudes are deemed wise in all prescientific wisdom literature, religious and secular alike.

Hence, what constitutes science is not exclusively a matter of interpersonal relations and attitudes. Certainly—as everybody will readily agree—curiosity about the nature of things is essential to science, and indeed the relations described in the fable are possible only between people curious about nature, though in different circumstances the same story could happen with a different topic of conversation and dissent. Also, the attitude the scientists exhibit towards a "crazy" idea (to use Neils Bohr's apt term) is not only disinterest, but also perhaps a mostly passionate interest—curiosity. Since the interpersonal aspect of science is not new, nor is curiosity, one may follow Popper and Polanyi together and consider science as the concentration of certain attitudes, personal and interpersonal, into specific social institutions and traditions. Of course, when the scientific attitude is institutionalized and has any measure of success, it has the fate of any other institutionalized arrangement; it accrues additional characteristics and draws different kinds of people—different in attitudes and in interpersonal relations—some useful, some useless. Science as an institution, then, is a mixed bag of honest and conformist curiosity.[6]

What, then, has happened to myth, magic, and all that? Do they vanish when the scientific attitude crystallizes, as Weber and Gellner have claimed? Is there a level of sophistication and critical attitude that disenchant the world? This is very questionable in view of the fact that science and magic do mix—even in the best scientific society. Yet if the scientific attitude is not only the readiness to be self-critical but also the readiness and the eagerness to entertain other people's views, I propose this in itself may very well cause disenchantment. Indeed, when social anthropologists exhibit this attitude towards the magical superstitions of prescientific cultures, they find that the very arbitrariness of so many views gets in the way.

To conclude, the addition of the interpersonal aspects of science to the personal and the social both helps solve old problems and raises new ones.

NOTES

1. For the egalitarian impetus of the Malinowskian philosophy, see I. C. Jarvie, *The Revolution of Anthropology* (London: Routledge and Kegan Paul, 1964).

2. See the concluding remarks in Emile Durkheim, *The Elementary Forms of the Religious Life*, trans. Joseph Ward Swain (Glencoe, Ill.: Free Press, 1947), and my discus-

sion of them in *Towards A Rational Philosophical Anthropology* (Paris and The Hague: Mouton, 1977), where both individualist and collectivist reductionism are criticized at length. See also Ernest Gellner, *Legitimation of Belief* (Cambridge: At the University Press, 1974) and *Cause and Meaning in the Social Sciences*, ed. I. C. Jarvie and Joseph Agassi (London and Boston: Routledge and Kegan Paul, 1973).

3. See J. W. N. Watkins, "Ideal Type and Historical Explanation," reprinted in an expanded version in *Readings in the Philosophy of Science*, ed. H. Feigl and M. Brodbeck (New York: Appleton-Century-Crofts, 1953), 723–43. Watkins claims that Weber had two ideal-type theories, one individualist and one collectivist. The reason the two cannot be merged is made explicit in the text to this note.

4. The case is studied in some detail in my *Science and Society* (Dordrecht and Boston: D. Reidel, 1981), a volume dedicated to the memory of Polanyi and that includes a detailed critical examination of his contribution.

5. Lord Acton's celebrated dictum, "Power corrupts: absolute power corrupts absolutely," refers to the power of the papacy. He was an ardent but critical Roman Catholic.

6. The point was made by George Bernard Shaw: every bandwagon has attraction to some rabble and mixed multitude. See, for example, the end of his preface to *Androcles and the Lion* (*Selected Plays*, 4 vols. [New York: Dodd, Mead, & Co., 1948], 1:848–49). It is an easily ascertainable fact that science militant speaks more of curiosity and science triumphant speaks more of achievement. It is also a fact that science triumphant is an unavoidable social nuisance, yet it has the same appeal as other successful movements. See, for example, George Orwell's comments on the appeal Stalinism has for intellectuals and Damon Runyon's discussion of the underworld complex. (Sheldon Richmond aptly refers to all this as "pistol envy.")

Polanyi's view of science as a tradition enables him to observe the existence of negative characteristics of science. Regrettably, he dismisses the matter, saying that these negative characteristics are unavoidable. They are also observed by Popper, but he cannot possibly ascribe them to science in the first place. On the whole, Popper's transition from the monism of his *Logik der Forschung* (1934) to the pluralism of his *Conjectures and Refutations* (1963) was not clearcut and awaits his putting his house in order. Clearly, his view of science as a tradition should make him notice the undesirable aspects of science—especially the triumphant accent on successful prediction (corroboration). I have discussed all this in my *Science in Flux* (Dordecht and Boston: D. Reidel, 1975), a volume dedicated to Popper and which includes a detailed, sympathetic, but critical examination of his contributions. It is a constant source of regret to me that he chose to ignore my writings altogether.

Science militant, I propose, should be demarcated differently from science triumphant; and their interaction begs to be studied.

How Does Biochemistry Mean?

BRUCE H. WEBER

California State University, Fullerton

Some years ago John Ciardi wrote a text on the analysis of poetry entitled *How Does a Poem Mean?*[1] To him, what is important about a poem is not "what" it means, its content *per se*, but rather "how" it means, how its images, music, form, its process fuse ultimately to its discovery, its meaning. To illustrate this fusion of process and content, he cites Yeats's famous couplet:

> O body swayed to music, O quickening glance,
> How shall I tell the dancer from the dance?

The medium is not the message, but rather meaning is to be discovered in the process.

In choosing as my title "How Does Biochemistry Mean?" I am, by analogy, focusing my attention not on the factual and conceptual content of biochemistry, but rather on the process of discovery and creativity of biochemists individually and as an intellectual community and on how they relate to the creativity of poets.[2]

This juxtaposition of the "two cultures" of poetry and biochemistry may seem unusual. Indeed, there is the image of the conflict of C. P. Snow's two cultures in C. S. Lewis's novel *Perelandra*, in the mortal combat of Dr. Ransom, the humanist, and Dr. Weston, the physicist. Rather than this confrontation, I wish to explore some possible connections in the spirit of the "other Lewis," C. Day Lewis. In a lecture given at Cambridge, he saw poetry and science as fraternal disciplines, sometimes at odds, but sharing the same parentage (ultimately magic) and many characteristics.[3] The tradition of seeing a connection between poetry and sciences goes back at least to Coleridge in English literature and to Boccaccio's use of the Prometheus

47

legend (Prometheus as both artist and scientist) in European literature.[4]

In attempting to understand the process of biochemistry, we need to draw on knowledge of how the field developed (the historical dimension), how biochemists work today (the sociological aspect), and on how they ought to proceed (the philosophical analysis). Historical, sociological, and philosophical studies of science are relatively recent disciplines, and it is only in the last decade that historical and sociological studies of biochemistry have begun. Most analyses of science, whether historical or philosophical, are based on the physical sciences. Analysis of the biological sciences is less developed, but enough is known that, putting aside questions of vitalism and teleology, it is reasonable to regard biology as an autonomous discipline and not as a derivative science. Biology is distinguished from physics in that biological systems are far more complex and contain far more information than inanimate nature, whether our considerations are at the level of an organism, a cell, an enzyme molecule, or the reactions catalyzed in a cell.[5] Biochemistry occupies the interface between the biological and the physical sciences and is the site of a complex interplay of concepts of each. Thus, a knowledge of how biochemistry means may help illumine both the biological and the physical sciences.

Before going any further, we need to review some of the models of how science works so that we can see how applicable they are to a description of the development of biochemistry. The models I describe are those of Thomas Kuhn, Karl Popper, Paul Feyerabend, and Stephen Toulmin. Although all these models are complex and resist accurate simplification, I will hazard a brief, if oversimplified, view of each.

Kuhn's model is presented in his *Structure of Scientific Revolutions* and has had a major impact, not only in discussion of the nature of the physical sciences, which was the focus of his study, but also in the social sciences.[6] The concept of the paradigm is central to Kuhn's thought. A paradigm most simply means a pattern or a way of seeing. For example, prior to Wordsworth, mountains were perceived as inconvenient barriers to be surmounted or circumvented, whereas after the romantic poets, they were primarily viewed as objects of beauty, grandeur, and inspiration. The act of artistic creation involves such patternings, as is reflected in Wallace Stevens's poem "Anecdote of the Jar," of which I quote the first part:

> I placed a jar in Tennessee,
> And round it was, upon a hill.
> It made the slovenly wilderness
> Surround that hill.
>
> The wilderness rose up to it,
> And sprawled around, no longer wild[7]

Paradigms not only give structure to perceptions, but they also define what observations are germane, what questions are relevant. To shift from poetry to biology I take the example of the studies of sudden infant death. The paradigm that guided research until recently was that there was a sudden metabolic change or a sudden closure of the airway; but a new paradigm was suggested that involved chronic prolonged periods of arrested breathing and predicted a number of specific resultant alterations. Now it was relevant to look for quantitative anatomical differences in the amount of heart muscle of the right ventricle between normal babies and victims of sudden infant death. In the thousands of previous autopsies performed no one ever thought to make such measurements, but as soon as the investigators looked, in the light of the new paradigm, they found the effect. Prior to this new paradigm, the observation of increased heart muscle would not have had meaning. In Kuhn's view, a mature science in its normal phase does not explore the complexities of nature at random, but selects puzzles to solve that are defined by the pervading paradigm. Scientific revolutions occur when a paradigm breaks down, becomes inconsistent with new information or ideas. During the revolution, there is a contest between paradigms and when the new paradigm is victorious, it supplants the old one completely, and provides the new definitions for the field; questions that were important to the old paradigm may no longer be relevant. The conversion from one paradigm to another is not a rational process, but more like a religious conversion; adherents of the old paradigm are not refuted, they merely die.

Kuhn's views were articulately and concisely presented and could be read with ease by practicing scientists as well as by historians, philosophers, and sociologists. Scientists could see Kuhn's model as a more apt description of their activities than the older positivist models. Further, the *Zeitgeist* on the campuses of the sixties and early seventies was favorable to a concept of progress through revolution. Indeed, the recent developments in bioenergetics, about which I will say more later, are discussed by most of the participants in terms of a Kuhnian revolution. This model emphasizes sociological factors in the development of science and is a reminder of how much the history of science and the content of the science itself are rewritten in textbooks. Of course, this model has been critically challenged; especially attacked are the sharp discontinuities implied and the nonrational element. The whole issue is further complicated by the fact that Kuhn uses the word *paradigm* in over twenty different senses, as has been pointed out by Margaret Masterman,[8] which cluster around three main meanings. A paradigm can be used in a metaphysical sense meaning a way of seeing, an organizing principle or governing perception; so used a paradigm is ideologically prior to theory and represents a world view. Changes in paradigm, in this sense, would be applied to, say, the Copernican revolution. Kuhn also uses paradigm in a sociological sense as a universally recognized scientific achievement and as a set of institutions, prior to and other than theory. Finally, Kuhn uses paradigm in the sense of a construct, such as a textbook, a classic experiment, instrumentation, or a conceptual analogy; in this sense a paradigm is something less than a theory, but rather is any aid to puzzle-solving. More recently, Kuhn has shifted emphasis from the dichotomy of normal science interspersed by an occasional revolution to a view in which revolutions are frequent and on a small scale, microrevolutions, occurring during times of normal science.[9] While the applicability of Kuhn's model to the physical sciences is often assumed, its usefulness for the biological sciences remains largely unexplored, despite Kuhn's own assertion that his ideas should hold also for biology. However, a few attempts to analyze the Darwinian revolution in Kuhn's terms have not been successful.[10] In point of fact, the problem may be that Kuhn has incompletely analyzed emerging preparadigm sciences and their transition through a competing conceptual stage to that dominated by a single paradigm; an unfortunate omission, since in the biological sciences there is a vigorous growth of new scientific disciplines.

In contrast to Kuhn, Karl Popper's starting point is that of the formal logician, and he examines not how scientists behave, but how they ought rationally to behave. In contrast to the logical positivists, he stresses falsification;[11] theories cannot be verified with certainty, but they can be falsified. Indeed, the best strategy for advancing knowledge is to seek to empirically falsify one's most cherished ideas. This gives a way of distinguishing science from other human activities. Thus, in science, there is a permanent right of challenge during normal times. Still, for Popper and his followers, conceptual change has been an anomaly to be explained. Popper's hypothetico-deductive scheme emphasizes the two different poles of scientific activity. Imagination and intuition can be important sources of new hypotheses, in what Peter Medawar calls "romantic science";[12] this is a process that can be seen as very close to the creation of poetry. Then the "worldly science," that of criticism and analysis, takes over, a process that Medawar suggests is antithetical to poetry. Medawar cites Shelley as having espoused both positions about the relationship of poetry and science, arguing in some places for the essential commonality of the imaginative act in poetry and science and in other places seeing the sciences' critical approach as being apoetical. But when we examine how poets actually work (*vide infra*) we see that there is also a critical phase in the creation of a poem. Both Popper and Medawar see this polarity of imagination and criticism as essential and interpenetrating, which by its process gives rise to new knowledge.

Paul Feyerabend agrees with Kuhn's concern with theory-laden observations but challenges formal models of discovery, asserting that scientists gain new knowledge only by breaking the rules, that there is no pattern to the process of progress, and that the framework of meanings changes constantly.[13] This view provides an anarchical antidote to taking models of science too seriously and should caution us as to how far we can progress in understanding the mystery of creativity, either poetical or biochemical. Further, Feyerabend sees science to be kindred in its actual processes to myth. More recently, Richard Rorty has extended the approaches of Feyerabend, Kuhn, and others, to criticize the concept of epistemology in science.[14]

Further, Rorty argues for the concept of science as a civil conversation and for the hermeneutic paradigm as the mode of change in science, thus blurring the distinction between the "hard" and "soft" sciences. It is interesting that some scientists are advocating a hermeneutic rather than strictly reductionist approach to some of the major current problems in the biological sciences, such as the embryological development of the brain.[15]

Finally, I wish to mention another view of science espoused by Stephen Toulmin.[16] In the dispute between Kuhnians and Popperians, Toulmin sees an analogy to the controversy in nineteenth-century geology between catastrophists and uniformitarians, and as with the catastrophists, Kuhn has modified his theory from major dislocations to microrevolutions. Toulmin goes on to suggest that these microrevolutions may not be units of transformation so much as units of "biological" variation and that concepts are under a selection pressure (due, in part, to empirical testing) such that those concepts most adapted to approach the problems deemed important at a given time will survive. The concepts in use define the field of inquiry and this field can expand, contract, or shift over time, in response to the selective process. Although most concepts are in a process of development or extinction, there is an occasional appearance of a novel concept. This model of science is explicitly based on the biological concept of evolution and can accommodate sociological and nonrational factors along with an overall rational view that focuses on historical development. Thus, Toulmin replaces the concept of revolution with that of evolution. However, if the field of concepts held should shift significantly in magnitude and speed, we might choose, for descriptive convenience, to view this extreme case as a revolution. Such discontinuities are consistent with the modern punctuational model of macroevolution.

Is the rise of biochemistry and molecular biology a revolution in the biological sciences or is it an evolutionary process? Certainly there has been a major advance in the knowledge of living systems since 1953 when James Watson and Francis Crick proposed the structure of DNA, and recently we have seen the potential for major changes wrought by the resultant technologies such as recombinant DNA, genetic manipulation, and cloning. But where exactly is the revolution? Was it in solving the structure of DNA? No, Watson and Crick were using the method of structural chemistry and model building developed previously by Linus Pauling and their results were rapidly accepted by the scientific community which suggested that their method was sufficiently orthodox. Was the revolution in looking for a molecular basis for heredity? Not really. This shift has occurred in a long process during the nineteenth and early twentieth centuries in the gradual triumph of reductionism over vitalism. However, one can claim that when Avery presented, in 1944, his observation that DNA was the genetic material, he muted his claims, since for geneticists the material basis of heredity was not a crucial question, even though he clearly understood the importance of his results. Perhaps the revolution resides in the microrevolution in which nucleic acid replaced protein as the biochemical paradigm. Even here we have trouble. After Friedrich Mischer's discovery of DNA in Felix Hoppe-Seyler's laboratory in 1869, there were numerous references in the literature through the end of the nineteenth century to the concept of DNA as the chemical basis of heredity; even a molecular code was suggested and the term *molecular physiology* was coined.[17] The problem at the time was an inadequate set of techniques to manipulate DNA properly without degradation or to test these ideas empirically. In the vacuum thus created the protein hypothesis remained, although it did not inspire a major research effort. Avery's work was not neglected, as a citation analysis has suggested,[18] but rather those studying viral and bacterial genetics were focused on other questions at the time; the biochemist Erwin Chargaff did start his key analytical studies on DNA because of Avery's work. What did transform biology was the theoretical extension that Crick made from the model of DNA, the development of the code concept and its decipherment, and the postulation of the central dogma (information normally flows from DNA to RNA to protein). This transformation was as much stylistic as conceptual. Before considering the question of the importance of style in the process of science, let us examine the background period during which the concept of the molecular basis of life developed.[19]

Biochemistry had its origin in the production of beer and winemaking as much as in medicine. The study of fermentation was a main impetus in the development of biochemistry in the nineteenth century. Indeed, the word *fermentation* is derived from the Latin *fermentum* or "yeast," the past participle of *ferveo* ("boil up"), reflecting the release of carbon dioxide. When it became clear that yeast made alcohol inside their cells, the term coined from the biological catalyst involved was *enzyme*, from the Greek ἐν-ζυμη, meaning "in yeast," ultimately derived from ζεῶ or "boil up." Actually, the possibility of catalysis in biological systems can be traced back to the alchemists of ninth-century Persia who sought to isolate this catalyst (the elixir) by distillation of wine, thereby discovering brandy.[20]

Early attempts to provide a chemical explanation of living organisms were based on the concept of an interpenetration of matter and spirit as represented by the thought of Georg Ernst Stahl, who was also a key figure in the development of the phlogiston theory. When Antoine Lavoisier overthrew the phlogiston theory, he extended his theory of chemical oxidation to include animal respiration as a process of slow combustion and viewed all living processes as being reducible to chemical events. Michael Eugene Chevreul, who founded biochemical analysis, extended Lavoisier's approach to a variety of chemical constituents of cells, started studies on the chemistry of biosynthesis (his term), and opposed all discussion of vital forces. Marie F. X. Bichat opposed this reduction and said that the living organism must be studied and that the vital force responsible for the organization of living things was not a spirit but a physical force like gravity; further, he said that although what gravity is is not known, it can be studied quantitatively, so by analogy, the vital force could be approached experimentally. In our own time, Max Delbrück started his Nobel Prize-winning research on viruses, hoping to discover a new physical force.

Some physiological chemists of the nineteenth century worked within both traditions, such as Justus von Liebig, who brought Lavoisier's type of analysis to a culmination and demonstrated that animal heat arises only from chemical combustion of carbon-hydrogen foodstuffs by oxygen. Yet he extended the concept of the vital force and opposed attempts to describe biosynthesis without this concept. In particular, he opposed the strict reductionist Theodor Schwann, who founded cell theory, and felt that the biological processes could be studied only from a chemical standpoint. Schwann coined the word *metabolism* to describe chemical changes in the cell, and linked respiration with cell metabolism. Chemists in this tradition felt that the chemistry of the cell had to follow the chemical reactions studied in the test tube by the concurrently developing organic chemistry. For example, Johann F. W. A. Von Bäyer suggested that glucose was converted in one step to lactic acid by yeast (as also in muscle) and then a further reaction converted the lactic acid to alcohol and carbon dioxide. The vitalists resisted this type of reduction and assumption of *in vitro* chemical pathways. A middle ground was espoused by the physiological chemists who sought to combine *in vitro* chemistry with *in vivo* studies and who stressed a realization of the complexity and organization of living cells.

In 1872, Hoppe-Seyler started the process of giving biochemistry its separate identity and stressed the need to isolate and characterize molecules of the cell before any further speculation. However, it was not until 1903 that Carl Alexander Neuberg coined the name of the new discipline and shortly thereafter started publishing *Biochemische Zeitschrift*, one of the first exclusively biochemical journals. In 1906 the *Biochemical Journal* was founded in England and in 1905 the *Journal of Biological Chemistry* was started in America. As Hoppe-Seyler's research program was carried forward, most successfully in Emil Fischer's laboratory, there was an increasing debate as to whether chemical reductionism or a rational vitalism, which stressed the organization of the cell, provided the best strategy for biochemistry. Eduard F. W. Pflüger was an exemplar of this sophisticated vitalism that used contemporary chemical thought yet conceived of the protoplasm as a single living catalytic molecule, energy-rich but dead when studied by biochemists.[21] The vitalist position was not so much refuted as abandoned when the reductionist position was modified by the concepts of Frederick G. Hopkins (and members of the German school such as Otto Meyerhof) early in this century. Hopkins stressed the multiple enzymic basis of metabolic change, the recognition that metabolic changes occur in many small steps, subject to the laws of thermodynamics, the notion that these steps are decipherable if one learns how to isolate and handle biological molecules, and the corollary that enzymes are not alive, but merely labile. On the other hand, Hopkins also stressed that the biochemist should not try to extrapolate from *in vitro* chemistry to the cell, but learn what chemistry the cell uses. By the time of World War II, not only was this viewpoint almost universally accepted, but the actual pathway for the metabolism of glucose to alcohol was elucidated, a process found to involve multiple enzyme-catalyzed steps, phosphory-lated intermediates, and coenzymes, such as ATP and one de-rived from niacin. During this time, it was known that enzymes are protein molecules of discrete structure and not catalytic forces imposed upon, or small molecules bound to, a colloidal particle. The details of this story not only involve a slow, com-plex set of conceptual changes (during a phase that Kuhn would probably view as pre- and/or multiparadigm), but the accumulation of the various techniques and strategies for han-dling labile biological molecules. Indeed, the eminent biochem-ist Erwin Chargaff has charged that a biochemist would try to figure out how a fine, delicate watch operates by smashing it with a heavy hammer, isolating the bits and then speculating on how the mechanism worked.[22] The nineteenth-century biochemists did not recognize that the pieces were broken. The first part of this century was spent developing smaller ham-mers and gentler ways to pry open the watch.

The process of the emergence of biochemistry as a distinct discipline from physiology and medical chemistry has been admirably chronicled in Robert Kohler's recent study.[23] The is-sues are complex and not as clear-cut as presumed by some previous writers.[24] It is interesting to note that because biochemistry was a graduate-level field of study in England and America prior to World War II, there were few biochemis-try books in England before 1945. Most of what we now call biochemistry was contained in textbooks of physiology or medical chemistry. English and American graduate students of biochemistry either used these textbooks (in English or Ger-man) or else employed the primary literature of journal articles and monographs. Only after World War II did a truly modern and influential biochemistry textbook appear. Ernest Baldwin's *Dynamic Aspects of Biochemistry* was published in 1947 and was appropriately dedicated to his mentor, Frederick G. Hopkins, who had founded the biochemistry department at Cambridge in 1914.[25] Baldwin's book codified for English-speaking stu-dents, several decades after the fact, the principles espoused by Hopkins in a series of papers and addresses that focused primarily on concepts of metabolism and the application of thermodynamics to living systems.[26] The emphasis on structure and the role of proteins and membranes that was articulated during the interwar years by David Keilin did not appear in textbooks until the publication in America of a text by Joseph

Fruton and Sofia Simmonds in 1953 and another by Abraham White, Philip Handler, and Emil Smith in 1954 (which is still widely used with a seventh edition published in 1983).[27] Since 1970 there has been a plethora of biochemical textbooks with much shorter lag times (just a few years) between the introduction of a concept in the field and its appearance in a textbook and much greater emphasis on the structural chemistry of biomolecules. This whole question of the codification of paradigms in biochemical textbooks needs further systematic study, especially in the light of the emphasis Kuhn puts on the role of textbooks for normal science.

I have arrived back where I departed, at that pivotal period after World War II. The complex path of discovery, competition, and creativity of Watson and Crick can be followed in Watson's autobiography or in an objective and balanced fashion in the recent superb history of Horace Judson, *The Eighth Day of Creation*.[28] The actual details of the process are not unique; actually, a similar sort of story could be told for the solution of the triple helix structure of collagen. What I wish to focus on specifically is Watson and Crick's style of approach and their style of presentation.

The style of discovery of Watson and Crick was one of model-building, taking all possible short-cuts and always focusing on the goal of solving the problem. This contrasts with the meticulous analytical and somewhat philosophical exploration of Chargaff and the methodical crystallographic procedures of Rosalind Franklin. Indeed, after discussing DNA structure with Watson and Crick at a Cambridge pub, where they speculated about helices but could not write down the structures of the component bases, Chargaff wrote in his diary that they were "two pitchmen in search of a helix" and not to be taken seriously.[29] Franklin had little use for their type of speculation and though she took the X-ray pictures that clearly showed the pattern of a double helix, she insisted on a systematic study and conventional methods of interpretation.[30] But the Watson-Crick style of working was not as important as the style of presentation, which was clear, concise, elegant, decisive, and pregnant with implications, especially since the model afforded a ready explanation of replication. Further, Chargaff's empirical base-ratio rules, which were not built into the model, were clear and direct consequences of the model. The impact of Watson and Crick's paper was at least as much psychological as scientific; it galvanized research in molecular biology and its funding. This spirit and style were kept alive with Crick's development of the "central dogma" and further codified by the Cartesian style of Jacques Monod, who extended the theoretical consideration to the control of gene expression and of enzyme activity.

It is reasonable to query if the creativity of Watson and Crick or of Monod and Jacob is related in any fashion to the creativity of the poet. One clear distinction exists. Usually in modern science basic problems are solved by a collaboration and frequently there are multiple independent discoveries of a basic pattern or multiple presentations of a theory. The poet's vocation is more solitary and although given forms and styles predominate at a given time, it is rare to have two different poets simultaneously and independently creating very similar poems. But examined more closely, the creative processes in poetry and biochemistry reveal some interesting parallels involving the inspiration and the style of execution.

Stephen Spender has written at length about craft and creativity in poetry.[31] Some of his comments on the compulsion to write poetry and the needed concentration are quite similar to the observations that Horace Judson has made about the creative process in science.[32] Although some poets have "immediate concentration," in Spender's terms, which is the facile conception of a poem in Mozartian completeness, most poets, he demonstrates, work by "complete concentration" in a Beethovian process of revision and growth. Spender states:

> Inspiration is the beginning of a poem and also its final goal. It is the first idea which drops into the poet's mind and is the final idea which he at last achieves in words. In between this start and winning post there is the hard race, the sweat and toil.[33]

Spender also describes the process of development of a poem and the transformation of its beginning materials and images.

Contrary to the way scientists report their research in the professional literature, they often work in a manner similar to that described by Spender. I. Bernard Cohen has studied the detailed history of the development of Newton's theory of gravity.[34] Rather than by a flash of insight from a falling apple, Newton came to his theory by a painful and slow process of hard intellectual effort in which he not only had to transform some of his starting notions, but in which there was a constant succession of comparisons of physical reality (as revealed by measurement and observation) and a simplified but abstract model of it. This slow, logical process, with many false turns, was also the method of the research of Watson and Crick and of Monod. Of course, there are examples in science of the "immediate concentration" when a problem is solved in a short time due to a creative, imaginative intuition. Certainly August Kekule's discovery of the tetravalency of carbon (the basis for modern organic chemistry) while riding on a London tram or Otto Loewi's discovery of chemically mediated neurotransmission (the basis of modern neurophysiology) during a dream have all the qualities of a sudden poetic inspiration.[35]

As the scientist struggles to make his theories more congruent with what he perceives as physical reality, more self-consistent and consistent with the conceptual framework of the relevant parts of science, so the poet works to make his words and imagery more precise and consistent with his vision. While the self-consistency of the imagery and the organic or formal unity of the poem are more aesthetically important than the congruence with physical reality, nonetheless the poet often works carefully to find the most apt "objective correlative" of the transphysical statement he is attempting to make. Jacob Bronowski quotes a comment that Niels Bohr made to Werner Heisenberg, "When it comes to atoms, language can be used only as in poetry. The poet, too, is not nearly so concerned with facts as creating images."[36] When attempting to describe events at the atomic or molecular level, one is not dealing directly with reality but rather creating images of sufficient precision and simplicity to guide our thought.

Another component of creativity in poetry and biochemistry involves getting more out of a poem or a theory than consciously went in. Poets frequently find meanings that exist in a poem of which they were not aware. Indeed, a good poet is a myth-maker as opposed to a fashioner of allegory;[37] different readers at a given time or, over a period of time, different generations find new meanings in poems of a mythic dimension whereas the meaning of allegory is intended by the author to be fixed. Similarly, a good scientific theory suggests more than went into its construction. The Watson-Crick model of DNA immediately explained Chargaff's base ratios, which were not part of the information used to develop the double-helical model. More important, the model at once suggested how gene replication could occur and ultimately how biology could be conceived in terms of information theory.

One can conjecture, as has Gunther Stent, what the scenario might have been if Watson and Crick had not teamed up or had gone off to another problem.[38] The structure of DNA would have been solved, probably mainly by Franklin, but the work would likely have appeared over several years, in perhaps a dozen papers from a couple of laboratories (with the inevitable differences in interpretation). The psychological effect would have been diffuse.

This type of what-if speculation is dubious at best, but it is instructive to compare a somewhat analogous situation. I choose to focus on an area of current interest to me: the development of the chemiosmotic theory, for which Peter Mitchell received the Nobel Prize in Chemistry in 1978. This theory seeks to explain how the cell captures energy from cellular respiration; that is, the slow combustion of carbon-hydrogen foodstuffs.[39] Electrons from the reduced carbon compounds are passed down a complex proteinaceous "wire" imbedded in the mitochondrial membrane (which is impermeable to water and to hydrogen ions) and ultimately reach oxygen, which is reduced to water. The question is, how is this electron-transfer process coupled with the synthesis of ATP, which is the metabolic energy currency of the cell? The paradigm, if you wish, that guided this research was the concept of chemical intermediates put forward by Slater, based in part on Efraim Racker's elucidation of an oxidation reaction coupled to ATP synthesis that occurs in the breakdown of glucose. Racker's work was a great conceptual triumph of the chemical-reductionist approach, and it was obvious to everyone that Slater's proposed intermediates *had* to be correct. There was one slight problem; in spite of thousands of people's efforts expended in the top laboratories around the world over several decades, no one ever isolated one of these intermediates. It was rather like the old Indian story of the man who escaped a lion by jumping on a boat that carried him across the river and who was so grateful that he carried the boat on his shoulder the rest of his life.

Alternative hypotheses were put forward in the sixties by Boyer and Mitchell. Mitchell, who was studying the transport of metabolites across bacterial membranes, found a connection between transport and the energy metabolism of the cell. In doing this, he brought together many strands of physiological research in addition to his own, including the study of ion transport across plant roots by Lundegårdh and by Robertson, the study of secretion of hydrochloric acid in the stomach by Davies, and the studies of the role of metal-ion gradients in metabolite transport by Christensen and by Crane. Mitchell fused these research traditions with that of mitochondrial energy capture and proposed that concomitant with the flow of electrons through the electron-transport chain was a vectorial release of protons or hydrogen ions producing a proton gradient that, in turn, as it was collapsed through the enzymic machinery of the coupling factor, helped catalyze the synthesis of ATP. Thus, the circuit of electron flow was coupled to a circuit of proticity.

Mitchell's creativity was in his confluence of several research traditions and apparently disparate phenomena and in his postulation of the role of hydro-dehydration reactions. The development of his ideas followed the slow, painstaking "Beethovian" approach.[40] Indeed, he can recall no moment of sudden insight but rather a continuous evolution and fusion of ideas and experiments. This is quite reminiscent of Spender's method of writing poetry. Knowing this does not lessen the mystery of Mitchell's or Spender's creativity, but it does suggest the need to allow individuals freedom to pursue a problem or a poem for an extended time. Mitchell's approach to publication was similar to that of Watson and Crick in that he published a brief theoretical paper in *Nature*;[41] but there the similarity of style ends. Mitchell's original paper, while correct in all the main principles, was wrong in some details and silent on mechanism. Over a period of years, he elaborated the details of his theory and developed explicit mechanisms in many papers and two books, continually modifying in a Popperian fashion his conjectures when confronted with apparent experimental refutation. However, the solution to one puzzle was the proposal of the "Q-cycle," which came to Mitchell in Mozartian swiftness and completeness.[42] His theory has become a complex, three-level affair with only the "physiological" level of proton coupling being widely accepted, even today. The other levels (the chemical and the metabolic), which deal with mechanistic details and which provide a broad conceptual framework for discussing other aspects of metabolism, are still hotly disputed even by his many supporters.

The response to Mitchell's theory, over time, can be measured crudely by just counting the number of citations of his work, which are increasing slowly but steadily. In contrast, however, an alternative proton-coupling model, proposed by R. J. P. Williams,[43] also in 1961, was achieved independently from considerations of chains of organic and biological catalysts and is more difficult to verify or falsify; only recently has it been noticed by the field. Even looking at citations more carefully with regard to acceptance or rejection of at least one level of the chemiosmotic hypothesis, the pattern of slow acceptance again is apparent, along with fairly steady opposition. If one looks a little closer at those individuals who have accepted at least some aspect of Mitchell's hypothesis, it becomes clear that there is a strong correlation to field of research rather than to age. This is due to the intertwined milieu in which biological research is conducted. The first supportive data for Mitchell came not from the biochemists studying the mitochondria, but from those studying photosynthesis and those studying ion transport across membranes. Not only is the Planck hypothesis (that is, the opposition dies rather than is converted) imperfectly applicable here, but there is no key, psychologically important, pivotal experiment. Analysis of the literature and interviews with dozens of the participants in the research reveals no clear-cut pattern of acceptance. Nor has it been possible to achieve a falsification of any of the competing hypotheses; in spite of the failure to isolate chemical intermediates, it is possible to account for almost all of the data cited in support of Mitchell by use of the intermediate concept, albeit with much less elegance and simplicity. Even at the chemical level, biological systems, because of their complexity, show this untidy disregard for the needs of a logic of discovery. The complexity of the phenomena, the complexity of Mitchell's hypothesis, and Mitchell's own somewhat unorthodox personal style of presentation have diffused the decisiveness of the impact of Mitchell's 1961 paper, major though it has been, compared to the impact of Watson and Crick's paper.

Those outside of science may not be aware and many scientists will not admit that style of work and presentation is an important component of the reception of a new theory by the field. This is especially true when several workers in a field are converging toward similar concepts. This effect of style may be likened to Pope's comment on wit:

> True wit is nature to advantage dress'd.
> What oft was thought, but ne'er so well express'd.

The importance of style in poetry is clear and reflects not only the conventions of the poet's time but also his unique individuality. Think how different the content of the history of English poetry might have been if Milton had died in his twenties or if Shelley had lived to be sixty. We will never know if Shelley might have produced an epic of the stature of *Paradise Lost*, although the development of his style in his last, incomplete poem, "The Triumph of Life," hints at the possibility; certainly, no poet could do it in lieu of Shelley. Similarly, the late quartets of Beethoven or Joyce's *Finnegan's Wake* are creations unique to their respective artist, despite the fact that they must be seen in their social and cultural matrices.

Both poetry and biochemistry involve a consistent, complex interplay of uniqueness and universality, though the poet more consciously focuses on the unique and individual, whereas the scientist, while not ignoring these types, puts more emphasis on the general and universal. As G. K. Chesterton (following Aristotle) has demonstrated, the poet's emphasis on the unique can have universal implications.[44] In contrast to artistic creations, the structure of DNA, the concepts of biological control, the role of protons in energy coupling, all would have come regardless of the existence of Watson, Crick, Monod, or Mitchell, but the impact of their unique personalities and styles has affected the rate and direction of development of molecular biology and biochemistry.

The problem of creativity in science and the arts, specifically in poetry and biochemistry, involves both the process of creating new metaphors and discovering new knowledge in both the individual and the social setting. Clearly, the study of poetry tends to focus more on the individual poet, though his or her social and literary environment must be considered. For the study of biochemistry, while the individual is important, one has to recognize that much of the most creative research involves a collaboration of at least two individuals, usually of different temperaments and backgrounds, such as Watson and

Crick or Jacob and Monod, where both are contributing to the creative search for a solution. In other scientific collaborations there is the theoretician working closely with the experimentalist, as with Mitchell and his associate, Moyle. In contrast, there are few examples of collaboration in poetry; Pound's revising Eliot's *Wasteland* and the collaborative efforts of some Elizabethan playwrights are among the rare exceptions. Biochemistry, like other sciences, is a less solitary vocation than poetry. The conditions that produce creative collaboration need more careful study, and it is necessary to examine with more scrutiny how the field, as a whole, works.

Bronowski has asserted that physics is the collective work of art of the first half of the twentieth century.[45] I would extend that assertion to the molecular biology and biochemistry of the second half of the twentieth century. If one accepts the classical definition of art that prevailed in the West, starting with the Greeks and revived in the Renaissance, then modern science can be viewed as an art form. The goal of the artist was to produce an "object" that represents the structure of the real of which we get only glimpses in the flux of experience. Modern science provides metaphors (or theories) of the atomic molecular reality that underlies the phenomena of the material and living world experience.

Although biochemistry is at an interface of the physical and biological sciences, it is clear that the biological component causes some problems in the application of the models derived from the physical sciences. Indeed, models that incorporate aspects of the arts and humanities may be just as relevant. The complexity of the subject and the phenomena, the complexity of the overlapping disciplines, the difficulty of designing a uniquely falsifying experiment mean that there are few clear-cut battles or clearly defined revolutions for the biological sciences, but rather what Judson called "multiple small-scale encounters—guerilla actions all over the landscape."[46] Biochemistry and molecular biology have grown by the opening up of research opportunities, by the unfolding of conceptual advance, rather than by overturnings. The Kuhnian approach can offer insights when applied judiciously, especially for sociological factors and the importance of new techniques or model experiments. Popper's philosophy is espoused by many biochemists, but more as a goal than as achievable in practice. Rorty's hermeneutic approach has great potential for examining, evaluating, and organizing the complex structure of the biological sciences and gives a convenient bridge to the disciplines in the social sciences, humanities, and arts. The idea of the unfolding of biochemical research suggests the original meaning of "evolution" from *evolutio* ("to unfold"). Toulmin's model, based upon an analogy to biological evolution, appears also to have great potential for organizing the historical development of biochemistry and the biological sciences in general, if not also the physical sciences, and for providing a framework for a more incisive analysis of how biochemistry means.

Having begun with Ciardi's concept of poetic meaning, I would like to close with a quotation from a recent book by John Gardner that I believe is as true for science as it is for art. Gardner claims that "art is essentially serious and beneficial, a game played against chaos and death, against entropy. . . . Art in sworn opposition to chaos discovers *by its process* what it can say."[47]

NOTES

1. John Ciardi, *How Does a Poem Mean?* (Boston: Houghton Mifflin, 1960).

2. This paper is an expanded version of a talk presented in the Outstanding Professor Series on 16 April 1980, sponsored by the President's Associates of the California State University, Fullerton. Current research described (on the historical development of chemiosmotic concepts) is funded by grants from the National Science Foundation and the American Philosophical Society. I wish to thank Professors David DePew and John Cronquist of the C.S.U.F. philosophy department and Professor James Woodward of the C.S.U.F. history department for reading and commenting on an earlier version of this manuscript. I am also grateful to Professor John Brugaletta of the C.S.U.F. English department for his helpful discussions and suggestions.

3. C. Day Lewis, *The Poet's Way of Knowledge* (Cambridge: At the University Press, 1957).

4. Owen Barfield, *What Coleridge Thought* (Middletown, Conn.: Wesleyan University Press, 1971), and Trevor H. Levere, *Poetry Realized in Nature: Samuel Taylor Coleridge and Early Nineteenth-Century Science* (Cambridge: At the University Press, 1981); Ernst Cassirer, *The Individual and the Cosmos in Renaissance Philosophy* (New York: Harper and Row, 1963), and Raymond Trousson, *Le Thème de Prométhée dans la Littérature Européenie* (Geneva: Libraire Droz, 1964).

5. For example, a very small protein composed of about a thousand atoms arranged as a polymer of about sixty amino acids (with twenty possible residues at each of the sixty positions) has 6×10^{79} possible arrangements of amino acids, each arrangement representing unique biological information. To give some sense of the size of this number, it is estimated that the total number of atoms in the whole known universe is about 1×10^{79}!

6. Thomas S. Kuhn, *The Structure of Scientific Revolutions,* rev. ed. (Chicago: University of Chicago Press, 1970).

7. Wallace Stevens, "Anecdote of the Jar," in *Collected Poems of Wallace Stevens* (New York: Knopf, 1954), 76.

8. Margaret Masterman, "The Nature of a Paradigm," in *Criticism and the Growth of Knowledge,* ed. Imre Lakatos and Alan Musgrave (Cambridge: At the University Press, 1970), 59–89.

9. Thomas S. Kuhn, *The Essential Tension* (Chicago: University of Chicago Press, 1977). Also see the analysis of Stephen Toulmin, "Distinctions Between Normal and Revolutionary Science," in *Criticism and the Growth of Knowledge,* 39–47.

10. See, for example, John C. Greene, "The Kuhnian Paradigm and the Darwinian Revolution in Natural History," in *Perspectives in the History of Science and Technology,* ed. Duane H. D. Roller (Norman: University of Oklahoma Press, 1971), 3–25.

11. Karl R. Popper, *Conjectures and Refutations: The Growth of Scientific Knowledge,* 2d ed. (New York: Basic Books, 1965); idem, *The Logic of Scientific Discovery* (New York: Basic Books, 1959 and revised 1968).

12. Peter B. Medawar, *The Art of the Soluble* (London: Methuen, 1967).

13. Paul Feyerabend, *Against Method* (London: New Left Books; Atlantic Highlands, N.J.: Humanities Press, 1975).

14. Richard Rorty, *Philosophy and the Mirror of Nature* (Princeton, N.J.: Princeton University Press, 1979).

15. For example, Gunther Stent, "The Rise of Molecular Biology" (paper read at the West Coast History of Science Society, Stanford University, 25 April 1981).

16. Stephen Toulmin, *Human Understanding: The Collective Use and Evaluation of Concepts* (Princeton, N.J.: Princeton University Press, 1972).

17. Alfred E. Mirsky, "The Discovery of DNA," in *The Chemical Basis of Life,* ed. Philip C. Hanawalt and Robert H. Heynes (San Francisco: W. H. Freeman, 1973); reprinted from *Scientific American* 218 (1968): 78–88.

18. H. V. Wyatt, "Knowledge and Prematurity: The Journey From Transformation to DNA," *Perspectives in Biology and Medicine* 18 (1965): 149–56.

19. The discussion below presents a brief outline of the recent historical development of biochemistry; a good, more complete treatment is given in Joseph S. Fruton, *Molecules and Life* (New York: Wiley-Interscience, 1972).

20. Since publishing was not demanded for tenure in those days (and perishing frequent), this key advance was not widely disseminated until it was rediscovered by some twelfth-century monks of alchemical bent.

21. The interplay of reductionism and vitalism and of chemistry and biology has been well presented in Fruton, *Molecules and Life.*

22. Erwin Chargaff, *Heraclitean Fire: Sketches of a Life Before Nature* (New York: Rockefeller University Press, 1978).

23. Robert E. Kohler, *From Medical Chemistry to Biochemistry* (Cambridge: At the University Press, 1982).

24. Wolfgang Krohn and Wolf Schäfer, "The Origins and Structure of Agricultural Chemistry," in *Perspectives on the Emergence of Scientific Disciplines,* ed. Gerard Lemaine, Roy Macleod, Michael Mulkay, and Peter Weingart (The Hague and Paris: Mouton, 1976), 27–52.

25. Ernest Baldwin, *Dynamic Aspects of Biochemistry* (Cambridge: At the University Press, 1947).

26. *Hopkins and Biochemistry,* ed. Joseph Needham and Ernest Baldwin (Cambridge: W. Heffer and Sons, 1949).

27. David Keilin, *The History of Cell Respiration and Cytochrome* (Cambridge: At the University Press, 1966); Joseph S. Fruton and Sofia Simmonds, *General Biochemistry* (New York: Wiley, 1953); Abraham White, Philip Handler, and Emil L. Smith, *Principles of Biochemistry* (New York: McGraw-Hill, 1954).

28. James D. Watson, *The Double Helix* (New York: Atheneum, 1968); Horace Freeland Judson, *The Eighth Day of Creation* (New York: Simon and Schuster, 1979).

29. Erwin Chargaff, as quoted in Judson, *Eighth Day*, 142.

30. For a description from Franklin's viewpoint, see Anne Sayer, *Rosalind Franklin and DNA* (New York: Norton, 1975).

31. Stephen Spender, "The Making of a Poem," in *Poetry: Theory and Practice*, ed. Laurence Perrine (New York: Harcourt, Brace and World, 1962), 138–46; reprinted from *Partisan Review* 13 (1946): 294–308.

32. Horace Freeland Judson, *The Search for Solutions* (New York: Holt, Rinehart and Winston, 1980).

33. Spender, "The Making of a Poem," 141.

34. I. Bernard Cohen, *The Newtonian Revolution: With Illustrations of the Transformation of Scientific Ideas* (Cambridge: At the University Press, 1980).

35. For Kekule see Herbert C. Brown, "Foundation of the Structural Theory," in *Selected Readings in the History of Chemistry*, ed. Aaron J. Ihde and William F. Keiffer (Easton, Pa.: Journal of Chemical Education, 1965); and for Loewi see Stephen W. Kuffler and John G. Nicholls, *From Neuron to Brain* (Sunderland, Mass: Sinauer, 1976), 147–48.

36. Jacob Bronowski, *The Ascent of Man* (Boston: Little, Brown, 1973), 340.

37. C. S. Lewis, *Letters of C. S. Lewis*, ed. W. H. Lewis (New York: Harcourt, Brace and World, 1966), 27.

38. Gunther S. Stent, "Prematurity and Uniqueness in Scientific Discovery," in his *Paradoxes of Progress* (San Francisco: W. H. Freeman, 1978), 95–113; reprinted from *Scientific American* 227 (1972): 84–93.

39. Peter Mitchell, "Coupling of Phosphorylation to Electron and Hydrogen Transfer by a Chemiosmotic-Type of Mechanism," *Nature* 191 (1961): 144–48.

40. Peter Mitchell, personal communication (1979, 1980).

41. Mitchell, "Coupling," 144–48.

42. Mitchell, personal communication (1979, 1980).

43. R. J. P. Williams, "Possible Functions of Chains of Catalysts," *Journal of Theoretical Biology* 1 (1961): 1–17.

44. G. K. Chesterton, *Tremendous Trifles* (London: Methuen, 1909).

45. Bronowski, *Ascent of Man*, 330.

46. Judson, *The Search for Solutions*, 612.

47. John Gardner, *On Moral Fiction* (New York: Basic Books, 1978), 6, 14.

Science, Discourse, and Knowledge Representation: Toward a Computational Model of Science and Scientific Innovation

WILLIAM FRAWLEY

University of Delaware

Science as Discourse

If we have learned anything from the failure of logical meta-science (the crumbling of observational terms, the possibility of antecedently meaningful theoretical terms,[1] and the fact that scientists do not reason wholly by either deduction or induction in their discoveries[2]) and from the secularizing of science through cognitive and sociological metascience,[3] it is that science is a contingent enterprise. In the wake of this relativism, there has arisen a semiotic/structural metascience based on the assumption that science is a sign system, a method of creating representations of the world and of institutionalizing these representations into coherent systems of extended talk: science is discourse.

Consider in this respect Richard Rorty's articulation of the discursive nature of science:

> Here is another way of looking at physics: the physicists are men looking for new interpretations of the Book of Nature. After each pedestrian period of normal science, they dream up a new model, a new picture, a new vocabulary, and they announce that the meaning of the Book has been discovered. But, of course, it never is, any more than the true meaning of *Coriolanus* or *The Dunciad* or the *Phenomenology of the Spirit* or the *Philosophical Investigations*. What makes them physicists is that their writings are commentaries on the writings of earlier interpreters of Nature, not that they are all somehow "talking about the same thing". . .[4]

Science is a bookish enterprise, and scientists deserve to be called such not because they are uncovering *facts* hidden in nature. A fact, or even a set of facts explicable in terms of a general principle or "law," is verifiable only insofar as it is made public. When scientific facts are put into texts and offered for the consumption of other readers—i.e., other scientists—then a fact or a scientific principle becomes legitimate. Only when it is legitimate can it ever be subject to further commentary and attempts at verification. Jurgen Habermas discusses this issue quite pointedly, and though his arguments are not specifically directed at science, they are worth noting here.[5] Legitimacy is a concept's claim to recognition, and recognition of a concept must precede a concept's validation or test of correctness. Legitimacy can be established only through verbal argumentation, through the verbal construction of good reasons for considering the validity of a concept. "But," says Habermas, "whether reasons are 'good reasons' can be ascertained only in the performative attitude of a *participant* in argumentation, and not through the neutral *observation* of what this or that participant in a discourse holds to be good reasons."[6] Good reasons are claims in discourse. As for the case of science, it turns out that discourse is the arena for establishing the legitimacy of facts. In this sense, scientific discourse precedes all factual knowledge; discourse is the first knowledge of science.

Consider the problem of Immanuel Velikovsky. His arguments that the development of the solar system was greatly influenced by astronomical cataclysms caused such a stir *not* because they were tested and proven to be either correct or incorrect (which, in fact, has never really happened). Rather, Velikovsky's ideas were so uproarious because they were permitted legitimacy; they were raised to the level of recognition by being allowed to be part of scientific discourse. Velikovsky's work was controversial not because it was empirical knowledge or empirical folly, but because it was allowed a claim to validation, because it was allowed to be discursive knowledge. And when this happened, its empirical stakes became very minor considerations.

Harold Brown documents this quite well when he discusses the incredible bother over this knowledge in manuscript form, ready to be made public.[7] He quotes Hadas as a pertinent indication of the discursive basis of the Velikovsky controversy:

As Moses Hadas argued with respect to Velikovsky: "what bothered me was the violence of the attack on him: if his theories were absurd, would they not have been exposed as such in time without a campaign of vilification?"[8]

The problem with Velikovsky was that he was allowed a position in the ongoing commentary known as "astrophysics," and this discursive legitimization of his claims could be countered only with opposing discourse. Thus, when Velikovsky's "facts" were legitimized even to the point of recognition in one of the highest "courts of knowledge" in the world, the American Philosophical Society, they were dismissed there with counterdiscourse as unorthodox, and Velikovsky's rebuttals to the counters were not allowed to be printed in the proceedings of the debate on his own theories, even though the statements of his opponents were allowed to be printed![9] But the APS was guilty of a tack taken by several other professional journals in disallowing rebuttal by Velikovsky. This demonstrates clearly that refutation and proof are properties first and foremost of discourse, and the ultimate refutation in science is not empirical falsification, but denial of access to the arena of scientific discourse: the labeling of knowledge as illegitimate and with no right to be propagated in texts or to generate commentary in the form of other texts. Proof, likewise, is permission of discourse and permission of commentary on that discourse. Thus, Velikovsky has never been disproven in the empirical sense, and some of his claims have even been validated in the empirical sense (such as his claim that planets emit radio waves).[10] But these empirical findings are superfluous since his texts remain illegitimate and, therefore, "wrong."

This notion of legitimacy and scientific knowledge as a property of documents is at the heart of Michel Foucault's well-known analysis of the structure and progress of systems of human knowledge:

> . . . science is not linked with that which must have been lived, or must be lived, if the intuition of ideality proper to it is to be established; but with that which must have been said—or must be said—if a discourse is to exist that complies, if necessary, with the experimental or formal criteria of scientificity.[11]

Scientific knowledge is not the experience of trained observers, no matter how their perceptions of the world are colored by "paradigms"; scientific knowledge is what an individual who has been inculcated into a particular mode of talking possesses. He learns a way of constructing connected statements. The various scientific disciplines are differentiated by their respective discursive practices, or the modes of discourse propagated by scientific readers and writers. Thus, scientificity is a characteristic of a group of verbalizations

> . . . formed in a regular manner by a discursive practice, and which [is] indispensible to the continuation of science, although [it is] not necessarily destined to give rise to one, [and] can be called *knowledge*. Knowledge is that of which one can speak in a discursive practice . . . there is no knowledge without a peculiar discursive practice; and any discursive practice may be defined by the knowledge it forms.[12]

In short, discourse provides science with the functions normally attributed to it as a body of knowledge: discourse defines objects and invests them with scientific status; discourse gives sciences their logics and their connectivity of statements; discourse accounts for the origins of sciences in emerging discursive practices and accounts for the propagation of sciences through the construction of, as Alisdair MacIntyre states, narrative accounts of the operation of the world, or re-tellings which subsume previous narratives.[13] In more philosophical terms, this progression of narratives, discourses, is called "building a better theory."

But if science can be viewed as discourse, why should science first of all be discourse? There are two reasons for this: the function of discourse in knowledge processes and the methods by which an individual becomes a scientist.

The function of discourse is that it provides what Richard Boyd has called "epistemic access," the means to knowledge of the world gathered by the mediation of language for parts of the world.[14] Imprecise scientific vocabulary affords access to the world prior to observation and refinement of such language. Metaphors, for example, function as such imprecise terms in the propagation of access to parts of the world. So, to call the "mind" a "computer," as a cognitive scientist might, is to provide a whole range of accesses to "mind" by means of components of the metaphor for it: "computation," "decision-making," "problem-solving," and so on.

Now one can easily see the relevance of epistemic access to the discursive basis of science. What discourse does for science, as the arena of the legitimacy of knowledge, is to provide epistemic access to other—even idiosyncratic—versions of scientific knowledge for readers, as for example, scientists. What discourse does for science is to allow language to extend the senses of the scientists by providing coherent articulations of terms which stand in lieu of, and often for only parts of, potentially observable phenomena.[15] Discourse provides scientists with epistemic access to all sorts of phenomena and explanations that are beyond their immediate circumstances, senses, or understandings. And this of course stands to reason since a scientist is a single person and cannot possibly explain, much less observe, all of the world himself. Discourse sets up possible systems; it fixes reference, to use Boyd's terms.

This entire function of epistemic access is nicely illustrated in the works of Thomas Kuhn, who describes, in the introduction to one of his books, his own grappling with epistemic access and the facilitation of his verbal reasoning and comprehension through his recognition of the function of scientific terms in discourse.[16] In *The Essential Tension*, Kuhn describes how he had difficulty coming to grips with what seemed to be Aristotle's wild misconceptions about motion, and he was puzzled not only because Aristotle seemed to be wrong in defining "motion" as "change of state," but also because he was convinced that Aristotle was normally an acute thinker (so how could he have been wrong?). As it turned out, Kuhn's expectations about Aristotle's acuity were correct, which forced him to rework his entire consideration of Aristotle's definition of motion to make Aristotle's acuity parallel his physics. But Kuhn resolves all of this in discursive terms:

> I all at once perceived the connected rudiments of an alternate way of reading the texts with which I had been struggling. For the first time I gave due weight to the fact that Aristotle's subject was change of state in general, including both the fall of a stone and the growth of a child into adulthood.[17]

In other words, Kuhn gained epistemic access to Aristotle's terms by comprehending the connectedness of Aristotle's discourse: his verbal reasoning about the term *motion* was facilitated by Kuhn giving himself over to the terms in the discourse that Aristotle produced.

A second value of epistemic access through discourse is that discourse allows scientists to make claims divested of any empirical commitments in the doing of their disciplines. For example, the introduction of a term such as *DNA* into a discourse evokes verbal reasoning about the relatedness of terms in the discourse without forcing scientists to test or experiment. This sort of verbal reasoning distances scientists from the world. As a result, through the logic of discourses, scientists can construct explanations regardless of the falsification or verification of the claims, which introduces astonishing leeway into the scientific enterprise. That is, epistemic access through discourse provides scientists with continual thought experiments, wherein imagined connections of terms have no immediate consequence for the world to be explained. Thus, epistemic access through discourse allows for the construction of possible systems and alternate ways of reading the world.

Just as the function of discourse in knowledge processes justifies viewing science as discourse, so the function of discourse in the development of scientists proper supports the notion of the discursive basis of science. Scientists are literally made, not born. But there are no self-made scientists, if indeed there ever were. A scientist is a credentialed individual, one who is licensed by the status quo as a participant in the social group called "scientists," and the only way for a person to gain such a license is to apprentice himself to other scientists, which involves spending a great deal of time in school.

Now this may seem rather obvious, but when one examines the function of schooling, the idea becomes less simplistic. The purpose of schooling is to introduce individuals to the universe of discourse. School is propositional knowledge, and the function of schooling is the inculcation of various ways of talking about the world. Science as discourse is therefore not unique; science is one type of propositional knowledge that permeates all schooling.

There is ample evidence from psychology and sociology for the discursive nature of school knowledge. David Olson, for example, has remarked that schools

> are tied to a specialized language and to a specialized form of knowledge as a consequence of our reliance upon written prose. Literacy is not only a primary goal of schooling, it is deemed necessary for the achievement of other goals. The advantage of that bias is that virtually every activity becomes an occasion for developing

competence with that use of language and that form of knowledge. The disadvantage of that bias is that all forms of knowledge and competence come to be translated into prose text.[18]

Moreover, the permanence and autonomy of school knowledge in texts give scientific knowledge its function since its seeming persistence in codified form and its immunity to alteration ("the meanings specified are lodged unalterably in the text itself"[19]) suggest that scientific knowledge, in texts, is objective.

Similar arguments have been made by Basil Bernstein, who has noted that

> educational knowledge is uncommonsense knowledge. It is knowledge freed from the particular, the local, through the various explicit languages of the sciences or implicit languages of the arts which make possible either the creation or the discovery of new realities.[20]

The language of schooling Bernstein calls the educational code, and the semiotic implications are pertinent since school instructs people in modes of symbolization through different discourses. These codes then "create new realities": the world is a derivative; fact is a construct, a selection. What precedes fact is the ability to construct a linguistic representation of the fact. School teaches this coding procedure through the construction of propositional systems, discourses, which splinter into disciplines through the natural dialectal differentiation of language.[21]

Science, then, is a by-product of this verbal process. One can easily see how the verbal reasoning so crucial to epistemic access is built into the structure of science as discourse. And one can further see how science is a peculiarly Western product since it is only in the West that explanatory discourse, science, is propagated, with verbal reasoning taking precedence over other lowly regarded forms of logic. Michael Cole and S. Scribner's work on cross-cultural logic, in fact, points this out.[22] They studied the abilities of indigenous African people (the Kpelle of Liberia, in particular) to solve verbal logical problems, hinging on the conjunctive logic of "and" or the disjunctive logic of "or." Simple logical problems turned out to be easily solved by Westerners but were enigmatic to the Kpelle, who solved logical problems incorrectly or gave conclusions based on what appear to Westerners to be irrelevancies. However, when Cole and Scribner gave such problems to Kpelle who had been to school—who had become familiar with discursive knowledge—the Kpelle answers improved markedly, so much so that there was a strong positive correlation between increase in formal education and swiftness and correctness of response to verbal logic problems. Schooling—verbal reasoning in discourse—allows such problems, simplified versions of the logical quandaries endemic to science, to be solved quickly and successfully.

Needless to say, indigenous African people have neither schooling nor Western science. But it is perhaps more appropriate to say that they have no Western science because they have no schools. The institutionalized problem-solving based on verbal reasoning in discourse is a product of the West and constitutes science in extended talk.

The Discursive Basis of Innovation

If the case has been established for the discursive basis of science, then the case for the discursive basis of emergent scientific knowledge must now be made. How does science advance? Naive metascience would have it that advances in scientific knowledge come from observations of new or inexplicable phenomena. No matter how theory-laden our facts turn out to be, naive metascience would tell us that new facts are the basis of scientific innovation. But if discourse precedes fact, as argued above, the place to look for innovation is obviously discourse.

Consider the case of biochemistry. How did it begin? That is, how did biochemistry emerge as a new form of science? One would imagine that biochemistry, a ruthlessly empirical science, began with observations of, and experimentation on, the chemical explanation of life. But this is an oversimplification. Biochemistry, it is generally assumed, can be traced to the publication in 1842 of Justus von Liebig's book *Animal Chemistry*.[23] This assumption indicates that scientific innovation is traceable not to phenomena and observation, but to the articulation of a coherent set of statements in a text. The problem of biochemistry as an emergent discipline bears this out nicely.

Liebig, quite frankly, founded biochemistry at the expense of data and fact and for the purpose of propagating a new discourse. When Liebig articulated the germ of biochemistry, it was in direct contrast to what was the trend of the day in organic chemistry: namely, the synthesis of organic compounds. Curiously enough, Liebig's book was originally commissioned by the British Association for the Advancement of Science as a state-of-the-art work on organic chemistry. But Liebig disagreed with the basis of that science, and "against the background of this factual development of organic chemistry, adherence to the goal of a chemistry of vital processes led to a special development": biochemistry.[24]

In his entire life, Liebig

> carried out one experiment on living animals, and that had been done more thoughtfully by Boussingault before him. As an organic chemist, he had never systematically directed his investigations toward biological materials. As an analyst, he had developed a highly successful procedure for the determination of carbon and hydrogen, but his method was of principal importance in the study of pure compounds. When applied to albuminous materials it would only prove misleading . . .[25]

And when he was at the height of praise for having founded a new experimental science, Liebig was offered a professorship at Munich, which he took on the "condition that he not be required to direct a laboratory."[26] What could be more accurate testimony to the unempirical nature of scientific innovation?

How, then, did biochemistry flourish in its early stages? It thrived chiefly through the word. The value of Liebig's work was that it retold the narrative of chemistry, to use MacIntyre's phrasing, in the biological mode. And although much of Liebig's text also presented his own ignorance or misinterpretation of the findings of other researchers,[27] his success as a polemicist and his prominent position in the scholarly community forced a new mode of discourse into the scientific texts of the day. The assertions that Liebig made (such as those on the relation between muscular work and protein consumption or those on the irrelevance of microorganic processes) were subsequently discredited empirically, but his asserting such things in discourse legitimized the concepts he was propounding: his assertions were all that counted.

Liebig's notorious expertise at rebuttal allowed for extended commentary in the journals on conclusions that would soon prove false (empirically), but the falsification was secondary to the appearance, in the journals of the day, of lengthy discourse on chemistry cast in the biological mode. Liebig, himself, "dealt out his own deck" in this matter by using his editorial influence—that is, by using his position in control of the production and dissemination of discourse:

> He held a dominant position in the *Annalen der Chemie und der Pharmacie* (the leading German chemistry journal and, at the same time, the leading international journal of organic chemistry), and thus he could give agricultural chemistry the backing of organic chemistry which was developing with extraordinary success.[28]

In other words, he could give biochemical discourse the legitimacy of organic chemistry through his position on the editorial board.

> To this end Liebig in 1840 modified the traditional classification in the *Annalen* (in which investigation in agricultural chemistry would have appeared only under the item "Mixed Notes") and had all relevant publications, including his own works and polemics with other scholars, appear in the *Annalen.* In addition, Liebig ensured that agricultural chemistry was given a prominent place in many of the handbooks and textbooks published.[29]

What Liebig did was to ensure the place of the discourse he founded in the discourses of his day; he reached both the established readership through the *Annalen* and the emergent readership through the textbooks. It mattered little that most of his claims were subsequently disproven, except that the failure of his claims had, with poetic justice, the consequence of preventing his own access to the discourse that he had begun and propagated years before. When his claims gradually proved groundless, his own discourse was discredited, so much so that ". . . the *Journal of the English Agricultural Society* refused to publish Liebig's answer" to reports contrary to his theories.[30] Liebig thus met a Velikovskyan fate in being disallowed participation in the discourse for which he was responsible.

The case of biochemistry is not unique, however. Research has shown that the sources for most scientific innovations are discursive. One finding of L. J. Anthony, H. East, and M. Slater's work on the production of physics literature is that chemists and physicists, when asked to list their sources for new ideas, gave not a single source that could in any way be construed as empirical or experimental![31] By far, the dominant sources for new ideas were journals and conversations with colleagues—two discursive sources.

H. M. Collins's study of innovation in laser design further supports the discursive source of scientific ideas, though he might object to this rendering of his findings.[32] Collins argues that the development of tacit understandings among scientists, so crucial to innovation in science since it provides presupposed knowledge, "is not like learning items of information, but is more like learning a language."[33] And his quotation of Peter Winch stands as explicit evidence that priority in scientific innovation must go to discourse:

> Imagine a biochemist making certain observations and experiments as a result of which he discovers a new germ . . . assuming that the germ theory of disease is already well-established in the scientific language he speaks. Now compare with this discovery the impact made by the first . . . introduction of a concept of germ into the language of medicine. This was a much more radically new departure, involving not merely a new factual discovery within an existing way of looking at things, but a completely new way of looking at the whole problem of the causation of diseases, the adoption of new diagnostic techniques, the asking of new kinds of questions about illness, and so on.[34]

In short, the introduction of the word *germ* into the discourse of medicine has more radical impact on science than does the factual observation. Why should this be so? To sum up the previous arguments: discourse provides the arena of legitimization of the innovation; discourse provides epistemic access to the innovation for other scientists/readers; discourse provides the means of propagating the innovation in the schooling of new scientists, in the institutionalizing of their verbal logical patterns. Discourse allows the innovation to be an innovation.

A Computational Model of Science and Scientific Innovation

Heretofore I have argued that science and scientific innovation are discursive. If this is granted, then a model of such knowledge and of such changes in knowledge is a description of the sorts of information that appear in discourses. The most complete method of representing discursive knowledge can be found in Artificial Intelligence and Cognitive Science, where considerable theoretical advances have been made in the representation of textual and discursive information by using computational-semantic formalisms.

Essentially, Artificial Intelligence and Cognitive Science view discursive information as an elaborate, encyclopedic lexicon structured into a network by means of a finite set of relations. Researchers in these areas focus their analyses on restricted semantic domains, or "frames,"[35] to use the AI phraseology, and they try to represent, in terms of a network, the total knowledge that individuals must possess in order to speak about—in other words, to produce discourses about—these domains. The classic example of this can be found in R. Schank and R. Abelson's work on the "restaurant frame," which is a representation of all of the information that an individual must know about restaurants cast in terms of a lexicon connected by logical relations.[36]

It is not my purpose to discuss Schank and Abelson's work, but simply to point out that the total information in a restricted semantic domain can be represented in a computational-semantic formalism (a lexical network) and that this representation forms the basis of a discourse understanding/ production system about the restricted semantic domain. (The reader is referred to their work for the details and the justification.)

Now if the information underlying ordinary language discourses can be represented in computational-semantic formalisms, and if science is discourse, then perhaps the model from Artificial Intelligence and Cognitive Science can be generalized and applied to the semantic domains of the sciences to provide a representation of scientific information. For the past few years, I have been working on just such a project; it involves the reduction of scientific lexicons to formal networks connected by a finite set of lexical relations. These networks, called in the AI literature "knowledge structures," are encyclopedic representations of the information in scientific disciplines; they are models of the knowledge underlying scientific discourse.

Of course, the crux of this project is the choice of the relations that constitute the network, which connect the lexicon. Fortunately, considerable work has been done in computational semantics on these relations,[37] and there now exists a fairly detailed list of relations for knowledge structures underlying discourse. Outlined below are twenty-three lexical relations that, at the time of this writing, have proven to be productive in the representation of scientific knowledge structures underlying scientific discourses. This does not mean, of course, that all of science can be captured in the twenty-three relations: if scientific knowledge could be captured in a set of one hundred relations, that would be a great feat. Thus, the twenty-three relations defined below and illustrated by means of scientific concepts represent a first step in the model suggested above.

The list that follows contains four types of relations: (1) the logical relations, which express the classic notions found in the structural semantics literature; (2) the syntactic relations, which describe basic case relations; (3) the processual relations, which represent basic verbal processes; and (4) the aspectual relations, which express the sorts of distinctions ordinarily found in verbal aspect systems. Furthermore, the "formulas" given as examples are to be read as follows: the first term is related to the second term by means of the relation in parentheses connecting the two terms. The terms used in illustration below are taken from the following sciences: geology, astrophysics, chemistry, mathematics, and biology.

LOGICAL RELATIONS	ILLUSTRATION
HYP: generic; taxonomy; class membership	elastin (HYP) protein
ID: synonymy; identity	pi (ID) 3.141
ANT: antonymy; opposition	electron (ANT) positron
ABS: absence of; lacks	xenoblast (ABS) crystal faces
LIKE: analogy; similarity	whipstock (LIKE) wedge
P/W: part/whole; is a part of	algae (P/W) cryptophyte
GRAD: gradience; occurs in a series with	orogeny (GRAD) postorogeny
PROV: provenience; is a source of	cubeba (PROV) cubeb oil
ATTR: is a nonconstituent attribute of	zero spin (ATTR) pion

SYNTACTIC RELATIONS	ILLUSTRATION
AGT: agent; does process	star (AGT) fusion
PAT: is affected by; is object of	positron (PAT) pair annihilation
INSTR: instrument; used for; used in	potassium cyanide (INSTR) alloys

PROCESSUAL RELATIONS	ILLUSTRATION
RES: promotes	acid catalysis (RES) novolaks
CAUSE: causes (directly)	downfault (CAUSE) inglenook

LIQU: destroys
DOM: dominates; controls; is
  central part
TRANS: transfers; give off
CHNG: becomes

lysis (LIQU) cell
insulin (DOM) carbohydrate
  metabolism
bacteriophage (TRANS) DNA
pion (CHNG) muon

ASPECTUAL RELATIONS
FIN: ends; stops; completes
INCEP: begins; starts
MULT: increases, addition of
DEGRAD: decreases; reduction
  of
AGGR: is unit, aggregate, or
  measurement of

ILLUSTRATION
auxin (FIN) fruit drop
ecdysone (INCEP) ecdysis
synthesis (MULT) enzyme
diakinesis (DEGRAD) chias-
  mata
skerry guard (AGGR) skerries

Given that the formalism for representation is sufficiently illustrated above, consider how science as discourse could be modeled by means of these mechanisms. Suppose that we ask a
biologist to tell us, in biological discourse, what "morphactin"
is and does. That is, suppose that we asked a biologist to produce a discourse about a concept in his or her discipline. The
biologist might respond with something such as the following:

Morphactin is a collection of compounds. It comes from, chemically, fluorinecarboxylic acid, and it works, mainly, on plants. Basically, morphactin controls plant growth; in fact, it prevents plant
growth. In particular, morphactin stops phototropism and geotro-
pism; it terminates seed germination and lateral root development
and completely eliminates apical dominance in the plant. What
results from morphactin is essentially a plant dwarf since plant
growth is controlled. This is quite unlike the effect of auxin on
plants, which promotes plant growth.

All of the information in this discourse can be captured by the
formalisms given above:

morphactin (AGGR) compound   *morphactin is a collection of com-*
                                pounds
morphactin (PROV)   *it comes from, chemically,*
  fluorinecarboxylic acid   *fluorinecarboxylic acid*
plants (PAT) morphactin   *and it works, mainly, on plants*
morphactin (DOM) growth   *basically, morphactin controls*
                                plant growth
morphactin (DEGRAD) growth   *in fact, it prevents plant growth*

morphactin (FIN) phototropism	*in particular, morphactin stops phototropism and*
morphactin (FIN) geotropism	*geotropism*
morphactin (FIN) seed germination ⎱	*it terminates seed germination*
morphactin (FIN) lateral root development ⎰	*and lateral root development*
morphactin (LIQU) apical dominance	*and completely eliminates apical dominance in the plant*
morphactin (RES) dwarf	*what results from morphactin is essentially a plant dwarf*
morphactin (ANT) auxin	*this is quite unlike the effect of auxin on plants*

This is a descriptive model, or a metascientific account, of a small piece of biological discourse. This formulaic knowledge structure is basically an encyclopedic definition of the term *morphactin,* but it is a definition quite unlike an Aristotelian definition in that it goes beyond simple genus and species and specifies the full range of the term's connectivity in biology. In order for biologists to speak legitimately of *morphactin,* they must know that the term bears distinct relations to other terms in the discourse: what is represented above is the tacit knowledge (following Polanyi) that biologists must have at their command in order to participate in biological discourse about this term.

But if the above discourse seems slightly contrived, consider the following discourse extracted from a larger piece of a study in theoretical mathematics. The essay concerns the use of differential geometry in representing heartbeat and nerve impulses; this section describes the relation between pacemaker waves and muscle fiber contraction:

LINE
1   Now the speed of P depends upon the conductivity of
2   the heart tissue, which is not the same in all directions.
3   Perhaps the best way to model this is to represent H by a
4   surface (with singularities) and represent conductivity by
5   a Riemannian structure on H. We can then define P to be the
6   solitary wave, of amplitude b_1—b_0, emanating from the
          pacemaker,
7   and propagating over H according to Huyghens' principle,
8   at speed determined by the Riemannian structure.
          Consequently

9   the wave front is given by the geodesic flow of H, emanating
10 at a given moment from the pacemaker.
11   We summarize the difference between the pacemaker wave
       P
12 and the muscle fiber contraction. The former is global and
13 the latter local. The former triggers the latter. Both depend
14 upon electrochemical mechanisms, but the former is
       primarily
15 electrical, while the latter is primarily chemical . . .[38]

The structure of the information in this discourse, too, can be represented in the computational-semantic formalisms given above (the lines are indexed):

REPRESENTATION	LINE
conductivity of heart tissue (RES) speed of	1–2
speed of P (ABS) same in all directions	2
H (ID) surface	2–3
singularities (ATTR) surface	4
conductivity (ID) Riemannian structure on H	4–5
P (ID) solitary wave	5–6
amplitude b_1—b_0 (ATTR) solitary wave	6
pacemaker (PROV) solitary wave	6
solitary wave (TRANS) over H	7
Huyghens' principle (DOM) solitary wave	7
Riemannian structure (DOM) speed	8
geodesic flow of H (RES) wave front	9
pacemaker (PROV) wave front	10
pacemaker wave P (ANT) muscle fiber contraction	11–12
global (ATTR) pacemaker wave P	12
local (ATTR) muscle fiber contraction	12–13
pacemaker wave (CAUSE) muscle fiber contraction	13
electrochemical mechanisms (RES) pacemaker wave P	13–14
electrochemical mechanisms (RES) muscle fiber contractions	13–14
electrical (ATTR) pacemaker wave P	14–15
chemical (ATTR) muscle fiber contraction	15

While it can be granted that the above representation misses the rhetorical connections in the discourse, the connectivity of the information is captured. Thus, this discourse, which is a legitimate statement (since it appeared in print within formal academic publishing) of the mathematical representation of electrochemical processes in the heart, is accountable to the

formalisms of a computational-semantic metascience. Represented above is the tacit knowledge that a mathematical physiologist must have in order to speak about—i.e., to know—the
physiological processes being described.

It appears, then, that structure of information in scientific
discourse can be captured rather easily in computational-
semantic formalisms. But since it was further claimed that innovations are also discursive, can those additions to scientific
discourse likewise be accounted for and represented by the
sorts of structures outlined above? To answer that question, we
must first know what it means to have an innovation in discourse according to the model proposed to account for discourse.

If innovation is effected through discourse, and if discourse
consists of elaborate formal knowledge structures, then an innovation is some change in the underlying semantic network.
The most common way for semantic networks to change is
through the filling of a "lexical gap," or a "hole" in the semantic
network. No network is ever complete. Any term in the network may have the full set of relations given above extending
from it, but that is an idealization. Every network has *gaps,*
points where certain relations do not come from a term. For
example, take the science of linguistics. What is the opposite of
the term *rule* in linguistics? There is none, and it seems rather
absurd to ask for it; it is like asking for the opposite of *table.*
Thus, the knowledge structures underlying the discourse of
linguistic science have the term *rule* in them, but there is no
term connected to *rule* by means of the relation ANT. The absence of this relation does not rule out the possibility that *rule*
could be antonymically related to another term; if researchers
in linguistic science were to come up with such an notion, then
an entire discourse would be generated legitimizing this new
lexical connection. In this way, an innovation would be effected
in linguistic science by the filling of the lexical gap between *rule*
and some other term connected to it by ANT.

We can find numerous examples of innovation in scientific
discourse generated by the filling of lexical gaps. For example,
when the positron was discovered, theoretical physicists reasoned, wholly in discursive terms (since no other such objects
had been discovered), that the other atomic particles ought to
have antimatter correlates. The entry of *positron* into the semantic network underlying physical discourse demanded that an

antonymic relation extend from the extant term *electron:* electron (ANT) positron. Such an antonymic relation, however, was absent from the term *proton,* and the precedent of the antonym of *electron* allowed physicists to see the gap in the semantic network and permitted them to augment the network through antonymies extending from other terms for atomic particles. Thus, a negative proton was posited—not yet observed—in the antonymic gap extending from *proton:* proton (ANT) negative proton. In this manner, the semantic network imposed a new distinction on the world for the physicists as a result of the semantic innovation in the knowledge structure underlying physical discourse. Granted, the negative proton was later observed, but it was first postulated as a theoretical semantic entity inferred solely from a gap in the knowledge structure.

Other examples of this phenomenon come readily to mind. Consider again the case of linguistic science. If, fifteen years ago, any linguist had been asked where syntax came from (i.e., what "syntax" bore a PROVenience relation to), the response would doubtless have been "What do you mean, 'where does syntax come from'?" No relation to PROV existed. Today, however, if certain linguists were approached with the same question, the answer would be: "From semantics." Over the past decade or so in linguistics, an entire discourse has emerged in elaboration of the relation of PROV for the term *syntax.* This discourse has come to be associated with the Generative Semantics movement in linguistic science; their texts (their knowledge) have as their priority the demonstration of semantics as the source of linguistic phenomena. And this whole process was the same as that which engendered "negative proton" in physics: the concepts were inferable from the semantics underlying the discourse of the science. Just as no physicist had ever seen a negative proton, so no linguist has ever seen syntax come from semantics, but that in no way demeans the validity of the provenience and antonymy relations since those relations are entirely system-immanent. The augmentation of the network and the production of new discourse in accordance with the augmentation were entirely within the bounds of the semantics available for the innovation: that is the only criterion for the augmentation.

One could continue with illustrations of this type of innovation, but it is perhaps best to see it occur in legitimate discourse with the formalisms representing innovations in the semantic network. Below is an excerpt from a recent article in *Scientific American* (1979) describing a new subatomic particle. The entire article is an explanation of a recent innovation in the knowledge of atomic physicists; this excerpt is a direct statement of the innovations:

> For now the solitons of particle physics are entirely the creation of theorists, and it may yet turn out that they do not exist in nature. On the other hand, if the equations that describe elementary particles are found to be among those that admit soliton solutions, then solitons should appear as net particles. They would be very massive, perhaps thousands of times heavier than the proton. A soliton particle would also have certain distinctive properties: for example, one theory predicts that each soliton would be a magnetic monopole, an isolated north or south magnetic monopole.
>
> Even if such particles do not exist, solitons may enter the realm of elementary-particle physics in another role, as objects confined not only to a definite region of space but also to a moment in time. Such evanescent solitons have been named instantons.[39]

The above is a discourse generated by the introduction of a new term into the discourse of atomic physics. The object described does not exist; the discourse is the legitimization of the term in its relations to other extant terms in the discourse of atomic physics. Solitons will "appear as new particles": soliton (HYP) atomic particle. Solitons "would be very massive": massive (ATTR) soliton. Solitons are "perhaps thousands of times heavier than the proton": soliton (GRAD) proton (gradience for weight). Solitons derive from equations for elementary particles: elementary particle equations (RES) soliton. Solitons are magnetic monopoles: soliton (ID) magnetic monopole. Solitons are instantons: soliton (ID) instanton.

Further in the discourse solitons are described as "waves that propagate without dispersing" (the relation [ID]), as deriving from hydrodynamics (the relation [PROV]), as a "transition between two states of a system" (the relation [ID]), and as a cause of a "pattern of particle masses" (the relation [CAUSE]).[40] In other words, the soliton is being described in terms of its completion of the semantic network possible for it. The entire article is an attempt to fix the innovation in the discourse of atomic physics; this is done by linking it to other terms in the existing knowledge structure. But what this illustrates, first and foremost, is that the innovation can be captured in terms of the computational-semantic formalisms postulated for the description of scientific discourse. The success of these formalisms in modeling scientific information and innovations suggests the possibility of a more complete metascience based on computational-semantic procedures for the representation of knowledge underlying discourse.

Implications of the Model

The claims that science is discourse, that the structure of scientific information can be represented in terms of computational-semantic formalisms, and that scientific innovation can be accounted for through lexical gaps may be interesting in their own right, but what do such claims suggest for the study of science and systems of human knowledge in general? There are three major implications of the computational model given above: (1) that a full descriptive epistemology might be developed; (2) that the processes of innovation might be studied in more detail; (3) that a general theory of systems of human knowledge might be constructed.

The first implication derives from Donald Campbell's argument that any metascience must be fully descriptive of the sorts of information possessed and transmitted by members of the scientific community.[41] Logical metascience fell considerably short of this goal in trying to describe the structure of scientific knowledge through a first-order logic and truth conditions; the result was a collection of rather trivial statements, in logical form, of the structure of scientific hypotheses. Cognitive metascience has addressed this problem of complete description, and although Kuhn's notion of "paradigm," with its subsequent revisions in terms of exemplars and disciplinary matrices, has been intuitively appealing, the model has not yet yielded any complete or detailed descriptions of scientific knowledge. The computational model given above is a good prospect for a complete description of scientific knowledge. What needs to be done is to completely reduce to computational-semantic formalisms encyclopedic lexicons of scientific disciplines. This is not such an unattainable project as it might sound. Work has already been done on reducing ordinary language lexicons to such formalisms, and the implementation of the project for specialized lexicons of the sciences is facilitated by the restrictive semantic domain that sciences embody. Thus, a complete descriptive epistemology is at least possible, given the precise tools of representation afforded by the model and the restricted semantic domain to be modeled.

The second implication suggests some interesting possibilities. If scientific information consists of an intensional semantic system underlying scientific discourse, then innovation in scientific knowledge might be investigated in terms of the process by which all intensional semantic systems are known to change. The process of filling in lexical gaps is but one means for a semantic system to change; the discipline of historical semantics has identified numerous other means by which change is effected. For example, the narrowing and broadening of meaning in semantic systems might be investigated insofar as they effect semantic innovation. Is it true, as is ideally thought, that sciences change information by making it more precise, by narrowing? This question could be answered by means of a thorough examination and description of the historical changes in the intensional semantic systems underlying scientific discourse. The process of semantic borrowing might also be investigated; this would show the means by which scientific discourses converge and diverge. For example, do all hybrid scientific disciplines emerge as a result of one discipline borrowing a considerable "piece" of the intensional semantic system of another discipline? Or is there something of a fifty-fifty trade-off across scientific disciplines as far as information goes? Why do some scientific disciplines subsume other scientific disciplines: is there a describable convergence of the two in their intensional semantic systems? Answers to these questions could easily be provided if the semantic systems underlying scientific discourse could be specified in detail; the processes by which scientific innovation comes about could likewise be documented and catalogued.

The third implication is perhaps the most intriguing: can a general theory of systems of human knowledge be developed? For years now, semioticians have been claiming that, from the point of view of discourse, there is really no difference between scientific knowledge and other sorts of knowledge traditionally considered less legitimate than science: literary and aesthetic knowledge, for example. If the arguments given above are correct, then all systems of human knowledge find their unity in expression, in their discursive base. There is no single type of knowledge that has priority in claiming correctness since all specialized forms of human knowledge are subject to the logic of their discursive practices for their legitimacy and correctness. Different types of knowledge result from different types of representations institutionalized into coherent expressions of those representations. If this is correct, then the computational model outlined above is a first step toward a general theory of systems of human knowledge since the model provides a representation scheme that is generalizable across all types of discourses. The computational-semantic formalisms can capture the information structure of any discourse; if very diverse types of human knowledge could be reduced to the computational-semantic formalisms and compared, then some conclusions might be drawn concerning the structure of human knowledge in general. I have attempted this project elsewhere;[42] what remains to be done is to augment the model with a richer set of lexical relations and apply the model to diverse discourses. This is not an insurmountable project, and even an approach to its completion would go a long way toward telling us what it means for human beings to know something.

NOTES

1. See *The Structure of Scientific Theories,* ed. F. Suppe (Urbana: University of Illinois Press, 1974).

2. See Ian Mitroff, *The Subjective Side of Science: A Philosophical Inquiry into the Psychology of the Apollo Moon Scientists* (Amsterdam: Elsevier, 1974); J. Larkin et al., "Expert and Novice Performance in Solving Physics Problems," *Science* 208 (1980): 1135–42; M. McCloskey et al., "Curvilinear Motion in the Absence of External Forces: Naive Beliefs about the Motion of Objects," *Science* 210 (1980): 1139–41.

3. For cognitive metascience see, for example, T. S. Kuhn, *The Structure of Scientific Revolutions,* rev. ed. (Chicago: University of Chicago Press, 1970); Stephen Toulmin, *Human Understanding* (Princeton, N.J.: Princeton University Press, 1972); and Donald T. Campbell, "Descriptive Epistemology: Psychological, Sociological, Evolutionary," The William James Lectures, Harvard University, 1977 (typescript). For sociological metascience see, for example, David Bloor, *Knowledge and Social Imagery* (London: Routledge and Kegan Paul, 1976), and Michael Mulkay, *Science and the Sociology of Knowledge* (London: Allen and Unwin, 1979).

4. Richard Rorty, "Philosophy as a Kind of Writing," *New Literary History* 10 (1978): 141.

5. Jurgen Habermas, *Communication and the Evolution of Society* (Boston: Beacon Press, 1976).

6. Ibid., 200.

7. Harold Brown, *Perception, Theory and Commitment* (Chicago: University of Chicago Press, 1977).

8. Ibid., 163.

9. Ibid.

10. Ibid., 163–64.

11. Michel Foucault, *The Archaeology of Knowledge* (New York: Random House, 1972), 182.

12. Ibid., 182–83.

13. See Alisdair MacIntyre, "Epistemological Crises, Dramatic Narrative, and the Philosophy of Science," in *Paradigms and Revolutions: Appraisals and Applications of Thomas Kuhn's Philosophy of Science,* ed. Gary Gutting (Notre Dame, Ind.: University of Notre Dame Press, 1980), 54–77.

14. Richard Boyd, "Metaphor and Theory Change: What is 'Metaphor' a Metaphor for?" in *Metaphor and Thought,* ed. A. Ortony (Cambridge: At the University Press, 1979), 356–408.

15. Ibid., 383.

16. Thomas S. Kuhn, *The Essential Tension* (Chicago: University of Chicago Press, 1977).

17. Ibid., xi.

18. David Olson, "The Languages of Instruction: On the Literate Bias of Schooling," in *Schooling and the Acquisition of Knowledge,* ed. R. Anderson et al. (Hillsdale, N.J.: LEA, 1977), 77–79.

19. Ibid., 77.

20. Basil Bernstein, *Class, Codes and Control* (London: Routledge and Kegan Paul, 1971), 215.

21. See Donald T. Campbell, "Ethnocentrism of Disciplines and the Fish-Scale Model of Omniscience," in *Interdisciplinary Relationships in the Social Sciences,* ed. M. Sherif and C. Sherif (Chicago: Aldine, 1969), 336.

22. M. Cole and S. Scribner, *Culture and Thought* (New York: John Wiley, 1974).

23. See A. Ihde, "An Inquiry into the Origins of Hybrid Sciences: Astrophysics and Biochemistry," *Journal of Chemical Education* 46 (1969): 193–96; W. Krohn and W. Schäfer, "The Origins and Structure of Agricultural Chemistry," in *Perspectives on the Emergence of Scientific Disciplines,* ed. G. Lemaine et al. (The Hague: Mouton, 1971), 27–51.

24. Krohn and Schäfer, "Origins and Structure," 36.

25. Ihde, "Inquiry," 194.

26. Ibid.

27. Ibid.

28. Krohn and Schäfer, "Origins and Structure," 48.

29. Ibid.

30. Ibid., 47.

31. L. J. Anthony, H. East, and M. Slater, "The Growth of Literature in Physics," *Reports on Progress in Physics* 32 (1969): 709–67.

32. H. M. Collins, "The TEA Set: Tacit Knowledge and Scientific Networks," *Science Studies* 4 (1974): 165–86.

33. Ibid., 168.

34. Ibid., 184.

35. See M. Minsky, "A Framework for Representing Knowledge," in *The Psychology of Computer Vision,* ed. P. Winston (New York: McGraw-Hill Book Co., 1974), 211–77.

36. R. Schank and R. Abelson, *Scripts, Plans, Goals and Understanding: An Inquiry into Human Knowledge Structures* (Hillsdale, N.J.: LEA, 1977).

37. See Y. D. Apresjan, I. A. Mel'čuk, and A. K. Żolkovsky, "Semantics and Lexicography: Towards a New Type of Unilingual Dictionary," in *Studies in Syntax and Semantics*, ed. F. Kiefer (Dordrecht and Boston: D. Reidel, 1969), 1–33; M. Evens et al., *Lexical-Semantic Relations: A Comparative Survey* (Edmonton, Alberta: Linguistic Research Corp., 1980).

38. E. C. Zeeman, *Catastrophe Theory: Selected Papers* (Reading, Mass.: Addison Wesley, 1977), 115.

39. C. Rebbi, "Solitons," *Scientific American* 240 (1979): 92–116.

40. Ibid., 92.

41. Campbell, "Descriptive Epistemology."

42. See William Frawley, "The Structure of Academic Knowledge: Theory and Application," Ph.D. diss., Northwestern University, 1979.

The Poetization of Science

JAMES WAYNE DYE

Northern Illinois University

Consider that on the one hand we praise and seek to encourage creativity in cognitive pursuits, such as science and philosophy,[1] while on the other hand we continue to speak of scientific "findings" and to insist that learning is discovering rather than inventing. In the most general terms, the problem inherent in talk of scientific creativity is that, of the three traditional cultural ends—truth, goodness, and beauty—few persons are willing to attribute to truth the same degree of subjectivity that they would ascribe to beauty or even goodness. Although standards of morality and aesthetics are widely supposed to vary with cultural setting, most persons probably feel uneasy in classifying truth or knowledge as cultural artifacts.

From one perspective this fact may seem to be little more than an accident of linguistic practice, in that "knowledge" and "truth" are terms signifying completion or perfection, as contrasted with mere "opinion" or "belief," whereas we have no such distinction for goodness or beauty and use the same terms to designate both imperfect and perfect forms of those values. However, more is at stake than that, for the issue posed by our contemporary search for scientific creativity is the way in which we are entitled to conceive knowledge, even in its most complete form. Accordingly, I should like to show how we commit ourselves to think of knowing by approving creative endeavor in cognitive pursuits. Assuming that the contemporary standpoint can best be illuminated in contrast to its cultural antecedents, much as one best discovers the distinctive biases of one's native tongue by studying foreign languages, I shall (1) sketch the relationship classically conceived to exist between cognition and creative work, focusing on the views of

Plato as the principal purveyor of this paradigm, and then (2) elicit the contrary conceptions underlying our attribution of creativity to cognitive enterprises.

The Greek term that most nearly approximates our concept of creative activity is probably ποίησις. Ποιεῖν means "to make." Another term, τέχνη, also designates productive ability, but it emphasizes application rather than creation. Although Plato can use it to refer to fields as grand as the whole of intellectual or physical "culture" (δύο τέχνα, *Rep.* 3.411E), he regularly uses it of a "discipline," such as medicine (e.g., *Phaedrus* 270B); and it can even be synonymous with "expertise" or "knowledge" (see *Pol.* 294D, 310A). Whereas τέχνη assumes established rules and methods, ποίησις alone captures the innovative, individual side of practical endeavor. For example, *Phaedo* 89D contrasts inspired poetry with poetry ἄνευ τέχνης, "by the book." A scientific investigator would never be said to be a ποιητής, save incidentally, as when Aristotle observes that Empedocles may be so called, not by virtue of what he does, but solely by virtue of his having communicated his theories in metrical form.[2] Of course, Plato most notably, or notoriously, views ποίησις as the antithesis of the search for knowledge. In the *Republic* he refers to a supposedly ancient disagreement between "philosophy," a relatively new term for inquiry, and poetry. The word he uses for disagreement, διαφορά, suggests a turning or carrying in different directions (*Rep.* 10.607B). He sees creative imagination (εἰκασία) as entirely opposed to that reasoned discourse that seeks understanding by searching out the permanent intelligble structures underlying everyday experience, as it were on the opposite end of a line diagramming our mental functions (6.511). The outcome of creativity, exemplified in poetry and painting but inclusive of all the cultured arts, is the production, through imagination's looking-glass, of a fascinating, entertaining, but entirely illusory realm of fictitious entities. Thus, far from leading towards truth, creative activity leads away from it; in terms of one of the ancient Greeks' favorite dichotomies, it replaces the natural objects whose contemplation is knowledge with purely conventional objects that please rather than enlighten. By thus substituting appearance for reality, it undermines intellectual culture and, ultimately, the whole of society.

In part, Plato doubtless focuses on poetry in his critique of creativity because of all the cultural arts it seems most capable of subverting the mind, its medium being not marble or paint but language.[3] If thought is nothing but "silent inner conversation" (*Soph.* 263E), language is the mind's own medium, in which all knowledge must be realized. Words and statements are properly (μάλιστα) the instruments of the scientist or true inquirer (φιλόσοφος), who uses them to obtain a vision of real existence (τοῦ ὄντος θέας), rather than allowing them to become themselves the objects to which he attends or through which he depicts an imaginary world (*Rep.* 9.582C-D). Much as Kant, two millenia later, holds that lying subverts "the natural purposiveness of the power of communicating one's thoughts,"[4] Plato sees the creative use of language as a misdirection of its natural purpose. Language is the medium of intellectual vision as light is the medium of physical vision; and in the *Phaedo* Plato has Socrates renounce mere observation to pursue the truth of things (σκοπεῖν τῶν ὄντων τὴν ἀλήθειαν) in theories or arguments (λόγους, 99E). In the *Theaetetus* Plato has his interlocutors agree that if perception were knowledge it would have to be τοῦ ὄντος ἀεί . . . καὶ ἀψευδὲς, "always about what really exists . . . and infallible" (152C). However, since only colors and shapes are revealed by light, the realities of nature are revealed only by language. If intelligence, our "eye of the soul," is to apprehend these things-in-themselves, language must be transparent or nearly so. It cannot be manipulated to project before the mind's eye the ephemeral fancies of the imagination, except at the cost of perverting its natural cognitive function.

Yet, even the dramatic poet, conjuring up a powerful, persuasive, and aesthetically pleasing make-believe world by unnaturally combining elements drawn from everyday sensible experience, is strangely admirable—a "holy, marvelous, and delightful" figure who merits our recognition, praise, and worship, although we could not allow him to display his art in a society dedicated to living in accordance with the truth about the world and human nature (*Rep.* 3.398A-B). In the *Ion* Socrates suggests that the poet and his interpreters are not in control of themselves but are possessed by a divine power (536A-D). When inspiration replaces insight and discourse is no longer regulated by the rational ideal of disclosing truth, our mental camera is effectively reversed, converted into a projector whose beam paints images of our own invention over the realities of nature. The poet talks skillfully about anything, as his inspiration may lead him, regardless of whether he has any expertise in the matters of which he speaks. He is not bound by the constraints of the practical craftsman, whose products must be functional and useful. He compounds his images as he wills and is nevertheless successful in his craft provided only that his product is believable and pleasing to an audience. This quasi-divine freedom from constraint is why Plato, as a Greek whose ideal of the highest personal achievement is a self-sufficient life, can admire the creative artist even though he obscures the true features of the objective world.

Just because the creator's activity produces a self-contained world whose significance lies in its own internal coherence rather than in its conformity to reality, he need not limit himself to telling a single tale. The imagination unfettered by utilitarian constraints is free to father many worlds. For Plato this power is reserved to "imitative" art. We shall see below that extending imaginative power to science and philosophy, as Goodman, Rorty, and several other contemporary thinkers have done, is a distinctive feature of another way to understand cognition. But Plato does not so extend imaginative power because it implies a liberty greater than that of the creator of the real world, whose knowledge and goodness permit him to make only the one best cosmos (*Tim.* 29A). Although there is only one reality, there is no one best poem, or best painting, or taking these as paradigmatic of creative products generally, best human creation. To the degree that works are creative, they are novel, indeed, unique. Since they are not bound to be like reality but only to seem real, there is no objective standard of comparison. Things are objectively comparable only insofar as they exemplify the actual relationships between real existences, which Plato calls "forms." However, creations do not purport to accurately represent forms. They are fashioned by the (literally) unruly imagination to the arbitrary tastes of specific cultures. No genuine superiority can be found between two incompatible fantasies, each of which satisfies its respective audience. In the realm of the imagination, it is *chacun à son gout.*

The search for knowledge, however, is governed throughout by the goal of seeing through the phenomena of sensuous experience to the invariant principles underlying their infinite variety. Expression that aims at saying the truth is guided entirely by the one set of principles that actually pertains. This leaves no essential role for our capacity to spin multifarious tales, since it can in nowise clarify or better communicate a vision of that single reality.[5] If there is only one reality, there is only one story to tell, the true one, and all the others are, from the scientific standpoint, wrong and perverse, however admirable they may be aesthetically. For this reason Plato's *Republic* attacks all that is "many" or "manifold" in human culture. To cite one extreme case, perhaps intended to be somewhat humorous, Socrates actually concludes that if only certain musical modes naturally reinforce the proper functions of human life, it is frivolous and dangerous even to possess many-stringed (πολύχορδα) and polyharmonic (πολυαρμόνια) instruments capable of a wider repertoire (3.399D). In this he echoes the language of Heraclitus, whose declaration that "learning many things (πολυμαθίη) does not teach intellectual insight" (Fr. 40), might well serve as the motto for this attitude, which holds the polymorphous excrescences of our imagination to be scientifically useless.[6]

I shall summarize the features of the Platonic view of the relationship of creativity to knowledge. (1) Knowledge is undistorted apprehension of what really exists independently of our beliefs and desires. (2) Knowing is more than just happening to have a correct belief. It is to possess certainty, by virtue of being able to show why that belief is true (*Meno* 98A). The overall effect of a correct scientific theory is to provide an intellectual vision of what really is, much as normal, nonillusory, vision is of visible objects really out there in visible space. (3) Human imagination is not under objective control, being productive of novel form rather than receptive of natural, archetypal form. (4) The products of imagination are self-contained constructions of images rather than concepts, bound by aesthetic rather than logical ties, gratifying perception rather than the intellect. (5) Whereas the value of scientific inquiry lies in truth, the value of creative activity lies in the person of the artist, with his mysterious, semidivine ability to manufacture verisimilitude. Inquiry is the worship of the real; creativity the exaltation of individuality, man's enchanting hybris.[7]

This Platonic perspective, although undeniably filled with persuasive insights, is apt to strike most of us as, on the whole, rather artificially neat. Yet, despite unease with it, its continuing power over the imagination and cultural institutions is evident in the common supposition that scientific and artistic endeavor constitute two distinct and competitive cultures within a common tradition. Some would like to find a physiological basis for this division in the functional asymmetry of the brain, although that conclusion is hardly warranted by present information.[8] Certainly most criticism of Plato has focused less on his separation of these faculties than on his apportionment of their relative importance, their alleged social effects, and especially his proposal to subject the fine arts to strict control. Yet it is the separation itself that is effectively challenged in modern scientific practice. Since it is possible to make a plausible case for slavery being a practice as damaging to master as to slave,[9] Plato's segregation of cognitive and expressive functions should affect the master intelligence as profoundly as the allegedly servile imagination. We need to see whether those consequences are really compatible with our dominant beliefs about art and science.

Perhaps the most outstanding feature of the history of science is that it seems to have as many heroes as does political history or the history of literature or painting. Even for those who would understand this history as a progressive discovery of truth gradually replacing misconception and error, it is undeniable that progress has been discontinuous and that the most significant discoveries have been accomplished by outstanding individuals. The greatest of scientific heroes seem to be those who initiate an interpretation of problematic phenomena with a theory so general that subsequent scientific activity in the relevant fields takes its bearings by reference to it. Obvious examples are Aristotle, Copernicus, Newton, Darwin, and Einstein, or in general, initiators of what Kuhn calls "scientific revolutions."[10] In fact they seem to be heroes for much the same reasons that revolutionary artists are heroes because they invent new styles of expression that effectively found different ways of hearing, seeing, or otherwise appreciating natural or artificial form. It is important to note that the scientific heroes remain such even if the point of view they establish subsequently yields to a different theory covering much the same explanatory domain, just as the status of artistic innovators outlasts the popularity of the styles they set. Since this fact rules out the possibility that we admire them for having discovered "the truth," it is hard to avoid the conclusion that we do so for their having produced conceptually distinctive interpretations that could not have been derived from continued application of previously dominant assumptions, and for having resolved or eliminated recognized problems, thereby opening avenues for research that led to more satisfactory explanations of the relevant phenomena.

For this reason, Toulmin finds the "central aims of science . . . to lie in the field of intellectual creation: other activities . . . are properly called 'scientific' from their connection with the explanatory ideas and ideals which are the heart of natural science."[11] This is not merely true of "activities," but even of those supposedly objective "facts" that many suppose to provide a firm, independent foundation for scientific theory. Within contemporary philosophy of science the first persuasive formulation of this insight was provided by Hanson's defense of the "theory-laden" character of observation. Hanson's point was anticipated in different terminology by the British idealists' and Whitehead's insistence that there are no uninterpreted experiences and by Peirce's arguments against the very possibility of any intuitive faculty in human beings whereby bare facts could be cognized. It is ultimately traceable to Hegel.[12]

As science has its creative side, art has its objective side, apparent if one substitutes terms such as *insight* or *appreciation* for the more scientific notion of *explanation*. P. B. Medawar even finds scientific inspiration more private than artistic inspiration and proposes that isolation as precisely the reason its existence has been doubted. "No one questions the inspirational character of musical or poetic invention because the delight and exaltation that go with it somehow communicate themselves to others. . . . But science is not an art in this sense; scientific discovery is a private event and the delight that accompanies it . . . does not travel."[13] He seems to make an opposite mistake by overlooking the fact that what travels in art is more than just delight and exaltation. There is a sciencelike objectivity to artistic imagination as there is an artlike invention in science. Although, as Plato claims, the arts manipulate the phenomena, they do not do so entirely capriciously. Is it not because they reveal relatively permanent structures of our capacities for perception and emotion that works executed in ancient styles retain a certain charm and practical relevance even when the form of life that occasioned their flowering no longer exists? Art of all periods must come to terms with the permanent possibilities in human nature for jealousy, envy, and ambition, and must provide satisfying expression for our feelings of sorrow, joy, and awe. Surely this capacity to illuminate the invariant bases of the common human experience is a significant condition of a continuing appreciation of old masterpieces of all sorts. The more an art form focuses on a contingent way of dealing with these perennial feelings, the less relevant it becomes once that therapy is forsaken. Most of us would not long mourn the loss of medieval morality plays, for example. The more an art is directly concerned with the passions and moral feelings, as in Greek tragedy, for instance, the greater its continuing value.

In a sense the objects of such art may even be more permanent than those of science, since much of the world of objects investigated by antique forms of science is forever vanished. There just is no transformation of water into air into fire, demonic possession, motion towards the center of the universe, changeless heavens, or a stationary earth to be explained. Plato is doubtless correct in insisting that the cognitive enterprise is to understand that which is; but "being" is the most abstract of concepts, and our positive characterizations of what exists have changed far more radically over the centuries than have the phenomena explored by painter and poet. Plato's error lies in his taking artistic expression to be the only use of imagination and an inferior substitute for scientific understanding. The repeated replacement of one schema of scientific explanation by another testifies to understanding's dependence on imagination, through which "disparate frames of reference" are merged to yield the quantum leaps of novel scientific insights. Thus the difference between art and science lies not in their respective use of imagination or reason but in their purposes.[14] Whereas science is the employment of imagination to construct a coherent and practical worldview, art strives to cultivate and communicate feelings of significance rather than to explain.[15] We comprehend through scientific inquiry; we cope through art. Considered as explanations of the emotions, successful art works may seem ambiguous and illusory, but considered as ways of structuring chaotic feelings and perceptions, they are far from arbitrary, since they deal with the natural foundations of affective experience in terms that are relevant and accessible, without being trivial.[16]

The monuments of creative achievement in artistic culture are just those works that have managed this schematization supremely well, as the monumental achievements in the history of science are those that most successfully have provided an explanatory ordering for important and problematic phenomena. In either case, their creators were necessarily acute observers, because, however mysterious the creative imagination, it does not operate *in vacuo*. Expressing oneself relevantly requires a mastery of technique and material and a cultivated awareness of what, in the light of previous accomplishments, can and should be tried. Creativity is never just doing something different. It is doing something different that is significant at that precise point in the cultural tradition. To achieve this the poet or musician must have a discerning familiarity with recent practice and patterns of expression in his craft as surely as the physicist or mathematician who makes an important contribution must know what needs to be done in his specialty. No innovation in either the arts or the sciences is creative unless it is also perceptive, and that cannot be achieved without "much learning," although expertise never guarantees creativity.[17]

Considering that all cultural activity takes place in a tradition, there is a curious asymmetry about the Platonic account of cognition and creation. Although he certainly recognizes that both activities address issues arising from the tradition, Plato thinks cognition aims at an end, the contemplation of the real, which stands above all temporal and social frameworks. This overlooks the social dimension of knowing. Occasioned by interests communally felt as worthy subjects of inquiry, it must ultimately come back to the community for judgment as to how adequately those interests have been satisfied. "The ideas of science represent a living and critical tradition. . . . progress can be made in science only if men apply their intellects critically to the problems which arise in their own times, in the light of the evidence and the ideas which are then open to consideration" (Toulmin, *Foresight and Understanding*, 110). This fact must color all our thinking about the "truth" that science has traditionally been supposed to uncover.

Assuming that the nature of truth is conformity of language to reality, it is easy to take the test of truth to reside in this same conformity, capable of being recognized, in the experience of certainty, by individual minds. The pragmatists, beginning with Peirce, have led some, although unfortunately too few, philosophers to feel more comfortable with a public test of truth. If truth is established by the continuing and ultimate agreement of competent investigators, there just is no knowledge without social corroboration.[18] Even with the Platonic caveats that knowledge must be of eternal forms and that it must include an awareness of necessary and sufficient conditions, it is always possible for an individual to be deceived in his conclusions by his unconscious and unquestioned presuppositions. Remember, for instance, the misplaced confidence with which Kant thought that eighteenth-century knowledge of logic and geometry was complete, since there had been no progress in those disciplines for centuries. Many contemporary theorists would now agree with Karl Popper's contention that scientific practice does not even aim at confirming hypotheses, since that is an infinite and unrealizable task. Instead, it tests hypotheses in order to refute the unsuitable ones.[19] Truth is approached asymptotically at best. Nelson Goodman is even less sanguine. He sees truth as a primary value only for the most literal and controlled scientific statements, which are inevitably surrounded by metaphorical statements and nonverbal depictions, so that to envision the project of understanding as a search for truth is "a perverse and paralyzing policy." If the Platonic goal of knowing as certain intellectual vision is not a viable one, the scientist's formulations cannot serve as transparent media through which to gaze upon the real. What, then, is their status? Goodman's suggestion is that the appropriate goals of science are "system, simplicity, scope," and that the common values of art works and theories are "their relevance and their revelations, their force and their fit—in sum their *rightness.*"[20]

Here creativity effectively becomes the lifeblood of science. Popper's view is that scientific claims are guesses, proposals that may be tested logically and empirically. Whitehead's often-quoted claim that "it is more important that a proposition be interesting than that it be true" also leaps to mind.[21] Goodman takes the scientific project to be only one among several modes of "worldmaking" (*Ways of Worldmaking*). Even if truth could be contemplated through the lens of language, something must first be said, and the saying is as much a human initiative as is the expression of the poet or painter. That the scientist's special interest is truth rather than beauty ought not to camouflage the fact that his project is possible only through appropriate symbolization. Inquiry presupposes the productive imagination's

positing of significant ideas and formulae if there is to be anything for the conscious processes of analysis and observation to
examine. Which imaginative proposals will be found interesting depends on the context of established interests already
generated by the patterns of behavior prevailing in that society.
As G. H. Mead put it over a half-century ago, "The causal effect
of the living organisms on their environment in creating objects
is as genuine as the effect of the environment upon the living
organism. A digestive tract creates food . . ."[22]

Goodman characterizes the specialized worldviews of the
physicist or artist as departures from "the familiar serviceable
world he has jerry-built from fragments of scientific and artistic
tradition and from his own struggle for survival." Since "reality
in a world, like realism in a picture, is largely a matter of habit,"
any one of the worlds that is right for the appropriate interests
is, in that context, *the* world (*Ways of Worldmaking*, 20–21). The
narrower interests that provoke specialized imaginative construction ultimately infect the common interest by making
more specific desires that were formerly vague and general.
Scientists create ideas that fulfill needs fathered by the institutionalized practice of scientific investigation. In turn,
scientific practice is itself an invention of a wider social practice
that recognizes its value and provides material support for such
activity. Useful novelty is the offspring of this relationship,
which, for example, makes it possible for us, unlike our ances-
tors, to consciously inhabit a world in which there are electrons
and to design useful devices to utilize them. The Platonic perspective views concepts as fixed realities that can only be discovered; a view based on contemporary scientific practice
would have to treat concepts more like tools, fashioned
specifically to handle particular problems that might not have
arisen in a different context of interests established by other
patterns of behavior.

This instrumentalist approach underlies one's praise of and
desire for more creativity in scientific inquiry. It further involves a complete rejection of the Platonic modeling of knowing on seeing, with its consequent separation from the making
characteristic of the arts. Although we continue to employ
metaphors derived from the perceptual model, we talk just as
frequently of problem-solving and of trying proposals to see
whether they fit. The two models are combined in the notion
that science is essentially a method of inquiry rather than a

body of knowledge.[23] It is commonly recognized that the most difficult task of a research project often is to formulate properly appropriate problems so that decisive results are reasonably expectable. The most creative part of inquiry seems to reside largely in generating the right questions. The question is the elemental, indispensable, scientific instrument.

Of course, the ancients, too, made much use of questioning. Plato, at least in his earlier work, champions the Socratic procedure of question, response, and refutation; Aristotle formulates the important principles of his logical (the categories) and physical (the causes) theories in interrogative form; medieval textbooks generally take the form of question and response. What they nevertheless seem to have overlooked is that the objects of knowledge are shaped by the questions the investigator puts to himself. Aristotle is careful to distinguish between the order in which one learns things and the order in which they are essentially related as real existences. The process of learning is indeed shaped by our specifically human and even by our individual abilities and experiences; but the true order of things is captured only in deductive proof, not in discovery. Here there is no inquiry, no making, but only contemplation of eternal truth. Thus, although ancient thought recognized the role of questioning in coming to know, the models of a direct intuitive recognition of concepts and of a finished system of geometrical demonstration dominated their idea of knowledge itself. It is just this that we have now given up, or are in the process of giving up, depending on our relative acquaintance with the object lessons of successive scientific revolutions. Taking its place is a concept of knowing as an inherently fallible process in which human invention does as much to shape knowledge as the other way round.

This is the epistemic necessity underlying the intimate connection of technology and science. With the overthrow of Cartesian, quasi-Platonic physics by the "experimental philosophy" associated with Newton, the scientific tradition turned its back (in principle, if not in vocabulary or explicit awareness) on what Dewey calls "the quest for certainty,"[24] to pursue, not a *vision* of truth, but an experimentally justified *interpretation* of the "book of Nature." Interpretation is not an apprehension of one thing (as generations sought the One, the Good, God, or just Truth), but rather a relating of at least two things in which the more familiar serves as a key for comprehending the less understood. Newton, for example, came to see falling apples, cannonballs, and the movements of the heavenly bodies as the same sort of phenomena; and since he knew something about the forces at work in projectile motion (which could be experimented with), he eventually could account for heavenly mechanics in the same manner, making the supposed uniqueness of superterrestrial matter a superfluous supposition. This hermeneutical procedure rests on the presupposition that we can perfectly understand only what we deliberately do or have made. Just because we have not made nature, the task of understanding it is a rather discontinuous and apparently infinite process of approximation. With something we make, we antecedently formulate the principles of its organization in the light of the goals we wish to implement. The purposes of nature, if there be such, would be intuitively accessible only to an author of nature. Since they are not available to us, our knowledge can only be founded on our artfully constructed guesses. Since we human beings make these guesses, they are in principle "many"—or in other words, expendable and replaceable. We "read" (although we may in the future "scan" or "process" as computer technology becomes more accepted as a source of illuminating metaphor) the phenomena of nature in terms of the familiar structure of our models, and when we encounter anomalies, we construct new models. If imagination cannot immediately generate a single synthesizing image, we do not hesitate to mix models; for example, considering electrons for various purposes as particles, waves, "clouds," or mere quantities—negative charges.

Of course, in practice even the ancients explained things in a similar way. Plato models causes on human purposes[25] and existences on geometrical structures; Heraclitus sees the universe as a conflagration and formulates what one would call the principle of conservation of matter and energy on the model of economic exchange; Aristotle understands conception as a sort of coagulation like what happens in cheese-making; and the Stoics interpret nature as ordered by laws like a city. For Plato, ironically, the adoption of a model of explanation as a direct intellectual "seeing" of rational form makes it impossible for him to comprehend how constructing such hermeneutical instruments is constitutive for knowing. He does not realize the general implications of his own practice because he, like many others, especially Descartes, is taken in by a seductive phenomenon, that mental experience which many, perhaps most, languages dub "seeing." Actually, the experience that feels like seeing is just the emergent quality of the operational process whereby the mind, after some trials, successfully fits some troublesome data into a conceptual template which that individual or his predecessors in a research tradition constructed. The case is similar to that of a pain—a backache, say—that seems simple to feeling, but that we know in fact to be composed of a complex set of bodily circumstances.

Ultimately, a genuinely contemporary perspective must rest on a different conception of human nature than that of the classical philosophers. They took the human being to be essentially a rational animal, *homo sapiens.* Unfortunately, if rationality is understood as a kind of direct perception of objective realities, then, as Kant observed, we have no acquaintance with such intellectual perception in ourselves. It belongs entirely to God (*Critique of Pure Reason,* B72). In the view implicit in present scientific and artistic practice, the distinctive character of being human is more plausibly located in invention than in cognition. Humanity is *homo faber* and even knowledge is among the artifacts it fashions. One tacitly affirms this distinctively human ability in praising and attempting to cultivate scientific creativity in lieu of disinterested intellectual insight. Nevertheless, the desire to be as gods dies hard, especially among philosophers, as is witnessed by the cloud of controversy that arose at the publication of Richard Rorty's masterful examination of the recent history of, and attack on, this old idea that minds can faithfully reflect the realities of nature. Although the attack itself has a clear lineage at least back to Hegel, and Rorty can cite contemporary philosophers as diverse and esteemed as Quine, Sellars, Strawson, Davidson, Sartre, and Heidegger as support for jettisoning all versions of the correspondence theory of truth, many philosophers seem surprised, even amazed, at the articulation of the overall view of cognition implied by the work of these thinkers. Rorty sees their "recoil" as a reaction to the threat to their authority to produce a critique of culture founded on a "permanent neutral matrix" providing "eternal standards."[26] But the changeless, omniscient deity they seek to emulate is concocted by philosophers, made to order to warrant their devotion to the "quest for certainty." Curiously, however, the dominant conception of God in the popular Western intellectual tradition has been God the craftsman, the artisan. The only wisdom to which we can confidently aspire is to be found in imitating that deity rather than Aristotle's eternal and self-sufficient contemplator.

NOTES

1. I shall hereafter refer simply to "scientific creativity" for brevity, although I mean "creativity in the search for knowledge," not all of which is restricted to disciplines conventionally identified as science.

2. *Poetica* 1.1447b12. He calls Empedocles a φυσιολόγος or "theorist about nature."

3. Other reasons are that poetry has a preeminent role in Athenian education and the aforementioned coincidence between the general and specific meanings of ποιησις.

4. *Metaphysik der Sitten, Ak.* 428; *The Doctrine of Virtue,* trans. Mary J. Gregor (Philadelphia: University of Pennsylvania Press, 1964), 93.

5. The *Republic* does propose to use poems and other images to communicate as well as possible with those incapable of more literal, rational thought, namely all children and that vast majority of adults who are not capable of handling exact, abstract concepts.

6. Heraclitus's terminology is explicitly invoked in the treatment of this same topic in *Laws* 7.812Aff.

7. As might be expected of the thinker of whom Whitehead said, "there seems hardly an insight that he has not had or anticipated" (*Dialogues of Alfred North Whitehead,* recorded by Lucien Price [Boston: Little, Brown, 1954], 110), another account of cognition can be extracted from the dialogues. Although it is not the account that has dominated the major span of our cultural history, it was reflected in the skeptical orientation of much of the academic tradition. Moreover, fairness to Plato obliges me to mention what we might today regard as his better idea. At *Phaedo* 85D our cognitive situation is characterized as one in which we take the best theory we can find and set sail with it as a sort of intellectual raft. At *Timaeus* 29 the whole of natural science, as distinct from exact science, is given the status of a "likely story." In Book 10 of *Laws*, the naturalistic worldview according to which everything occurs by chance and necessity is contrasted with the teleological worldview, which sees reality as rationally structured. Although arguments are marshalled for the existence of the gods and the logical priority of intelligence to random motion in the world, these strike me as rather weak or viciously circular. The most impressive point is, rather, the Athenian Stranger's conviction that only a theistic interpretation of things is compatible with the rule of law and order in human society. Nonpurposive naturalism is seen as the ultimate presupposition underlying the justification of the supremacy of arbitrary power in human affairs. Collectively these lines of thinking suggest a view of knowledge more like that implicit in modern scientific practice as interpreted by our better philosophers of science, namely that the best we can do is to work out the implications of alternative worldviews and adopt the one that best satisfies those needs conjointly constituting our currently greatest concern. Since any reasonably coherent worldview satisfies some interests and skillfully handles some of the experiential data, any choice is historically conditioned, comparative, and pragmatic. Apparently Plato never took the next step to

acknowledging that truth is what works rather than what is mentally seen; but he came enticingly close.

8. See, e.g., Howard Gardner, *The Shattered Mind: The Person After Brain Damage* (New York: Knopf, 1974).

9. A point made by Hegel in his famous analysis of the master-slave mode of awareness in the *Phenomenology of Mind*, long before it was made by social historians studying the institution as actually practiced.

10. *The Structure of Scientific Revolutions* (Chicago: University of Chicago Press, 1962; rev. ed., 1970).

11. Stephen Toulmin, *Foresight and Understanding* (Bloomington: Indiana University Press, 1961), 38.

12. Norwood Hanson, *Patterns of Discovery* (Cambridge: At the University Press, 1958), esp. chaps. 1–2; F. H. Bradley, *Essays on Truth and Reality* (Oxford: Clarendon Press, 1914), esp. chap. 5; A. N. Whitehead, *Process and Reality* (New York: Macmillan, 1929), chaps. 7–8; C. S. Peirce, "Questions Concerning Certain Faculties Claimed for Man" and "Some Consequences of Four Incapacities," *Journal of Speculative Philosophy* 2 (1868): 103–14, 140–57; G. W. F. Hegel, *Phaenomenologie des Geistes*, ed. J. Hoffmeister (Hamburg: Felix Meiner, 1952), Vorrede; Sec. A, "Bewusstsein."

13. Peter B. Medawar, *The Art of the Soluble* (London: Methuen, 1967), 155.

14. See G. B. Madison, *Understanding: A Phenomenological-Pragmatic Analysis* (Westport, Conn.: Greenwood Press, 1982), 235–38. Madison also reminds us of other works in which the arts and sciences' common reliance on imagination is argued, including Max Black, *Models and Metaphors* (Ithaca, N.Y.: Cornell University Press, 1962), and Jacob Bronowski, *Science and Human Values* (New York: Harper and Row, 1965), and of a survey of literature on this topic in W. H. Leatherdale, *The Role of Analogy, Model, and Metaphor in Science* (Amsterdam: North-Holland, 1974). He clearly errs, however, in concluding (235) that "scientific entities . . . are . . . convenient fictions," not significantly different from "witchcraft substance." Not every fabrication is a fiction, and no sound one is.

15. Aristotle's assessment of tragedy in the *Poetics* marks the beginning of this understanding of artistic expression. He sees that drama is valuable for its cathartic effect on feeling rather than for its informational content. R. G. Collingwood's idea of art as emotional language, despite its obvious difficulties, captures both the objective, universal character as well as the subjective content of art works; see *The Principles of Art* (Oxford: Clarendon Press, 1938).

16. Of course there is always what Collingwood (*Principles of Art*, chap. 5) calls "art as amusement." Science too has its trite forms, as anyone who watched an episode of the teledocumentary *Cosmos* knows.

17. See Austin Porterfield, *Creative Factors in Scientific Research* (Durham, N.C.: Duke University Press, 1941), passim, esp. 101.

18. See C. S. Peirce, "How to Make Our Ideas Clear," *Popular Science Monthly* 12 (January 1878): 299: "The opinion which is fated to be ultimately agreed to by all who investigate is what we mean by the truth, and the object represented in that opinion is the real."

19. Karl Popper, *Conjectures and Refutations* (New York: Basic Books, 1963), chaps. 1 and 10.

20. Nelson Goodman, *Ways of Worldmaking* (Indianapolis, Ind.: Hackett, 1978), 18–19. Compare this to the view propounded in Stephen Pepper's *World Hypotheses* (Berkeley and Los Angeles: University of California Press, 1948), chaps. 3–4, in which "scope" and "precision" determine the "strength" of a "world hypothesis."

21. Alfred North Whitehead, *Adventures of Ideas* (New York: Macmillan, 1933), chap. 16, sec. 3.

22. G. H. Mead, "A Behavioristic Account of the Significant Symbol," *Journal of Philosophy* 19 (1922): 158.

23. Plato also emphasizes method; indeed, he introduces μεϑοδος into the vocabulary (*Soph.* 218D). However, his emphasis on the utter separation of knowledge and opinion had the more pervasive cultural effect.

24. John Dewey, *The Quest for Certainty* (New York: Minton, Balch, and Co., 1929).

25. See my "Plato's Concept of Causal Explanation," *Tulane Studies in Philosophy* 27 (1978): 37–56.

26. Richard Rorty, *Philosophy and the Mirror of Nature* (Princeton, N.J.: Princeton University Press, 1979), passim, esp. chaps. 4, 7, 8. The quotations are from p. 179.

The Dialectic of Technology and Culture

EDMUND DEHNERT

Truman College

In the effort to study and pursue purity of expression, we very often find ourselves splitting off humanistic concern from concern for technical efficiency.[1] Saarinen's Sydney Opera House is admirable despite the architect's structural miscalculations that caused massive cost overruns. Pei's Hancock Tower in Boston was receiving the highest awards for excellence in design at the very time that poor engineering was causing its windows to fall out.[2] Our legacy from the traditions of humanistic ideas and methods manifests itself in two perspectives. One has to do with the value of conceptualization and the other with the value of completeness and closure. Writers of the Middle Ages were fond of saying that "theology is the queen of sciences and philosophy is her handmaiden." The degree of conceptualization required by an activity or a field of study became the mark of its dignity as an art or a science. We are so accustomed to studying the history of painting and architecture in print and slide reproductions that we become more interested in abstract balance and shape than in questions of texture, technique, and execution.[3] We discuss musical scores as though they were only problems in mathematics or logic, forgetting that a chord when orchestrated and performed has an emphasis, balance, and quality that Rameau's abstractions by necessity have ignored.[4] Architects begin to think of their buildings as only visual phenomena and of themselves as sculptors, as designers and not engineers.[5] Painters and sculptors join the flight from the physical in the refuge of conceptual art. Conceptual artists feel no need to execute art objects. Their function is to invent ideas for art objects. Some people would prefer that their ideas in fact never become actualized works of art.[6] If it ever is executed, the idea, the concept in the artist's mind, is the exemplar. It is a matter of indifference whether or not someone "performs" it; the execution only documents the existence of the idea.[7]

Ever since the Renaissance people have felt a need for ordering their fields of knowledge so that they are totally subject to conscious analysis and management. But technology operates with concrete situations and materials. Unlike the forms of knowledge of greater abstraction, technology cannot devise ideal universes of investigation wherein all variables are controlled. It must function with all possible variables, even those not understood or not anticipated. Gothic buildings had to be stable under the load the wind brought to bear upon them, even though their architects never analyzed wind loading. Abstract sciences use "clean" models; technology's models are "dirty."[8] A musicologist can analyze a sonata in terms of Rameau's harmonic theories, but the pianist who performs it must consider the acoustics of the concert hall, the attention of the audience, the economic marshalling of his or her emotional resources and muscular tension, and the differences between the Steinway used for practice and the Steinway on the stage. One cannot "logically" collate all these factors. Technology does not achieve closure. Methods of conscious surveillance apply to only a limited extent. Beyond that the pianist has to be intuitive or lucky, as were the Gothic architects whose buildings the wind did not blow down.

In the efforts to distinguish and dissect, to find the last abstraction and the basic principle of a field of inquiry, we must not leave behind the concrete world and the living reality from which these abstractions came and in which the principles operate. In abstraction there are hierarchies and queens. In this world the abstractions, entered into action, are beings in time and space. When isolated, fields of study are two-dimensional, studying the principles in the content area they define. But the concrete world is a multidimensional prism of mutual influences. Each abstract field sees through only one facet of the prism. The multiplicity of perspectives reveals that these principles become involved in other content worlds and that the content we abstracted interacts with other principles.

If we distinguish principles in order to unify the conception of this looming chaos of involvement and interaction, there is no problem. The method used does not become the model of the reality to which it is applied. But humanistic perspectives have evolved toward having primarily a negative value: they are the last bastion of defense against the encroachment of dehumanizing technology. It lacks dignity because of its low degree of conceptualization and because it leaves our need for the perfect closed system unsatisfied. Technology, instead of being part of our culture, is seen by many as confronting and challenging it. It is "basically destructive."[9] It is "out of control."[10] It is the "enemy of human life and social interaction."[11] We are reluctant to accede to those who see technology as a force for the better, since they seem to offer hope only if we abandon our former concept of freedom to govern ourselves.[12]

We must overcome this adversary relationship. My work in educational television and film has revealed to me the beguiling intrusions of technology. Awareness begins at a very practical level. The shape of the television screen dictates that paintings oriented vertically cannot be presented as well as those oriented horizontally. The effect of Seurat's pointillism is impossible to duplicate on a television screen. The bold outline and color areas of a Picasso can be presented much more faithfully, not only on television but also in every other form of art reproduction used: books, prints, slides, film.[13] Television is a sight and sound medium. Music heard in such a context is not music heard in a traditional manner: something visual must appear on the screen to accompany it. The music is heard on only a four-inch speaker. Its dimensions, just as those of a painting, must be accommodated to the new medium. Thus the rhythms of Stravinsky can be presented more clearly than the colors of Debussy. Rock music, both in its sound, which by its nature is created and amplified electronically, and in its visual boldness, is much better suited to the television medium.[14] The techniques of color print reproduction enhance some painting styles and diminish others. Musical composition begins to aim at the recorded sound; painting begins to aim at the printed reproduction. But I do not believe this is merely a struggle for survival and coexistence. There are deeper questions. Artists have stimulated technological discoveries and fostered their development as often as they have been forced to react to them. The Greeks could not cast bronze in large sizes, such as that of the seven-foot tall statue of Poseidon hurling a spear (c. 460–450 B.C., National Museum, Athens). In order to produce metal sculpture of heroic size they had to invent welding to join together the smaller cast sections. The first use of electricity, in 1837, was decorative: works of art were printed

with electrotype plate. Nuclear fission began with radiant ex-
posures on photographic plates in the 1880s and 1890s. There
was no idea at the time that any of these technologies would
have military consequences. The Spartans used to say, "The
best dancer is the best soldier."[15]

There is a dialectic of technology and culture. Poland, for
example, has risen in the last forty years to international leader-
ship in graphics and poster design. Its iconography is an art of
quick associations, sometimes absurd, sometimes with double
or triple meanings, but always universal and easily read, always concrete and immediate, utilitarian, in simple flat compositions and avoiding realistic depiction of objects, people, or
facts. Some of this iconography was dictated by political necessity in an occupied country, where written words of protest
could mean death. Some of it flows from the technical purity of
the printing procedure, which avoids photography and mixed-
media techniques. Some of it is prescribed by the context in
which the works are given. Their gallery is the walls and fences
of the dreary city streets of a ravaged country. Some of it was
caused by the rapid rise in the level of communication technology that Poland, a culture quickly evolving from the premod-
ern to the postindustrial, strove to achieve after World War II.
The Polish poster evolved as an anonymous, pragmatic vehicle
of public expression of ideas and communication of information, visually illustrating possibilities and hopes within political
and social constraints. It speaks a unique language of mass
communication based on Poland's history and national traditions. Its metaphors and iconography draw deeply from folk
culture, which, like the country's political history, is a study in
contrasts and contradictions: in politics Poland is a nation that
is not on the map, has freedom under tyranny, is where Chris-
tianity thrives in a communist state; in folklore dark is light,
strong is weak, God is a baby.[16] In 1982 simple images juxtapos-
ing winter and spring speak clearly to Poland's latest oppres-
sors: a melting snowflake next to a flower.[17] No other mass
medium, which can still be considered art, has the same vast
appeal. But this is not a simple case of adapting to technological
forces. Rather, the poster iconography and the technology are
born of the same political, economic, and cultural needs.[18]

Reason and sense, form and matter, concept and reality,
theory and practice, abstract and concrete—one should avoid
all attempts of whatever school of thought to depreciate one

member of any of these pairs in favor of the other. The point of departure should stress their total interdependence. Two principles emerge that provide a basis for interdisciplinary organization of a broader scope than that of the categories of philosophy, history, and the arts. It offers a way to see these fields, science, and technology all as humanistic expression.

First, the study of the dialectic of technology and culture begins by isolating what Aristotle would call the material cause: the media of art, the means of communication of ideas. A culture is a means of coping with present existence. Traditions are active, not static. Cultural monuments are not relics, but manifest and reinforce values that grow from present needs. Art represents and embodies philosophy, history, personal and social identification, and ethical and intellectual ideals. A culture is not a set of categories; it is an organic whole. It is the way in which human beings define themselves and their relations to the persons and things outside of themselves. It flows from their conception of the world. Because such conceptions persist, human beings preserve the culture that embodies them. The preserved tradition establishes a continuity and an identification. It is the way human beings understand and cope; it is their means of survival. Technology has always been part of the practice of human culture, but it has not always been examined in its theory. To study the material cause is to study neither the essence nor the principle of a culture's existence, but the way of its being in the world, the circumstances of its activity, and its processes of communication.

Most cultural awareness of the history of art today, for example, comes not from paintings, sculpture, and buildings, but from pictures of these works of art. This change in the material cause of experience is an expression of the change in our temporal and spatial sense of when and where art exists, of the changed self-conception of those who are the deliverers of culture, and of the change in the audience for art. In the past the interaction of artist and audience was close physically, psychologically, and socially. Now the audience is larger but more distant from the artist and thinks of historians and critics, not of artists primarily, as deliverers of culture. Many strata of society have now entered into the cultural mainstream for the first time. This growth is valued. But this cultural need cannot be satisfied without new communication systems, which in turn evoke new modes of expression in the visual arts. The new media, forms, and cultural patterns interact to create the milieu of this new consciousness. The case is similar in music. Phonograph recordings finally allow musically illiterate persons to "perform" a piece for themselves just as one reads a novel to oneself.

It is often more obvious that material causes change than that human expression and the forms it takes are changing. The temptation would be, then, to say that reproduction has changed our consciousness.[19] A deeper insight affirms that changes in the material cause, in the technology, are self-reflexive: they themselves are expressions of the cultural dialectic of continuity and change. The effect of this approach to cultural analysis is to posit technology as a mode of translation and reinterpretation. As in the instance of Polish posters, technology is one factor in a tension of several forces and its development is an expression of that tension.

This hypothesis attempts to avoid fixing the concept of technology at one or the other end of a hierarchy of inquiry. For example, Aristotle notes the material cause but emphasizes the maker, the form, and the purpose. In theory and contemplation humans are more divine; in practice they are more animal. Aristotle excludes practice itself from the realm of the objects of contemplation.[20] Marx inverts this structure by making the material cause the primary one. The prevailing relations of production give form to the economic basis of society, and this in turn determines the entire cultural superstructure.[21] My hypothesis tries not to prejudge Aristotle or Marx but does avoid beginning with their premises because they—or at any rate Aristotelian and Marxist aestheticians—tend to make technology into an alienating principle: Aristotle because matter is a principle limiting reason and aspiration, and Marx because reason and aspiration are consequences of material circumstances.[22] The alternative thrust of the hypothesis serves to emphasize that all levels of culture and endeavor, including technology itself, are revelatory and expressive.

A second principle takes all of the humanities to be forms of communication. The humanities are all involved in a dialectic search for a definition of what "human" means. That is their principal message. The urban technological culture of the present struggles after the definition in a new context. We are in a holoscopic technology. This pervasion is a function of a new dialectic, a new fusion of expression and the means of expression. Analysis of this dialectic search is derived from information theory. Every communication involves:

SENDER $\not\rightarrow$ CODING $\not\rightarrow$ CHANNEL $\not\rightarrow$ DECODING $\not\rightarrow$ RECEIVER

The sender (an artist, a philosopher, a director of television commercials) codes the message for transmission through the channel (the work of art, an essay, a commercial). The receiver (the audience) decodes the message within a cultural framework of expectation and knowledge. In ordinary conversation, for example, literary or historical allusions are the shorthand of educated people. These frameworks are meant to ease interpretation. They require cultural awareness lest they create communication problems between the sender and the receiver. In this context, rather than speaking of literature, painting, architecture, and music, one speaks of verbal, visual, and musical communication that uses oral, literate, or electronic media. Aestheticians speak so often of "the artist" and "the artifact" that we lose sight of art's interdependence with its world. Disciplinary histories that speak of artists only as influenced by the work of other artists are operating at a level of abstraction a step or two removed. Works of art are fashioned in a context wherein artists are contingent upon an interplay between themselves, their culture, and their audience. This principle of communication is the clearest way to focus on the humanities as fashioned within a culture and as meaningful only in their cultural context.

Found art seems to contradict the principle of communication and the principle of art as organizing and making. By found art I mean anything from an attractive piece of driftwood to Duchamp's *Fountain* (1917), the urinal he chose for an art exhibition, or John Cage's *Imaginary Landscape No. 4* (1951), a musical work that consists of the chaos of twelve radios, each controlled by two persons, one changing stations and the other changing the volume level. These art objects are visually and aurally indifferent; there is no visual or aural syntax. They have sensible form, but there is no concern for their origin, for the manipulation of materials, or for sculptural or musical meaning. The "music" of Cage's *0' 0"* (1962) is the sound of the artist on stage cutting vegetables, preparing them in a blender, and then drinking the juice, all amplified throughout the concert hall. Duchamp and Cage have been called madmen, their works nonsense, nonart, or antiart. At least people do not say that when they see the driftwood I put on my coffee table. Let's begin with that.

People do not experience reality directly. They experience it through the communication networks, the systems of messages that regulate behavior and understanding in our culture. The cultural codes learned from artifacts and rituals teach a way of seeing even that part of the world that is not fashioned and conceived of by human beings. The point was made by Proust, writing of Swann's realization that his beloved Odette bore a striking resemblance to a figure painted by Botticelli:

> . . . . the similarity enhanced her beauty . . . and rendered her more precious in his sight. Swann reproached himself for his failure, hitherto, to estimate at her true worth a creature whom the great Sandro [Botticelli] would have adored.[23]

Just as Proust's Swann does not praise every woman's beauty, so people do not single out every piece of driftwood they see on the beach. We select that one whose shape is accommodated to our way of seeing—that is, to the coding learned from our culture. I *have* made something when I put the driftwood on my coffee table. My creation is a context of communication wherein the cultural framework explains to my visitors what it is about that particular piece of driftwood that is so visually interesting that I singled it out.

Setting up impersonal mechanisms to generate works of art is not a contradiction of a communication theory. In principle, all art is subject to chance, either in discovery or in execution. Stravinsky described composing as aimlessly improvising at the piano "the way an animal grubs about. . . . I suddenly stumble upon something unexpected. This unexpected element strikes me. I make note of it. At the proper time I put it to profitable use."[24] Hayden confessed that skilled performers "often discover beauties which the composer himself did not suspect."[25] Sculptors let the grain of the wood guide their carving; violinists "let the instrument speak." Art is not totally foreseen, nor are Duchamp and Cage abdicating all control. These artists are setting up parameters of the chance events possible. They have carefully chosen the context. The audience's expected reaction to what happens by chance appropriately illustrates the artists' idea and makes their point.

There is no name for this art form. It is not visual art; the elements are not colors, lines, and shapes. It is not music; the elements are not melody, harmony, and rhythm. But it is not mindless. Duchamp's and Cage's art object is a performance set in a gallery or a concert hall, with viewers or listeners attending to the urinal or the chaotic radios, all of this in a situation created by the artist. The urinal and the radios are not syntactical themselves. They do not embody meaning, or at least no more than in traditional art a single word, a single chord, or a single shape embodies meaning. The performance situation embodies it. It is meta-art: art about art. It is a statement about cultural frames and codes and about aesthetic principles, using the idea of sculpture or music as a metaphoric element, carefully calculated to achieve an intended effect. What we know and expect about what is given and received in such contexts in ordinary gallery or concert hall life is the syntactical principle of the interactional event. The audience is meant to observe not the urinal or the radios but rather the context and the meaning of its own behavior in the staged performance. It is a performance about themselves with themselves as actors. It has elements, form, and content; the circumstance encodes the statement, the point Duchamp and Cage want to make. Men and women do not usually reflect upon themselves and the context of their aesthetic events. Our critical disciplines stress artists and art works. Duchamp's and Cage's interactional events are closer to folk ritual, where the audience is the actor and not just a witness. At a wedding I am expected to dance, but when the dancers are isolated up on a stage I must only sit and watch. High culture and popular culture maintain between artist and audience a distance that is physical, psychological, and social. Folk ritual lessens these artist/audience distinctions.

Ordinarily, in the received view of the arts, the viewer takes the object into account. In this alternative way of "doing art" the viewers must take themselves into account. What Duchamp and Cage *make* is the circumstance wherein a meaningless object is presented for aesthetic contemplation. Sculpture and music were expected, but they did not happen. The event is a metaphor that embodies the idea that art is interactional. Their art remains a language for the communication of values. The same point is made by the principles that all the humanities are forms of communication. It is as significant to understand the cultural frame and the distancing between creator and audience, in art, life, and philosophy, as it is to understand the message. Communication is prismatic. The message, the frame, and the distancing are all functions of each other. In this light philosophy and history function as means of cultural frame analysis.

The two principles of the material cause and communication are crucial when ideas and works are translated from one context to another. Before the twentieth century, for example, listeners had to be always somehow in the presence of musicians—in a place, usually a building, where they could see what was going on. Music was situated and visual. Today for every hour of live music experienced we undoubtedly listen to dozens of hours of the radio and the phonograph. I am speaking of purely instrumental music, not just of combinative forms like opera or ballet, where it is obvious that the radio and the phonograph abstract from a work's formative visual elements. In every earlier musical culture there had always been a conception that music was somehow a visual art. Athena, Aristotle related, once found a pair of flutes but threw them away because of the ugly way in which her features were distorted when she blew them. The lyre was preferable.[26] C. P. E. Bach stressed the visual aspects of keyboard art:

> . . . the revealing of [the performer's] own humor will stimulate a like humor in the listener. In languishing, sad passages, the performer must languish and grow sad. Thus will the expression of the piece be more clearly perceived by the audience. . . . in lively, joyous passages the executant must again put himself into the appropriate mood. . . . Those who maintain that all of this can be accomplished without gesture will retract their words when, owing to their insensibility, they find themselves obliged to sit like a statue before their instrument . . . fitting expressions help the listener to understand our meaning.[27]

Friedrich Marpurg said of C. P. E. Bach's father, "I know a great composer on whose face one can see everything that his music expresses as he plays it at the keyboard."[28] Stravinsky wrote in his autobiography:

> I have always had a horror of listening to music with my eyes shut, with nothing for them to do. The sight of the gestures and movements of the various parts of the body producing the music is

fundamentally necessary if it is to be grasped in all its fullness. All music created or composed demands some exteriorization for the perception of the listener. In other words, it must have an intermediary, an executant. That being an essential condition, without which music cannot wholly reach us, why wish to ignore it, or try to do so—why shut the eyes to this fact which is inherent in the very nature of musical art?[29]

In radio and the phonograph the visual elements of music disappear and an unexampled distance intervenes between performer and audience.

Music composed for live performance in the acoustic environments of cathedrals, opera houses, and concert halls is altered by the limitations of pitch transmission and the range of decibels possible to commercially available radios, television speakers, and stereo phonographs. Under controlled conditions, where expense is not a factor, stereo disks have ranges within 30 to 15,000 hertz (or cycles per second), the entire range of human hearing, and volume ranges within zero to 75 decibels. But although record companies proclaim "pristine clarity," "absolute fidelity," and "complete dynamic range," no commercial recording is a faithful reproduction of orchestral sound. Equalization and time delay equipment correct the sonic deficiencies of the halls where the recordings are made. In the case of dynamic range one would not want fidelity. In the space of an average living room, if a symphonic orchestra's pianissimo were barely audible, then its fortissimo would be intolerable. Neither the listener nor the plaster walls would survive. In disk recordings and in both the transmission and reception of commercial radio and television broadcasting, the fidelity of the pitch range below 300 hertz (middle C) is, in practice, weakened. Live music from pianissimo to fortissimo has a range of 75 decibels. Ordinary receivers have a range of only 30; in practice, recordings reach 45 or more. Sound engineers for radio and television broadcast adjust the dynamic range of recordings so that it is nearly a constant mezzoforte.[30]

The opening double bass pedal C (the first thirteen seconds) of Richard Strauss's *Also Sprach Zarathustra* is at a pitch so low (the lowest sound possible in the orchestra) that its fundamental cannot be reproduced by ordinary radio transmission. If anything, one hears the overtones of the pitch. The psychology of hearing is such that the overtone pattern is interpreted as the low C of the basses. Those who know this work only as the theme of *2001: A Space Odyssey*, as it has been heard on television and radio and even on most home stereo systems, have never heard the beginning of the piece. Generally the basses are heard as a rumble, confused as surface noise or the "white noise" of the medium. But the C is essential. The trumpet call that follows is a response to the low C, which is rich in its suggestion: higher sounds must follow, rhythmic patterns and color diversity must begin, and melodies must take shape. The trumpets define the C acoustically by sounding its overtone series. They make clear what it is and relate it to triadic tonal harmonic movement and to orchestral practice. Together the basses and trumpets establish anticipation and musical space.

The television medium provides a visual substitute for the C that it cannot broadcast. The Earth, surrounded by the vast distances of space, for example, is shown. Music and image are joined to form musical-visual art peculiar to the twentieth century, an art first seen in film.

The visual elements of music are of four kinds. They are sometimes associative: either as the stimulus of a composition—the paintings that originally accompanied Mussorgsky's *Paintings at an Exhibition;* the vistas of the Grand Canyon, which inspired Ferdé Grofé's *Grand Canyon Suite*—or as a visual response to music—album covers for rock music. Neither of these is necessarily concomitant with the act of performing the music. Some visual elements are consequential: the movements of which Stravinsky spoke result directly from the technical requirements of playing instruments. Some are interpretative: the gestures that C. P. E. Bach described are emotional responses not called for technically. Notice sometimes how an audience for a piano recital divides itself into those who sit on the left to watch the consequential movements of the pianist's hands, and those who sit on the right to watch the interpretative gestures on the pianist's face. Some interpretative gestures psychologically extend consequential visual elements: Artur Rubenstein's high release of his hands in his performance of De Falla's *Ritual Fire Dance* or the trick of violinists who extend the length and softness of a terminal pianissimo by holding the bow in position a few moments longer than the sound that has ended.[31] Some gestures are formative, such as the movements of conductors as they control orchestral balance and tempo. One of the greatest losses in the translation of live string quartets to recordings is the sense of ensemble communication that must go on between the players. It is also found in ballet, in theater ensemble acting, and in certain sublime moments in team sports. On a record the absence of the tension and release of formative ensemble communication deprives the listener of a dimension of anticipation and involvement. It is like the difference between watching a football game live and seeing the reruns on the late evening news.

The visual elements that television or film add are formative. The power of the image is such that music is not the dominant element. Film directors have long known that an actor is made more important and that what he says is emphasized and even seems subjectively louder and more distinct if the camera zooms in on him and holds only his face on the screen. Sometimes this distorts the music. In a 1980 telecast of Ravel's *Daphnis and Chloe* by the Northwestern University Symphony Orchestra conducted by Robert Marcellus, the television director chose to focus on the fingers of the clarinet player as he performed a virtuoso passage. Difficult as it was, it nevertheless was intended as a musically subordinate theme. On television the visual interest of the clarinet overpowered everything else.

Films of paintings are transformations of another kind. The scene in Georges Seurat's *Sunday Afternoon on the Island of La Grande Jatte* is static, but *Seurat's "La Grande Jatte,"* a television film I wrote for the Art Institute of Chicago, is constantly in motion, panning details.[32] The painting becomes temporal art. Moreover, in film a painting's excerpts and details become more important than the work as a whole because the whole is not shown on the same scale as the details. The painting as a whole is relatively less distinct and intense than its parts. This is especially true of a painting the size of *La Grande Jatte.* The whole, a 7- by 10-foot painting, is reduced to a square foot or two on a television screen, but its details are shown sometimes twice their original size. The paintings William Alexander creates on his programs for Public Television are more successful because they are always not much larger than their image on a nineteen-inch television screen.[33]

The filmed image sometimes enhances music but replaces it as the dominant element. We have always been able to see conductors, usually only from the back. What in the past was interpretative facial expression becomes a new art form on television. A videotape of Bernstein's or Giulini's conducting demonstrates that they are not just musicians interpreting in the manner of C. P. E. Bach; they are actors. Their gestures and expressions are made so powerful a focus of attention that one might say that, rather than these visual elements being interpretations of the music, it is the music that is interpreting them. The principal element in artistic communication becomes visual.

Composers are no longer the chief artists. Composers have always fought for control over the performance of their works, particularly after printing and general musical literacy made them dependent upon notation to communicate the ideas of their music to performers. The written score is not a visual equivalent of music. Rhythmic notation is at best only an approximation of what it intends.[34] Tempo indications, even metronome markings, are only rough guides to what performance requires in the particular space and acoustical environment of a concert hall. Verdi scrupulously noted metronome markings in his score for *La Traviata*. But what seemed correct in his studio where he sang and accompanied himself at the piano is generally impossible in an opera house where the singer must project into a vast space over a full orchestra.[35] In the rehearsals for a performance of Ravel's *Bolero*, Toscanini and Ravel argued over the interpretation of the music. Toscanini went on to perform the piece faster than the score indicated and, ignoring Ravel's protestation, accelerated the climactic ending. Ravel was livid. Toscanini responded, "The real problem is that you don't understand your own music."[36]

In literate musical contexts there are only arguments about how best to put over a piece. But television and film give the performers a presence they never had before. In the film *Bernstein on Beethoven: Ode to Joy from the Ninth Symphony* Leonard Bernstein, as writer, actor, critic, and conductor, is not simply performing the last movement of Beethoven's *Ninth Symphony*.[37] He is creating a visual essay in which the music is only one aspect of an expression of the conceptual grasp that Bernstein has of the meaning of brotherhood. Schiller, Beethoven, Bernstein, singers, and musicians all contribute to this exposition. But the formal organization and emotional content are controlled by Bernstein. He manipulates critical remarks, poetry, music, and visual image. The others are contributory artists; Bernstein is the chief artist. When visual, musical, and verbal media are integrated, one medium tends to become dominant over another. New cultural frameworks are created, and the distancing between artists and audience is realigned. The chief artist is the person who controls this integration. He or she is the sender of the message.

In television and film presentations of musical performances, the director enters actively into the communication process. In background music for films, music is strictly ancillary.[38] The sound engineer, particularly in recordings, has decisive control. In "Fattening Frogs for Snakes" Charles Keil studies an oral musical culture that is abruptly thrust into a literate and electronic milieu.[39] Keil consistently implies that record companies and the broadcasting media exploit Blues singers. Tensions exist; Keil's raw data reveal them. But they are due not so much to motives of exploitation as to the technological differences between oral, literate, and electronic cultures. In the oral Blues culture there is no distinction between composer and performer. The singer is the chief artist. But in a literate culture the composer assumes this status. A musically illiterate Blues singer cannot write musical arrangements and thus Joe Scott, who writes all of Bobby Blue Bland's musical scores, is the chief artist for Bobby's stage shows. As is the case with the introduction of every new technology (in this case, musical notation), the resultant new social structures tend to be interpreted in terms of the values of the old frames of reference. In this transition from oral to literate, Scott is therefore not acknowledged as chief artist; Bobby Blue still is. Scott is "the omniscient and somewhat mysterious figure behind the scenes."[40] In literate musical cultures the model of fixity is the score and the composer is chief artist.

With electronic technology a new chief artist emerges: the sound engineer or the artist and repertoire man (the producer-director of the recording session). Recording technology calls for a whole new set of skills that A and R men and sound engineers have but that oral Blues singers and composers do not. Composers who retain control do so not in virtue of their literate ability to write music but only by becoming sound engineers. In the transition from the literate to the electronic musical culture twentieth-century composers have lost the traditional sense of architecture as the situation for music. They write instead for electronic environments, tailoring their compositions to the new acoustical parameters of radio, film, and recordings and exploiting the new opportunities electronic media present: microtones, rhythms, and sonorities that human beings cannot produce on traditional instruments. As sound engineers, composers finally achieve the same control over the execution of their works that painters have always had over their canvases. The model of fixity in the electronic culture is the recording.[41]

Recordings are no more like live music than a film is like a play in the theater. The etymology of the term *record* supports what Harry F. Olson wrote:

> The main purpose of sound reproduction is to provide the listener with the highest order of artistic and subjective resemblance to the condition of live rendition.[42]

Although this is true in terms of the engineer's goal of eliminating the distortions of the medium, it is false in terms of the new cultural framework that recording evokes. Recordings are a completely new art. Technological change of a medium does not immediately yield an insight into either the cultural needs that have evoked it or the cultural transformations the new media produce. Records could never truly be documentaries of performance, nor would we want them to be.

Popular music has embraced this principle more quickly than has serious music and with none of its ambivalence. Sound engineers and A and R men have a creative control readily acknowledged by the popular music industry. Their names go on every label. The producer-directors of the Beatles and of the Mamas and the Papas, George Martin and Lou Adler, respectively, are known in the industry as "The Fifth Beatle" and "The Fifth Mama." The band Cream insisted that it could not record without Felix Pappalardi engineering its sound.[43] A technique used especially with the Fender Bass gives excellent creative control to the engineer. Instead of using a microphone to record the bass's sounds as electronically colored by the performer, the engineer records only its melodic patterns by direct pickup through the control board. Thereupon the engineer, not the performer, determines the electronic coloring. The guitar's sound is so completely under the engineer's control that the Fender Bass player does not even hear the sound that the tape records.[44] Each instrument and each voice is recorded on its own track or tracks. Twenty-four or more tracks may be mixed into the final two stereo signals. The balancing, electronic modification, and editing of the ensemble's sound are all in the engineer's hands. Rock music is so much a recording art that it is impossible to duplicate it in live performance.[45]

Popular singers have had a generation or two more time than Blues singers to make the transition to electronic media. They have done this so well that they have evolved a new art of singing that is not architecturally relevant. The microphone and the camera enable them to achieve low ranges without weight, an emphasis on consonants instead of vowels, a rhetorical rather than a lyrical and melodramatic style, and a consummate integration of acting and singing that never before existed. The best of them are so aware of the prerequisites of their art that they have become their own A and R men. They, not composers or arrangers, are the chief artists of popular music.[46] In typical recording practice the singer tapes only with a rhythm section, the chorus may tape its part in Nashville, the strings in New York, and the final mix might be done in Hollywood. It is a recording of music that never existed as a live performance.

Popular culture embraces new technology. It is conscious of and exists only in the present. It has no consciousness of a past. Its consumers find the past irrelevant. But the elite culture reveres the past and the history of the ideas it expresses. It stresses continuity with a heritage. And so it is ambivalent about recordings. Stravinsky called recordings "ersatz" music,[47] just as the fifteenth century called printing "artificial writing."[48] Just as film criticism clung to the auteur theory, so serious music clings to a composer-conductor theory of electronic media in spite of the fact that films and recordings are team products that composers and conductors do not control. The film is not like literature; recordings are not like traditional music. Yet elite culture analyzes recordings in terms of old frames of reference.

Musicians do not fear tools. They are using tools constantly. The best woodwind players are also the best able to maintain and repair those instruments. Their practice studios are repair shops. In their traditional technologies musicians speak of their instruments as animate and personal, as an extension of the artist's hand. A standing joke among orchestra players satirizes singers as "half-way" musicians, as incompetent because they have no mechanical instrument which gives them more measured control over vibrato, pitch, and rhythm. But musicians do fear tools that they have not subsumed as extensions and expressions of themselves as human beings. The objective measures and controls of sound engineers are far more precise and subtle than human perception. But these tools are called "impersonal mechanisms" and engineers who organize and shape music with them are "non-musicians." They, like Joe Scott, Bobby Bland's arranger,[49] seem to be alien intruders and are not acknowledged as the chief artists of a new communications medium. We trust the human ear.[50] Record jackets and orchestra publicity show Stokowski and Solti sitting in an engineer's control room listening to tapes to be released. He who molded the orchestra according to the old frame of reference must appear to be in control.

The major symphonies pretend that their primary identity is as live performing groups. But recordings are not "records of performances." Deutsche Grammophon experimentally processes the tapes of the Chicago Symphony Orchestra to remove the dryness and tubby midrange effects that are produced by the acoustics of Orchestra Hall in Chicago.[51] The primary identity of the Chicago Symphony is on its recordings and the tapes it releases for broadcast and telecast to over two hundred stations across the country. In 1976 a Ford Foundation study concluded that only 4 percent of those living in the metropolitan area of Chicago had ever seen a live performance of the Chicago Symphony. The symphony survives not because it performs live. The live performance is a cultural coding that serious music maintains in its transition from the literate to the electronic culture. Nonetheless, major musical organizations orient themselves toward recording and broadcast, not toward the situation of the live audience. For example, the classical concert arrangement put first violins on the left, seconds on the right, and violas and celli in the middle. This gave more clarity to the string lines. Early in radio broadcasting technicians discovered that the best distribution of the orchestra for microphone pickup was to place first and seconds next to each other. Today the latter distribution is common in live performance. Dry concert halls were found to be better recording studios because monophonic radio and phonographs increased the impression of reverberation. Such acoustics are better for recordings, worse for live performance.[52] When Unitel televised live performances of the Chicago Symphony, the members of the

Civic Orchestra, the symphony's training orchestra, were given tickets for the front rows so that the television audience would get the impression of a youthful, alert audience. When opera is taped for television at the Lyric Opera in Chicago, the audience is instructed not to leave its seats, to refrain from its normal behavior of applauding at the ends of arias, and to ignore the obtrusive cameras and lights. The final tapes are edited from different performances. The audience becomes an actor in a staged event that exists for the sake of reproduction and broadcast.

Some performances on records could not possibly exist as live music. For Deutsche Grammophon's 1976 recording of Saint-Saëns's *Organ Symphony* Daniel Barenboim conducted the Chicago Symphony in the United States, Gaston Litaize recorded the organ part in Chartres Cathedral, and the tracks were mixed in West Germany.[53] Columbia's 1976 recording of the *Rhapsody in Blue* is a collage of a piano roll Gershwin made—the holes on which the piano played the orchestral parts were covered—and a newly recorded orchestra performance of the score Ferdé Grofé wrote for symphony orchestra in 1942, five years after Gershwin's death.[54] In recording practice the sound engineer, much like a film director, edits tapes of several versions of the various sections of a work and enhances certain characteristics of the performance electronically. The result is a precision and control well beyond what is possible in live performance. The pianist Artur Rubenstein and one of his conductors were once reviewing the final tapes of a concerto they had recorded. The conductor turned to Rubenstein and said, "Maestro, if only we could always play it that well!" Rubenstein, realizing that what they were hearing was a collage of the tapes of the best moments of several takes, responded, "No, my friend . . . if only we could *ever* play it that well."

There are four categories of interaction between technology, as a principle of aesthetic organization, and culture.

First is technology as the physical medium and its potential. Carved sculpture, for example, is more introverted than modeled sculpture because of the way the materials dictate that shape must be conceived. Working in marble the artist carves from the outside in; the more general primary shapes will *contain* the specific details that are latent within them. Working in clay the artist models from the inside out; the more general primary shapes will *support* the specific details.[55] Matter, the physical medium, is understood here in two ways. The first is as a product of nature. In this sense the law of gravity is a principle of architecture. The second is matter as it is altered and specified by culture and accommodated to our way of seeing things. The poet, for example, is subject to certain cultural constraints. Not every combination of sounds human beings can make is possible content for poetry, but only those specified as material that can be active in particular syntactical systems. Other constraints are psychological. Poets, musicians, and painters are subject to the principles of pattern perception. Together, a culture's stylistic systems and the principles of human pattern perception determine what its members intuit as the potential of the material. The matter of art is anything that can exist as an object of the senses, but specified by culture and human psychology. A composer could juxtapose any number of sounds and violate no physical principles of acoustics. But this first sense of matter is, in art, always conditioned by the second. Composer Alexander Tcherepnin, my composition teacher, used to tell me, "Don't rape the music!" Composers often test their constraints and invent new syntactical systems. But one cannot force music to do what it does not want to do.

The second category of technology as an aesthetic principle is technology as control over a medium. Technology in this second sense is knowledge about the physical medium and its potential and the ability to analyze and organize it so that its meaning can be grasped in sense perception. One value of art is the artist's display of this knowledge and ability. Thus people admire Rembrandt's virtuosity in achieving chiaroscuro effects. But almost anyone who sees a Mondrian for the first time will say, "I could do that." This does not mean "I could conceive of and execute a Mondrian." It means merely "I could control paint well enough to paint the red rectangle and the black lines." It is only this second value of technology that Mondrian abandons, though not completely, because he does make something.[56] Any felt reluctance to call Rembrandt a technologist is only a hangover from the notion of the values of conceptualization. Heidegger said that we are all technicians, that making is the perfect expression of human rationality in its calculative and active modes.[57] Heidegger is only restoring meaning to a principle of human life that we have forgotten in our abstract categories. The first meaning of τέκτων was a worker in wood, a carpenter. The Greeks extended this to mean a master of any art. Hence masters of the art of poetry were τέκτονες ὕμνων or makers of song. Then, by extension, τεκτων meant a planner or an author. These are not analogies. Poets and painters all exhibit a knowledge of their media by what they make.

These first two categories become clear by analyzing the differences between Archaic Greek marbles and cast bronzes in terms of both the potential of their physical media (marble versus bronze) and the techniques required for controlling the media. Technology can be seen to be a factor in the stylistic evolution of the depiction of the human face. Marble sculpture from the Middle Archaic period such as *Standing Youth from the Island of Naxos* (c. 560 B.C., National Museum, Athens) or *The Rampin Head* (c. 560 B.C., The Louvre, Paris) consistently exhibits what is called the "Archaic Smile," a curious deep accentuation of the corners of the mouth. But bronze statues of the same period very seldom show it. How is this related to the materials from which the statues were made? Experiment with pointed and flat chisels made of an alloy of 20 percent tin and 80 percent copper, such as the Greeks used up to 500 B.C., demonstrates that one can work in limestone with chisels at a fairly shallow angle to the stone surface but that this technique is impossible on marble because the chisels invariably skip and slide. The only way to have an effect on marble is to work with the pointed, not the flat, chisel at right angles to the surface. Eventually, finer pricking yields a surface of minute pits. By careful polishing one achieves a surface similar to the Greek examples. The smile, one must conclude, is the product of the bronze pointed chisel technique, which produces a deep accentuation of the corners of the mouth. It is clear that beyond this feature the simple and severe designs of these works are very strongly influenced by the technique required.

Steel chisels came into general use about 500 B.C. Flat or pointed, they can work marble at shallower angles and pitting is unnecessary. But examples of marble sculpture made with steel chisels up to 470 B.C. show the same smile. It had become desirable as an expression of liveliness even though the technique did not require it.[58]

Questions of aesthetic value cannot be separated from questions of "how to do it."[59] The artist must understand the material conceptually or intuitively. There must be something that can be made to exist for perception by the senses, something that can enter into a process of communication. The conceptual artist, who renounces making in a physical medium and communicates only by stating a concept of a work, is still a painter or musician, if the concept, like an unperformed musical score, is about something that *could* exist. After all, there have been many works planned but never executed. Frank Lloyd Wright's concept of a mile-high building is architecture if it is something that could be built. His plans exhibit knowledge about a medium and an ability to realize his concept. But what of Paolo Soleri's arcologies? Let us assume that to put these concepts into execution is technologically impossible. If so, they are not architecture. They are art of a different kind: a form that combines literature, architectural models, and drawings and that uses architecture as a metaphor—a kind of Platonic exemplar—to clarify a sociological and philosophical ideal. It is illustrated poetry. Conceptual art still makes something.

The third category of technology as an aesthetic principle is technology as the psychic model for the creative act and for the analysis and understanding of expression by the critical audience. In the discussion of technology as physical medium and as control over the medium, "intuition" and "perception" were key words. Artists and their audiences do not know the whole potential of the medium in terms of concepts they can articulate. They know it in large part in terms of internalized modes of perception, recognition, and response.[60] Art as a medium of communication is sensory material that is immediate and concrete in the audience's perception. The artist's knowledge and control of this is partly intuitive and partly conceptual. Artists like Mussorgsky or Henri Rousseau are almost wholly intuitive. Others, like Berlioz and Cézanne, know all the conceptual rules but break them when another solution seems more expressive. It is more important to do than to explain. But many twentieth-century artists—Schoenberg and Albers—feel compelled to have a logical explanation for all of their choices. Thus, although composers for generations had resorted to free atonality as an expressive device, it was not until 1923 that Schoenberg published the first atonal composition (Number 5 of *Five Pianoforte Pieces*, Op. 23) in which the twelve tones of the scale were related "by method." He insisted that the twentieth-century brain as well as the nineteenth-century Romantic heart must be part of the musical creation.[61]

The paintings and theoretical writings of Georges Seurat are profound examples of science and technology becoming an artist's psychic model of precision and control. The scientific discoveries of the nineteenth century, particularly those concerning the laws of optics and color, prompted Seurat to assiduous study and experiment in order to find formulae for color and design that could control and sharpen his expression. Eventually painting became for him the product more of applied science than of sensation and intuition. This is evident in his work not only on the relations of light and color to the human eye, but also in the relationship between the real objects he painted, the preliminary sketches he made (hundreds in the case of *La Grande Jatte*), and the final composition.[62] Mondrian, Klee, and Kandinsky, each in his own unique way, sought, like Seurat, to determine a set of rational principles that could determine the processes of creation and expression.

Artistic communication has always been concerned with the nature of appearance. What was important was what could be sensibly perceived. Gluck wrote in his preface to *Alceste* (1769) that "there is no rule that I have not felt justified in sacrificing readily in favor of an intended effect."[63] But with technology as their psychic model artists set for themselves the goal of conceptually understanding the essential nature of a structural reality underlying their art's appearances. Luck or being carried away is of no value unless the artists and the audience know why. To produce a work that is effective and expressive is not enough. The work must be shown to embody an integrated abstract form. The history of art is replete with mathematical theories of artistic order: Pythagoras's theories, the Golden Mean, cancrizans canons, and fugal techniques. Although in its act of perception the audience could often discover the operation of these principles, it could never grasp all the nuances of their activity. But with precision and control as a psychic model, the possibility of the analytical reduction of a work of art to symmetrical mathematical formula becomes, for a critic like René Leibowitz, the first criterion of its value.[64]

In the twentieth century much art becomes more like empirical science. Artists struggle for conceptual control over their own intuition. In an age of information we need data for "truth" because the appearances of the work may be deceptive. They are neither a necessary nor sufficient condition for artistic truth. Truth and beauty are established in analysis that reveals that the work reflects an underlying structure, hidden from sense perception. Schoenberg's "Mondfleck" from *Pierrot Lunaire* is a vocal line accompanied by a double canon played in cancrizans fashion and a simultaneous three-part fugue. It is absolutely impossible to grasp this complex abstract order in the listening experience. But for Leibowitz it is not important that this be known in aesthetic perception. The pleasure is not in such discovery but in the rational justification that demonstrates the operation of a precise, fluid, and measured principle.[65] In the Baroque period hidden logical order was felt to enhance aesthetic pleasure. In the twentieth century some critics take more pleasure in the analysis than in seeing or hearing the work. Conceptual art has its roots as much in this flight from intuition as in a flight from the physical. Leibowitz does in music what Robert Mark does in analyzing the structural principles of historic architecture. As a psychic model technology leads to an aesthetic of analysis, what Mark has called the "engineer's aesthetic."[66] The judgments about art are made according to the manner in which judgments are made about technology.

The fourth category is technology as the thematic or metaphoric content of a work. In Henry Reed's *The Naming of Parts*, for example, the dismantling and cleaning of a rifle serve as a metaphor for fantasies of sexual play. Just to enumerate such images does not explain much. After all, every painting with a house or a windmill reflects the existing technology of the artist's culture. Some film genres simply substitute cars and airplanes for horses and trains. But images reveal not simply by their passive presence. We see technology and culture interact when the images manifest new expectations and changing values. In *Zen and the Art of Motorcycle Maintenance* or in the film *Easy Rider* a motorcycle becomes an instrument in a rite of passage and a means of self-expression. The machine exhibits the need for self-determined options.[67] Motorcycles, cars, and railroads all have become cultural codes for the themes of change, power, and freedom.

Does our culture's involvement with technological metaphors amount only to a difference of degree, or is it a difference of kind? Clearly technology has revolutionized culture before: the invention of the printing press is an example. Ever since then, to enter into the communications networks of Western civilization one has had to become literate. One hardly ever thinks of reading and writing as technologies. Education toward literacy is felt to be every child's birthright, a necessary expression of the human self. Once I found my children watching an old television Western. The Indian chief was demanding that the schoolmarm stop teaching his son to read. "If he learns to read, he will not be fit to be Chief." How silly, I thought. But field work done by the Chadwicks and others has shown that oral cultures in urban settings believe that reading and writing threaten to destroy their cultural psyche.[68] Oral cultures cannot store knowledge in abstract categories. Their knowledge is preserved in terms of events as heavily patterned stories about types of heroes.[69] Oral storytellers must use striking imagery so that they can effectively retain their epics. They pursue the image not simply as beautiful but also as technically necessary for storage and recall.[70] The formulaic image is their primary form of thinking. Emerging into a literate culture means moving away from thinking in terms of narrative conflict and heroic types. An oral culture must move from assimilation of images toward reflection upon orality and speech—that is, toward rhetoric. From thinking in terms of the whole it must move toward abstract analysis. From "What do people say?" it must move to "I think." From rhetoric, cultures move toward reflection upon abstract categories, that is, toward philosophy. All of this is wedded to the technological change from oral memory to the craft of the written text.[71]

This society does not honor the Indian chief's complaint. It seems bizarre for a culture to claim it has a right to resist literacy. Nonetheless, something is lost for what is gained. Plato's ejection of the poet from the republic expressed the need to move from visualization to abstraction, a need to organize information more fluidly and in greater detail for the purpose of reflective analysis and conceptualization. What Plato did, he did with regret. The poet was welcome to return from exile, once it was clear how his techniques and his way of knowing differed from those of the philosopher.[72] The evolution of consciousness was more important. Consciousness had to extend to areas of life until then preempted by the unreflective method of visual imagery.[73]

Today we turn on technology as enslaving the human spirit. George Lukács sees us helplessly accepting mechanistic determinism; Herbert Marcuse sees us being swallowed into the lonely crowd.[74] We are so greatly concerned not only because we are more self-conscious than were the ancient oral poets. We are also in the throes of another evolution of consciousness.

This is the first culture to define itself in terms of its tools. Technology has become paradigmatic. Although we, somewhat like the Indian chief, may resist this, all forms of human activity, all products, and all values are expressed in terms of a single root. Technology is the power that controls this civilization. In the mental universe this late-twentieth-century civilization creates, technology is the basis for meaning. It is the model to define what is, yet most of us know little more than which button to press in order to use the tools by which we participate in the physical and historical environment of the present. We live by computers, television sets, photocopying machines, and cars, yet we cannot manage them. Machines are not trusted to our care. We are told that computers and television sets are "not serviceable by owner." The copying machine orders, "Call Key operator." For every modern man or woman who can take apart a carburetor for cleaning and repair there are a hundred who would not dare to touch it and a thousand who have no idea what it is for. Yet all the millions of us need computers, television sets, copying machines, and cars in order to participate in this culture. Everyone who has survived a Chicago winter knows that when cars stop, city life stops. It is unthinkable that all machines would ever stop.

Being with machines is our way of being in this world. Technology verges on becoming for us what the mystery of Divine Being was for the Middle Ages. What was meant as our means of control has become a control over us. The question is not simply one of quantity. Every culture has had to resolve the dilemma of power, reason, and magic that its iron-maker evoked by transforming the products of the earth into something that never existed before. Each technological change is a challenge to traditional gods. In past cultures the gods have always met the challenge. When Prometheus stole fire from Olympus, the gods punished him to demonstrate that traditional order prevailed. The universe had not become suddenly mechanistic. Humans acting on nature had released power for change. But the myth proclaimed that this power was still subject to a conscious order and purpose in the universe.

In this century there is a qualitative change in the power of myths to do this. People have always wished to be like the gods. In *Civilization and Its Discontents* Freud pointed out the great dilemma of the present time. Technologies have given us all the powers to mold, fashion, and create that once were magical perquisites only of gods. Yet society still is unhappy and dissatisfied.[75] But we are still myth-makers and must be in order to reconcile the rational and the demonic in the reordered environment. The new metaphors that the interaction of technology and culture has prompted move toward establishing new modes of coding and decoding. Every culture encounters a clash between its models of behavior and the realities of life wherein the models are seen to fail. In response every culture develops narratives that are offered as resolutions or at least explanations of the dilemma.

The modern response is a theme that pervades twentieth-century works, particularly after World War II, and the fourfold theme includes:

1. Massive evil: genocide, concentration camps, dehumanized behavioral engineering, total annihilation. The consequences of this evil cannot be escaped. It transcends all reason and purpose.
2. Psychic and physical distance between perpetrators and victims. Not only do no human ties exist between the two, not only are the perpetrators and victims so far separated that they do not know or understand one another, but they do not even recognize one another as human.
3. Mass guilt: whole nations and races are guilty; even the victims themselves are guilty.
4. No redemption: there is no saving catharsis.

The theme is found

in paintings: Picasso's *Guernica* (1937); Orozco's *Dive Bomber and Tank* (1940)
in films: Resnais' *Hiroshima mon Amour* (1959); Lina Wertmüller's *Seven Beauties* (1976)
in novels: Jerzy Koszynski's *The Painter Bird* (1965); Anthony Burgess's *A Clockwork Orange* (1963)
in music: Penderecki's *Threnody for the Victims of Hiroshima* (1960); Schoenberg's *A Survivor from Warsaw* (1947)
in plays: Robert Shaw's *Man in a Glass Booth* (1971); Bertolt Brecht's *The Resistible Rise of Arturio Ui* (1941)
in popular media: the made-for-TV film *World War III* (1982); the TV series *Battlestar Galactica* (1978).

This fourfold theme embodies the contradictions in our culture's value system, which is the dilemma of our own power.

All change is difficult, but technology is its own universe of discourse. It is not subsumed within a universe controlled by a god. People turn against technology not for its own sake. We have always needed and embraced tools. We object to tools that we cannot control and that therefore seem to control us. But have we ever had more control than now? Are we more controlled by technology than we were by fate and the mysterious gods of the past? It is not just a horrible fate we fear. The monsters of ancient folklore stirred as much horror as these machines do now. Evil and injustice, too, have always been present. Many cultures resolve the problem of good and evil with myths of trickster gods who unconcernedly cause human misfortunes. How is this much different from the benevolent god whose actions leave us befuddled about the good of an innocent's pain and suffering? Our dilemma's uniqueness rests not on tools, control, horror, or evil.

Human mythology everywhere seeks a humanly motivated and directed universe, not a mechanistic one.[76] But in the twentieth century the reason and motivation are not those of a mysterious god. The dilemma is that we see, for the first time, our own culture, our collective selves in control. The process of myth-making happens *ab origine.* We are at a new point of origin. A new cultural psyche awakens, and with it is born a new myth that embodies our greatest fear: the sterility of our own power. Christian mythology reconciled the sin of Adam and Eve as a "felix culpa": although it was a sin, it was "felix"—a lucky, happy, and fruitful event—because it had a power that gave birth ultimately to the Christmas and Easter myths. The fourfold massive evil theme marks the end of the fecundity myths. It is emerging as a myth born of holosopic technology. We see it now in its first evolving expressions; as yet it only states the dilemma but does not resolve it. The mature myths of the past are constructions by people who have ordered and come to terms with their environment. We have not done this yet. We are still hoping to find that, as in Genesis, our looming tragedy will be a source of fecundity. Our "felix culpa," if that is what it is to be, will grow out of our myth's focus of attention on ourselves: on our power, which can turn against us, on the distances created between ourselves, and on the identification with one another as all equally victims and aggressors. The coin has a reverse side. The possibility of being freed by technology to do only those things that human beings alone can do is the first step toward human self-redemption.[77] Technology and culture are not antinomies. They act together as a crucible for change.

NOTES

1. This paper is an expanded revision of one presented at the final convocation of the National Humanities Institute at the University of Chicago, which was funded by a grant from the National Endowment for the Humanities. I am indebted to my colleagues at the Institute, especially Professor Jane Upin, who worked with me on "Technology and Culture: Arts and Ideas," another NEH project.

2. Robert Mark, "The Structure of Historic Architecture" (Paper delivered at the conference of the American Association of State Colleges and Universities, Boston, 1–4 May 1979. Cf. also Michael Cohalan, "Tension in the Cathedral," *Science 81* 2 (1981): 41.

3. Cf. Cyril Stanley Smith, "Art, Technology, and Science: Notes on Their Historic Interaction," *Technology and Culture* 11 (1970): 497.

4. In the last movement of his Ninth Symphony Beethoven wrote a chord (meas. 208) that, on the piano, is a mess; it simultaneously sounds all the notes of the D-minor scale. But in the orchestra it is a combination of three consonant chords, one in the strings, another in the woodwinds, and a third in the brass. It is still truly dissonant, but the consonant relations of the orchestral timbres qualify the dissonance in a way impossible to the piano.

5. James Marston Fitch, "The Aesthetics of Function," in *People and Buildings*, ed. Robert Gutman (New York: Basic Books, 1972), 4.

6. For example, Douglas Huebler, *Ideas and Image in Recent Art* (exhibition program), Art Institute of Chicago, 23 March–5 May 1974, 36.

7. *Idea Art*, ed. Gregory Battcock (New York: E. P. Dutton, 1973).

8. Robert Mark, lecture given at the National Humanities Institute at the University of Chicago, October 1976. Cf. Robert Mark, "The Structural Analysis of Gothic Cathedrals," *Scientific American* 227 (1972): 91, 96, and 98.

9. Jacques Ellul, *The Technological Society*, trans. John Wilkinson (New York: Knopf, 1964).

10. Bernard Gendron, *Technology and the Human Condition* (New York: St. Martin's Press, 1977).

11. Philip Slater, *The Pursuit of Loneliness* (Boston: Beacon, 1970).

12. For example, B. F. Skinner, *Walden Two* (New York: Macmillan, 1948).

13. Edgar Wind, *Art and Anarchy* (New York: Vintage Books, 1969), 76–77, 164ff.

14. Don Ihde, "Bach to Rock, a Musical Odyssey," in *Technics and Praxis*, Boston Studies in the Philosophy of Science, vol. 24 (Dordrecht and Boston: D. Reidel, 1979), 93–100.

15. Cyril Stanley Smith, "Technology and Human Possibility" (lecture series given at the National Humanities Institute at the University of Chicago, 7–8 December 1976). Cf. Smith, "Art, Technology, and Science," 494.

16. From the Christmas hymn "Bóg się rodzi." Cf. Jerzy Strzetelski, "History of

Polish Literature" (lecture series given at the Jagiellonian University in Cracow, 27–28 June 1974); and Jerzy Strzetelski, *An Outline of Polish Literature* (Cracow: Jagiellonian University Press, 1974).

17. The slogan of the Solidarity movement in 1982 was "Winter yours, spring ours."

18. Edmund Dehnert et al., *Gallery in the Streets: Polish Poster Design* (Washington, D.C.: GT-70 Consortium, 1974). Cf. also Jerzy Wasniewski, *Plakat Polski* (Warsaw, 1972).

19. Cf. Walter Benjamin, "The Work of Art in the Age of Mechanical Reproduction," in *Film Theory and Criticism*, ed. Gerald Mast and Marshall Cohen (New York: Oxford University Press, 1974), 612–20.

20. Aristotle, *Nichomachean Ethics* 1.3 (1094b–1095a) and 2.2 (1103b27–29); *Eudemian Ethics* 1.6 (1216b21–25); and *Metaphysics, Book E* 1 (1025b18ff.).

21. Karl Marx, foreword to *Critique of Political Economy*, in Karl Marx–Friedrich Engels, *Werke*, 39 vols. (Berlin: Dietz, 1961). 13:8. Cf. Bernard Gendron, "Marx and the Technological Theory of History," *Philosophical Forum* 6 (1975): 397–422.

22. Nicholas Lobkowicz, *Theory and Practice: History of a Concept from Aristotle to Marx* (Notre Dame, Ind.: University of Notre Dame Press, 1967), 36–46, 373–99, and 416–17.

23. Marcel Proust, *Swann's Way*, vol. 1 of *Remembrance of Things Past*, trans. C. K. Scott Moncrieff (New York: Modern Library, 1928), 321.

24. Igor Stravinsky, *Poetics of Music*, trans. Arthur Knodel and Ingolf Dahl (New York: Vintage Books, 1960), 55.

25. Joseph Haydn to the French musicians, Paris, 10 August 1801, in *The Collected Correspondence and London Notebooks of Joseph Haydn*, ed. H. C. Robbins Landon (London: Barrie and Rockliff, 1959), 189.

26. Aristotle, *Politics* 1341b. Visual elements may have had a part in the Greek theory of musical ethos. Singing in very high and low tessituras caused uncomely facial contortions, either too strained or too relaxed. The melodic modes with a middle tessitura were more moderate and settled, and therefore more appropriate in their affective ethical character. Aristotle, *Politics* 1340a–b. Cf. Curt Sachs, *The Rise of Music in the Ancient World, East and West* (New York: W. W. Norton, 1943), 248–52.

27. C. P. E. Bach, *Essay on the True Art of Playing Keyboard Instruments*, trans. William J. Mitchell (London: Cassell and Co., 1951), 152.

28. Friedrich Marpurg, *Der Critischen Musicus an der Spree* (Berlin: A. Haude and J. C. Spencer, 1750), 9 September 1749.

29. Igor Stravinsky, *An Autobiography* (New York: Simon and Schuster, 1936), 114.

30. Cf. Harry F. Olson, *Music, Physics and Engineering* (New York: Dover, 1967), 248–51, 260–61, 319–21, 382–84; David Hall, "Stereo: Genuine and Simulated," *Hi-Fi Music at Home*, October 1957, 168; and James Moir, *High Quality Sound Reproduction* (London: Chapman and Hall, 1958), 553.

31. Cf. H. C. Hart, M. W. Fuller, and W. S. Lusby, "Precision Study of Piano Touch and Tone," *Journal of the Acoustical Society of America* 6 (1934): 80–94.

32. *The Shape of Our Vision: Seurat's "La Grande Jatte"* from *Man and His Art* (1971), six 16mm films, research and script by Edmund Dehnert, distributed by Great Plains Television Library, Lincoln, Neb.

33. William Alexander, *The Magic of Oil Painting*, a television series produced by KOCE-TV, Chicago.

34. Aaron Copland wrote, "It seems unlikely . . . that a scientifically exact

scheme of rhythmic notation will ever be devised. Much of the delicate rhythmic variety we are accustomed to hearing in first-rate performances is simply not written in our present system of notation" ("Shop Talk: On the Notation of Rhythm," *Copland on Music* [Garden City, N.Y.: Doubleday, 1960], 279).

35. Boris Goldovsky, *High Fidelity*, April 1961, 28.

36. Cf. Rollo H. Myers, *Ravel: Life and Works* (New York: Thomas Yoseloff, 1960), 83.

37. *Bernstein on Beethoven: Ode to Joy from the Ninth Symphony*, Leonard Bernstein and the Vienna State Opera Chorus and the Vienna Philharmonic, BFA Educational Media, produced by CBS News in association with Amberson Productions.

38. Irwin Bazelon, *Knowing the Score: Notes on Film Music* (New York: Van Nostrand Reinhold Co., 1975), 8–12.

39. Charles Keil, *Urban Blues* (Chicago: University of Chicago Press, 1966), 68–95.

40. Ibid., 115.

41. Only three hundred copies of a new record of contemporary music are produced for the whole country and not even that many are sold nationally. There is no profit motive in being recorded. But getting into the *Schwann Catalog of Recorded Music* has the same aura for electronic culture that getting into print had for the literate musical culture. I refer to the remarks of Ilhan Mimaroglu, president of Finnadar Records (Atlantic Recording Corp.), at the symposium "The Composer and the Media," Region V Annual Conference of the American Society of University Composers, Chicago, 10 November 1979.

42. Olson, *Music, Physics and Engineering*, v.

43. Paul Hirsch, *The Structure of the Popular Music Industry* (Ann Arbor, Mich.: Institute for Social Research, University of Michigan, 1979), 26.

44. Tom Bruner, *The Arranger/Composer's Complete Guide to the Guitar* (Studio City, Calif.: Greso Publishing Co., 1972), 116–18.

45. Ihde, "Bach to Rock," 94–96. The halls where rock music is performed live are the slums of sound. The architectural settings are hockey arenas, large movie houses, cow palaces, and gymnasiums. In Chicago the International Amphitheater echoes bass figures back and forth. The reverberation time of the Uptown movie theater and of the Aragon Ballroom makes everything sound muddled. The Chicago Stadium loses bass frequencies. This inverts the relationship that existed between serious music and architecture. Live serious music, created for an architectural setting, cannot be duplicated on recordings; rock music, created as a recording, cannot be duplicated in live performance.

46. Henry Pleasants, "The Art of the American Popular Singer," in *The Great American Popular Singers* (New York: Simon and Schuster, 1974), 33–48.

47. Stravinsky, *An Autobiography*, 211.

48. Susan Noakes, "Reading Before Gutenberg" (Paper delivered at the National Humanities Institute, University of Chicago, Fall 1976).

49. Keil, *Urban Blues*, 115.

50. Robert Marsh, "Sage of Skokie Blazes Paths with his Advanced Amplifiers," in *Stereo/video, Chicago Sun-Times*, 8 November 1981, p. 2.

51. Thomas Willis, "Recordings Sound Notes Not Heard Live in Orchestra Hall," *Chicago Tribune*, 10 October 1976.

52. A. E. Robertson and K. R. Sturley, "Radio Transmission," *Groves's Dictionary of Music and Musicians*, 5th ed. (1954).

53. *Saint-Saens' Organ Symphony* (DGG 2530–619).

54. The original orchestration of *Rhapsody in Blue* was for a jazz band of twenty-three instruments, scored for the premiere by Ferdé Grofé in 1924.

55. Cf. James J. Kelly, *The Sculptural Idea* (Minneapolis, Minn: Burgess Publishing Co., 1974), 47–75.

56. Many electronic music composers, on the other hand, embrace this second value exclusively. Leonard B. Meyer has called such music "Mahler without any syntax whatsoever." Cf. his "Exploiting Limits: Creation, Archetypes, and Style Change," *Daedalus* 109 (1980): 205. Such composers are primarily exhibiting a joy in their ability to create and manipulate unimaginable sequences of sound. Their work has meaning primarily as a sensuous wonderland of effects. Its cultural coding is the mass, climactic surges and the play of sonic variety that find their paradigm in Mahler's postromanticism.

57. Martin Heidegger, *An Introduction to Metaphysics*, trans. Ralph Manheim (New Haven, Conn.: Yale University Press, 1959), pp. 16–17, 158–160. Cf. Harold Alderman, "Heidegger: Technology as Phenomenon," *Personalist* 51 (1970): 535–545.

58. H. J. Etienne, *The Chisel in Greek Sculpture*, trans. Denis R. O'Beirne (Leiden: E. J. Brill, 1968).

59. Cf. Charles W. Morris, "Science, Art and Technology," *The Kenyon Review* 1 (1939): 409–23.

60. Meyer, "Exploiting Limits," 179–80.

61. Arnold Schoenberg, *Style and Idea*, ed. Dika Newlin (New York: Philosophical Library, 1950), 102–43, 180–95.

62. William Innes Homer, *Seurat and the Science of Painting* (Cambridge, Mass.: M.I.T. Press, 1964), 112–64, 250–57.

63. Translated from Gluck's dedication to *Alceste*, 1769.

64. Cf. René Leibowitz, *Schoenberg et son école: l'étape contemporaine du langage musical* (Paris: Janin, 1947), 106; and idem, *Introduction à la musique de douze sons* (Paris: L'Arche, 1949), 224–29.

65. Leibowitz, *Schoenberg et son école*, 106.

66. Mark, "Structure of Historic Architecture."

67. Robert M. Pirsig, *Zen and the Art of Motorcycle Maintenance: An Inquiry into Values* (New York: Morrow, 1974); *Easy Rider* (1969), Swank Motion Pictures (starring Peter Fonda and Dennis Hopper).

68. H. Munro Chadwick and N. Kenshaw Chadwick, *The Growth of Literature*, 3 vols. (Cambridge: At the University Press, 1932–40). Cf. Walter J. Ong, "Writing and Print as Technology" (Lecture given at the National Humanities Institute, University of Chicago, 11 January 1977).

69. Walter J. Ong, *The Presence of the Word* (New Haven, Conn.: Yale University Press, 1967), p. 203. The motifs and types of oral literature are indexed in Stith Thompson, *Motif-Index of Folk-Literature*, 6 vols. (Bloomington: University of Indiana Press, 1955–58); and in Antti A. Aarne and Stith Thompson, *The Types of the Folktale*, rev. ed. (Helsinki: Suomalainen Tiedeakatemia, 1961).

70. Ong, *Presence of the Word*, 25; Eric A. Havelock, *Preface to Plato* (Cambridge, Mass.: Harvard University Press, 1963), 188–89.

71. Ong, *Presence of the Word*, 33–34, 231–33. Cf. Havelock, *Preface to Plato*, 171, concerning the development of the Greek mind in its transition from orality to literacy.

72. Plato, *Republic* 10 (605–607b).

73. Walter J. Ong, "Milton's Logical Epic and Evolving Consciousness," *Proceedings of the American Philosophical Society* 120 (1976): 296–97.

74. George Lukács, *Geschichte und Klassenbewusstein* (Berlin: Der Malik-verlag,

1923); Herbert Marcuse, *One-Dimensional Man: Studies in the Ideology of Advanced Society* (Boston: Beacon, 1964).

75. Sigmund Freud, *Civilization and Its Discontents*, trans. and ed. by James Strachey (New York: W. W. Norton, 1962), pp. 38–39.

76. Ruth Benedict, "Myth," *Encyclopedia of the Social Sciences*, ed. Edwin R. A. Seligman (New York: Macmillan, 1937): cf. Victor W. Turner, "Myth and Symbol," *International Encyclopedia of the Social Sciences*, ed. David L. Sills (New York: Macmillan, 1968).

77. Cf. George Miller, *The Psychology of Communication* (New York: Basic Books, 1967), 118–23; and Lobkowicz, *Theory and Practice*, 316.

Scientific and Artistic Creativity According to Kant's Philosophy

STEPHEN BARKER

Johns Hopkins University

For most people the term *creativity* carries strongly favorable connotations. Creativity is considered somehow the source of what is most valuable in the achievements of those who advance civilization by means of their skill, taste, or genius. We perhaps think of creativity first of all in connection with the humanities, especially the arts and literature. But creativity is also present in other areas of life, notably in the activity of scientists. However, in today's culture the sciences have moved far apart from the humane pursuits of art and literature, which may well make us wonder whether there can be anything in common between creativity in the arts and creativity in the sciences. Does creativity have various essentially different forms? What is creativity in the arts and what is it in the sciences? This difficult and elusive notion needs to be clarified.

Two general comments are useful here; they may or may not be borne out by later discussion. First, notice that *being creative* is not the same as *being productive.* People can be productive and can bring into being great quantities of good work (as on a well-run assembly line) without being creative. Where the production is a matter of routine hard work, done unimaginatively, there can be neither need nor scope for creativity by the workers. They build mechanically, repetitiously producing items of a standard type in a standard manner. Creativity, in contrast, involves originality. When people produce things creatively, they devise novel products or novel ways of making products. It is not the quantity or quality of what they produce, but its originality, that marks their activity as creative.

A second point is that creativity is by no means limited to

situations in which products are being made. Creativity can be regarded as having to do with *new awareness of structures;* these structures may or may not be brought into existence by the creative person. Where these structures did not exist before, the person who with imaginative insight first succeeds in bringing them into existence thereby shows creativity, of course. But where these structures already are what they are, the person who newly recognizes and interprets them may well be displaying creativity too. The latter kind of creativity is no less genuine and important than the former kind. The decipherer of the Rosetta stone, for example, was perhaps more creative than were those who wrote its inscription.

The structures mentioned above may be composed of physical objects or of more abstract elements; and their value may be practical or scientific or aesthetic, or some combination of these. Tools, buildings, and machines are physical objects whose value is mainly practical. Paintings, sculptures, and gardens are physical objects whose value is mainly aesthetic. Engineering techniques, social institutions, and scientific theories are structures of more abstract elements having practical scientific value. Literature, music, and dance are structures of abstract elements with mainly aesthetic value. The variety of types of structures with respect to which creativity can be displayed is unlimited.

A creative person, then, is one who has an imaginative talent for devising new structures or for newly recognizing ones already in being. His or her achievements excite surprise and admiration in the rest of us who lack this talent because we cannot understand how he or she does it.

These preliminary points do not go very far, however. A theory of human creative thinking would point out the similarities and differences between scientific and artistic endeavor, as regards their respective forms of creativity.

One way of trying to grasp a difficult concept like creativity is to look back at what a great thinker of the past has had to say about it. Even if one does not, in the end, fully agree with his views, still one is likely to learn from him, and our own thinking may well be aided.

In this essay I want to consider the views concerning creativity of Immanuel Kant (1724–1804), a towering figure in eighteenth-century thought, whom many regard as the greatest of the German philosophers. While Kant did not use any word

exactly equivalent to the English term *creativity,* his philosophical system does include striking views about the nature of
creative thinking in the sciences and the arts. It is these that I
want to discuss. Kant's system as a whole is intricate and technical, and so to give any sort of full consideration here to his
philosophy in its entirety is out of the question. But my hope is
to be able to present his views on creativity without going into
detail about his whole philosophy.

Kant's three most important works are *Critique of Pure Reason,*
Critique of Practical Reason, and *Critique of Judgment.* The second
of these books deals with ethics, so I will not discuss it here. I
will consider certain ideas from the first and third books, since
they relate to creativity in science and in art. Kant works out
the most fundamental of his views about the character of
scientific thinking in the *Critique of Pure Reason* and in the second half of the *Critique of Judgment;* his opinions on art are in the
first half of the *Critique of Judgment.* In these works Kant under-
takes a critical examination of the faculties of the human mind
in order to determine to what extent the human mind is able to
attain genuine knowledge.

By "reason" Kant means the thinking capacity at its most
abstract: the kind of thinking that endeavors to arrive at the
truth about reality without making use of sense-experience.
Kant's conclusion in the *Critique of Pure Reason* is that such
thinking is not able to achieve any genuine knowledge of what
is the case.[1] To this extent, his critical inquiry reaches a negative
result, destructive of traditional rationalistic philosophy. He ar-
rives at this result because he holds that human minds are so
constituted as to be capable of awareness of things only as they
are presented through the senses. He holds that we can have
no justification for supposing that the way things appear to us
in sense-experience need resemble at all the way they are in
themselves (indeed, Kant believes he can prove that things in
themselves cannot be either spatial or temporal,[2] and therefore
that they have to be utterly unlike our sensory experiences,
which are necessarily spatial and temporal in form). We cannot
have knowledge of things as they are in themselves; they are
"suprasensible" and forever inaccessible to us.[3]

Does this mean that we can have no knowledge of what is
the case? No, Kant's view is not so skeptical as this. Human

awareness results from the cooperative functioning of sensibility (the capacity to receive sensations) and the faculty of thinking (which Kant calls "understanding," rather than "reason," when he wants to describe thought-activity as cooperating with sensation, rather than as trying to proceed independently of it). We human beings all have the same type of sensibility and the same type of understanding, and therefore in principle the way things appear to us will have the same structure for all of us human beings. This structure is something objective (interpersonal) that we can study and agree on; it is not subjective, in the sense of being merely arbitrary and personal. The spatio-temporal world—what unphilosophical persons think of as the "real" world—is just this orderly and objective structure of "phenomena": of the way things appear to us, as filtered through our sensory and intellectual faculties. According to Kant, this is what science is about. Scientific knowledge of what is the case is knowledge of the orderly ways in which things appear to us. It is not, and must not pretend to be, knowledge of things as they are in themselves.

When we survey Kant's philosophy with the question of creativity in mind, we find that among the types of human mental capacities that he recognizes and distinguishes there are four that are especially relevant to creativity. Two of these have to do with what one would call aesthetics:[4] *genius,* the power by which the inspired artist creates beautiful or sublime works of art; and *taste,* the power by which the cultivated observer recognizes and appreciates the beauty or sublimity of things. Two others have to do with science: *determinant judgment,* the capacity to apply universal and necessary scientific principles to particular cases; and *teleological judgment,* the capacity to see complicated structures as purposive and goal-oriented even when there is no way of verifying that they are so. These four types of capacity do not all involve creativity in the same way, but each is relevant to the question of creativity.

Genius

Probably the most obvious examples of spectacular creativity are provided by great artists, writers, and composers. We do not comprehend the mental processes by which Michelangelo or Shakespeare or Beethoven produced their works of art, literature, and music. How were they thinking? By what miraculous strategies did they devise such products? Any attempts to explain this are utterly inadequate.

We say that great artists have genius, that they are inspired. These words hark back to the ancient view that gods or demigods work in and through such remarkable men, guiding the tongue of the poet, the chisel of the sculptor, and the brush of the painter. According to this ancient theory, the artist himself has little or no comprehension of any plan, according to which he is working, for he is in the grip of supernatural powers. The poet is merely a mouthpiece for his muse; the sculptor or painter lets some nonhuman force direct his hand. Such artists are, as it were, hypnotized or bewitched tools of superior beings. On this view, they exercise no creativity themselves, since it comes from above.

This ancient theory of course does not provide a fundamental understanding of how creativity can occur. It merely transfers creative power from the human artist to a supernatural being without explaining the thought processes by which this supernatural being is able to devise works of such beauty or sublimity. Kant must have regarded this ancient theory as superstitious; he did not think we can have any evidence that gods or demigods work through the artists. He continues to use the word *genius,* however. For Kant, genius is a power of the imagination, a power possessed by some human beings but not by most of them.

Imagination is a faculty of the mind that lies between sensibility and understanding, partaking partly of the character of each. Kant distinguishes between reproductive imagination (memory), which brings back into consciousness elements of experiences previously sensed, and productive imagination, which recombines elements drawn from sensation into new combinations. Genius is a type of productive imagination, of course. By this power of productive imagination the artist is able to create works of art whose intricacies of structure and harmonies of proportion give inexhaustible aesthetic pleasure to cultivated observers.

But where does this power come from, if it does not come from gods and demigods? It does not seem to come from any normal operation of ordinary human capacities, as we know them in conscious thought. Kant's view is that genius is "an innate mental disposition, through which nature gives the rule to art" (*Crit. of Judg.*, 46).[5] That is, Kant holds that the artist of genius does not create primarily through processes of his conscious mind, but instead that there is some natural process (Kant may have thought that it would be some natural physiological process within the artist's body) that stimulates and directs his creative imagination. The richness and complexity of nature (the phenomenal world) can thus find their way into art.

Suppose that physiologists were to learn more about those natural processes that "give the rule to art" in artistic creation. Information about this could be valuable, since it might lead to measures that could enhance creativity in people; for instance, perhaps a certain diet, by enriching the nervous system, could make people more creative. Nevertheless, artistic creativity would remain mysterious to an essential and important extent.

For Kant, to comprehend a process is to capture it in terms of conceptual thinking, to bring it under the concepts of the understanding, by finding a recipe, rule, or principle that fully spells out and accounts for its details. A full comprehension of genius would then provide a rule telling in full just what it does and how and why it works. In principle, then, great works of art could be produced by mechanical application of the rule, without needing to wait for genius to operate naturally. Great works of art might then be mass-produced cheaply in profusion (not merely reproduced or copied) and society would have no further use for natural artistic genius. But this is an impossible fantasy, as Kant would see it. His position is that the making of great works of art can never be reduced to any recipe or rule.

Crude works of art sometimes do follow rules. The novelist who writes pot-boilers perhaps has a formula calling for certain fixed features and certain predictable variations; the same may happen with a painter or composer who is cranking out uninspired works. Such inferior works Kant dismisses as lacking in "spirit" (Geist) (*Crit. of Judg.*, 49). They are too regular in form; once observers have grasped the formula, such works hold no surprises and seem mechanical and stiff. "All stiff regularity . . . is inherently repugnant to taste," he says (*Crit. of Judg.*, 22, Gen. Remark). In contrast, a great work of art is a source of endless challenge and surprises. The more we study it, the more we discover the unexpected in it. Of course, we also discover much that we did expect to find, but the interplay between the expected and the unexpected rivets interest and delights contemplation.

What is fully understood cannot surprise. Great works of art always retain the capacity of surprise and therefore retain an essential element of mystery; they outrun and partly defeat the intellectual power of comprehending them under rules. But if the product of genius, great art, has an essential element of mystery, so too must genius. For there can be no comprehending the creative power apart from comprehending its products.

What is most suggestive about Kant's remarks concerning genius seems to me to be his emphasis on the mystery, the transcendence of conceptual understanding, which genius and great art share. In addition, his theory strikingly underlines how even the human artist himself often has little comprehension of the mental processes operative within his creative consciousness, and how he can feel himself to be moved by a power that is not his conscious self.

Determinant Judgment

By "judgment" Kant means, roughly speaking, the cognitive capacity to tell whether a particular thing falls under a general rule or concept. By "a judgment" he means an act of thought exercising this capacity. Judgment is an activity of the mind that sometimes involves creativity, but often it does not. What Kant calls "determinant judgment" does not involve real creativity, but we need to consider why it does not.

Kant introduces the term *determinant* to describe those judgments that are "based on definite concepts" (*Crit. of Judg.*, Introd., 4). He seems to hold that in all areas of human experience where firm knowledge is attainable, one is able to make determinant judgments. This would include mathematics and the pure part of natural science.[6] A determinant judgment, Kant says, is one in which a concept is antecedently available and a particular is subsumed under it. This is a rather scholastic way of stating the matter, but the point can be interpreted along the following lines.

The simplest type of determinant judgment is that in which a particular phenomenon is classified under a general heading. Thus, for example, when I judge that something I perceive is a square and that something else is a mountain, what I am doing is subsuming these phenomena under the concepts of the square and the mountain, respectively. Other logically more complex kinds of judgments would have to be explained in relation to this simple paradigm.

But what does it mean to subsume a particular phenomenon under a concept? Kant seems to believe that to have a concept is to know a definition (one might also say a general rule or criterion) establishing the necessary and sufficient conditions for a thing to be of the specified kind. My concept of the square is perhaps that of an equilateral rectangle. Here the definition of squares as equilateral rectangles proves a general rule for identifying squares as equilateral rectangles when one encounters them. When I see a phenomenon that I can tell is both rectangular and equilateral, the rule tells me to classify it as a square; that is, through an act of judgment, I subsume it under the concept of the square. Or my concept of a mountain is perhaps that of a piece of terrain of much higher altitude than most of its nearby surroundings. Here too I have a definitional rule for identifying instances. If I experience the phenomenon before me as terrain of much higher altitude than its nearby surroundings, then I can see that it fits my criterion; that is, I subsume it under the concept of a mountain.

Along with his view that to have a concept is to possess a definitional rule of this kind, Kant seems to suppose that it will always be possible to know for certain and to prove that a particular thing is of the given kind. To prove that the shape before me is a square, I need only verify that it fully satisfies the rule. Here the proof can be formulated in deductive form: "All and only equilateral rectangles are squares; this is such a figure; therefore, this is a square." In this way, I think, Kant's notion of what it is to have a definite concept is connected with his view that judgments can embody knowledge, and that knowledge rests upon proof, and that proof is deduction.

Human judgment is able to subsume phenomena under a concept only if the conditions stipulated in the definitional rule are ones that we can connect with sense-experience. (Kant, in one of his most famous sayings, declared, "Thoughts without content are empty, intuitions without concepts are blind."[7]) At this point the faculty of imagination must come into operation. Imagination mediates between concepts and sensations by developing imaginative procedures to go with concepts. One must have a regular way of imagining rectangles and sameness of length if one is to be able to apply the definition of a square. The procedure that imagination uses Kant calls a "schema" of the imagination: "This representation of a universal procedure of imagination in providing an image for a concept, I entitle the schema of the concept."[8] The schema that goes with the concept of square is simple and definite: it involves imagining four straight lines of equal length, joined at right angles. But the schema for the concept of a mountain would be less specific: it allows leeway for the imagination to picture a ragged or a smooth contour, a steep or a gentle slope, and so on. The schema has to be a complex rule for the imagination, prescribing just how much leeway is open and in what respects.[9]

Imagination has to be at work when the mind imagines an instance of a concept, as for instance when one mentally pictures an imaginary square. Here the imagination synthesizes a mental image in which sensory qualities are combined in a way conforming to the definitional rule of the concept. In addition, the imagination is at work when the mind recognizes phenomena encountered in experience; here the imagination would have to run through the schema, comparing it point for point with the structure of the encountered phenomenon, so as to tell whether the phenomenon measures up to what the definition requires. Furthermore, sensations of a physical thing usually are very incomplete (one visually senses only part of the outer surface of the mountain), and imagination, working in an unconscious manner, must synthesize further images to augment what is sensed, so that experience becomes that of perceiving a solid mountain having a far side and insides. As it carries on this activity, the imagination is guided always by definite rules of schematism, laid down in advance. These rules specify exactly what leeway the imagination is to be permitted in its synthesizing of images.

In a larger sense, the activity of imagination is what produces one's experience of nature (and correlatively self-consciousness). This happens as follows. The sensations coming into the mind are structureless and unrelated (a mere "manifold," Kant believes). The imagination must run through them, must hold them together, and must supplement them, in order to build up consciousness of a natural world. In this activity, the imagination works in conformity to the rules of the understanding, which prescribe certain general rational requirements. These have to do especially with causality and substance (the categories or "pure concepts of the understanding"). Nature, as our minds organize it in consciousness, must be structured so that every event belongs to a thoroughgoing network of causes and effects and must involve underlying substance that does not come into being or pass away. Because the understanding lays down these requirements, Kant says that our minds are "law-givers to nature."[10] That is, we ordain the orderly structure that nature must exhibit (and without which we could not become aware of nature).

What does this mean for creativity? Does it mean that nature is a creation that our minds freely spin out, just as artists of genius freely create their aesthetic structures?

To be sure, these rules of the understanding do provide a structure that we impose upon an alien material consisting of sensations that are not of our making. This material is forced upon us, not created by us. But is the structure that human imagination and understanding impose upon this material an expression of our creativity? No, to suppose so would be the wrong interpretation. The rules of the understanding, which govern the operations of the imagination here, are regarded by Kant as exactly the same for all human beings (indeed, for all "sensuously affected" rational beings). They come from the universal character of rational thinking, which is the essence of our being. There is nothing personal or individual about them. So my imposing these rules upon my experience cannot be an action of choice, whether conscious or unconscious. There is no scope for orginality here, no opportunity for individual self-expression. Consequently, this activity is not at all creative in the sense in which the activity of artists can be.

Determinant judgment, then, is not a creative activity in the sense with which we are concerned. As Kant sees it, it is a routine activity in which the human mind brings phenomena under concepts (or general rules) in a cut-and-dried manner. Much of scientific thinking, for Kant, consists of this routine process. For example, in the science of pure mechanics, general laws are laid down by the understanding as such,[11] and through determinant judgment we apply those laws to particular cases; there is only one correct way for human beings to do this. If there is a type of judgment that involves individual human creativity, it must be sought elsewhere.

Teleological Judgment

In the *Critique of Judgment* Kant presents a doctrine that he had not mentioned in his earlier works: not all judgment is determinant; there is another type of judgment, "reflective" judgment. Kant says that in reflective judgment one does not have a definite concept under which one decisively subsumes particular phenomena. Instead, upon encountering a particular phenomenon, one seeks a concept (a definition, a rule, a regularity) under which to subsume it. With reflective judgment, one imaginatively constructs some hazy rule to which the phenomenon seems to conform, and one judges (guesses, hypothesizes, or inductively infers) that this is the rule governing it—but one cannot tell for certain whether this is so.

For Kant, reflective judgment is of two types: judgments of taste and teleological judgment. Let us consider the latter first.

In the world around us are some phenomena known to be purposive; for instance, buildings, which are always intentionally made by human builders for the purpose of providing shelter. But with the vast majority of phenomena (such as the motions of the planets, the eruptions of volcanoes, the growth of a blade of grass) we cannot verify that they are designed by any intelligent being, nor can we know what purposes they serve, if they are designed by anyone. (To know such things would require access to suprasensible reality, which human beings cannot have.) Should scientists regard these phenomena as merely mechanical?

Kant was well aware that the new science of the modern period tended to denigrate attempts to see purposes in unconscious nature and tended to advocate the abolition of teleology from science.[12] Kant did not go along with this. He agreed that in the study of pure physics teleology has no place; there, mechanical laws reign supreme and there is no room for thinking in terms of purposes. But elsewhere in science he found teleological thinking to have a legitimate and indeed a necessary role. He had two lines of argument about this.

Kant's more specific line of argument has to do with biological science. He holds that living organisms cannot be understood or explained mechanically. We need to think about them teleologically, Kant holds, focusing on the purposes that the parts of an organism seem to serve in benefiting the whole. We invoke the notion of an organism as a "fully organized system":

a system in which every part is completely attuned to all the rest and in which each part functions fully in the service of the whole. Using this notion as a "leading thread," Kant thinks that we shall be led to make many new, verifiable discoveries about the observable operations of organisms. Kant's line of thought here is pragmatic; teleological thinking proves to have indispensable value for biological science, he thinks, and so it must be engaged in, even though there can be no proof that organisms do embody any such purposes. This biological argument will seem outdated and wrong-headed to today's readers, who are familiar with the successes in recent years of non-teleological biology. So let us turn to Kant's more general line of argument.

Kant's other argument in favor of the teleological viewpoint relates to the logic of scientific reasoning. He holds that we can know for certain those *a priori* universal laws of mathematics and pure physics that our minds impose on nature, but the rest of the laws of nature have to be reached by shrewd guesswork, based upon observation. Cases constantly arise in science where observational evidence concerning a group of phenomena is insufficient to enable us strictly to deduce the governing laws. In chemistry, for example, suppose we observe, within a margin of error of 1 percent, that twice as much hydrogen as oxygen is consumed in forming water. This leaves open (within that same margin of error) the possibility that the true ratio might be anywhere between 1.98 and 2.02 to 1. Of course we could do more experiments and perhaps narrow down the margin of error, but we can never eliminate it altogether. As long as there is a margin of error, a range is left open within which infinitely many different precise hypotheses fall. Our observations are logically compatible with all of them. How can we choose which hypothesis to accept as scientifically best?

In practice scientists unhesitatingly prefer the simplest hypothesis compatible with their observations. In the example, the ratio of 2 to 1 would be regarded as the best hypothesis. Here, and in many other connections, scientific thinking employs simplicity as one criterion for judging what is to be accepted scientifically. Without such a criterion, scientific thinking would fall into disorder and would not be able to cope with the profusion of competing hypotheses. And in relation to somewhat different types of examples, Kant also advocates parsimony and continuity, along with simplicity (*Crit. of Judg.*, Introd., 5).[13]

Kant is not claiming that we can know nature to be simple (or parsimonious or continuous); evidence can never establish this. But in scientific thinking we must proceed as if nature is simple; only by so regarding nature can thinking have coherent guidelines. And what are we presuming about nature when we regard it in this way? Kant thinks it is evident that we are presuming nature to be designed by a supernatural creator who intended it to be simple (and parsimonious and continuous) in its laws.

When a world is in every respect under the control of an intelligent creator, what character can we expect this being will impose on it? Kant holds that an intelligent creator with absolute power is going to produce an organic whole, every element of which mirrors the structure of the rest, combining simplicity with diversity in a pattern of maximum coherent articulation (parsimony and continuity will belong as well).[14] The result is that scientists are to regard nature as if it is an organic whole, created by an all-powerful intelligence, with empirical laws of nature forming a pattern that manifests the metaphysical purposes of the creator. This means that scientific thinking has to be teleological. Outside of pure mathematics and pure physics, science constantly needs to rely upon judgments about purposes underlying unconscious elements of nature.

In this connection, Kant speaks of "purposiveness without a purpose": by this he means purposiveness in the sense that phenomena are to be viewed as thoroughly organized by intelligent design. By "without a purpose" Kant indicates that we cannot verify what purposes, if any, they really do serve (*Crit. of Judg.*, 58). This notion of purposiveness without a purpose is an "indefinite concept" that we employ in reflective judgments. Unlike the concepts involved in making determinant judgments, it is essentially imprecise. Also, unlike them, it can never be proved to apply to phenomena, yet it can never be proved to be inapplicable either, and it gives indispensable coherence to our thinking about phenomena.

In the making of determinant judgments one uses concepts whose schemata spell out exactly how much room for maneuver is allowed to the imagination. With determinant judgments it is always a cut-and-dried matter whether a particular phenomenon falls under a specific concept. And hence, creativity, which has to involve originality and freedom of choice, cannot be involved in the making of determinant judgments. In reflective teleological judgment the situation is different. Here there is no definite concept that can be proved to fit. Instead, there is the indefinite notion of purposiveness (and the simplicity that it involves) by means of which we seek to understand phenomena. When confronted by a need to choose between competing hypotheses that are equally consistent with our observations, we try to choose the simplest hypothesis, but there is no easy way to determine which is simplest. Our minds have room for free maneuvering in trying to devise hypotheses that will creatively tend to maximize the simplicity, parsimony, and continuity of our overall theory of the material world. Thus there is scope for a type of genuinely creative thinking. Yet this thinking is not arbitrary and subjective, either; once one thinker has creatively devised a new hypothesis, others should be able to agree with him on how it compares with available competing hypotheses for simplicity, and so on, which it will impart to the overall theory. To be sure, there can be no mechanical proof to determine which of two competing hypotheses contributes more to simplicity, and so on, since with indefinite concepts deductive proofs do not operate. But because all human beings have the same cognitive faculties, we should be able to come to agreement about this sort of point. It would seem that, for Kant, this claim to universality must be of the same type as that for judgments of taste.

Judgments of Taste

Kant's other type of reflective judgments are what he calls judgments of taste. These are judgments on what is beautiful or sublime. For the sake of brevity, I concentrate on beauty and neglect the sublime.

Kant states that "the judgment of taste is not based on concepts" (*Crit. of Judg.*, 56). He seems to be suggesting that judgments on what is beautiful cannot state scientifically verifiable facts, which seems to imply that there is no objective truth on what is beautiful; if one person considers an object beautiful and another person regards it as not beautiful, neither appraisal can be any more correct or any more mistaken than the other. In support of this thesis, Kant insists that no judgment concerning beauty can ever be proven or disproven ("There is no disputing about taste"). That is, no matter how much one learns about the verifiable properties of a phenomenon, nothing logically follows as to whether it is beautiful or not.

On the other hand, Kant insists that in making judgments on beauty we do claim objectivity and think it legitimate to do so. In making such judgments we cannot regard them as merely subjective and arbitrary. Kant emphasizes the difference between saying "this is beautiful" (a judgment of taste) and saying "I happen to like this" (an expression of one's subjective preference). In the former remark one is claiming that others are mistaken if they disagree with one's appraisal, but such a claim is excluded from the latter remark.

According to Kant, judgments about beauty are those that human beings make as a result of a special kind of functioning of two cognitive faculties, imagination and understanding (no other faculties are involved). Kant believes he is entitled to presume that all human beings have the same kind of cognitive faculties. Therefore, it is legitimate to suppose that all human beings must be able in principle to reach agreement in their judgments concerning beauty. The agreement will not be achieved through deductive proofs, which logically compel assent as to what is beautiful and what is not. But because all human beings have the same kind of cognitive faculties, all of us should respond in the same way to any observed object—provided that each of us allows his imagination and understanding to function in this special way, undisturbed by other faculties of the mind; that is, provided each of us attends to the object with what may be called a purely aesthetic attitude.

When a person judges that something is beautiful he claims to be appraising it on the basis of this special attitude. One can be mistaken about one's attitude, however. Thus, for Kant, disagreements about beauty, when they do arise, must always come from undetected (but detectable) impurity in our attitudes. For example, suppose that two people see a tiger; one judges that it is beautiful and the other judges that it is hideous. According to Kant, they are contradicting each other; each is claiming that everyone ought to agree with him (though this is not an ethical "ought"). The explanation of the disagreement must be that at least one of them has not adopted the appropriate attitude. Perhaps the second person has allowed his judgment to be contaminated by his fear of the animal, whereas the first person has adopted a purely aesthetic attitude in his contemplation of the rich color pattern of the tiger's coat and the elegance of its movements.[15] The first person has abstracted himself from all consideration of the harm associated with the object of his attention and has achieved a properly aesthetic appraisal of it; his judgment is the correct aesthetic one, and his opponent has made a mistake through inattention to his own attitudes.

The aesthetic attitude, according to Kant, is an attitude in which one disinterestedly contemplates the patterns of one's sensations of shape, color, sound, and so on (*Crit. of Judg.*, 2). Disinterestedness involves setting aside all one's "interests": all sensuous interests (self-centered, subjective concerns about the pleasure or pain that the object may cause), and also all rational interests (objective concerns about the ethical rightness or wrongness of allowing the object to exist). To cultivate one's taste is to learn to adopt this attitude in which all interests, whether sensuous or rational, are set aside. Of course many people do not succeed in cultivating their taste: as Kant writes, "Taste that requires an added element of *charm* and *emotions* for its delight, not to speak of adopting this as the measure of its approval, has not yet emerged from barbarism" (*Crit. of Judg.*, 13). But, in principle, every human being is capable of learning to perform this abstraction. And so it is proper to presume agreement in principle about beauty among all human observers, because for people who do make this abstraction, the only faculties that will then be operating in forming their appraisals about beauty will be cognitive faculties common to all human beings.

But how do these cognitive faculties operate when one is disinterestedly contemplating beautiful things? Kant says that cognitive powers are then "in free play" (*Crit. of Judg.*, 9), which somehow is related to the "form" of the object rather than to its "content." This "free play" can lead to a "harmony" between the imagination and the understanding (*Crit. of Judg.*, 35), which provides "entertainment for the mental powers" (*Crit. of Judg.*, 22, Gen. Remark) and yields disinterested pleasure.

These points are suggestive, but what do they add up to? We need an interpretation of Kant's cryptic remarks, which will spell out what is supposed to be going on when human beings experience beauty. Various scholars writing on Kant's account of beauty have provided much valuable commentary. However, they have not offered as much as one would like to have on this problem of interpreting the process supposedly going on in the experience of beauty.[16]

In trying to work toward an answer to this question, let us first notice that the things which humans judge to be beautiful exhibit organic structure, just as do those aspects of nature that teleological judgment deems to be purposive. It is a question of the thoroughgoing relationship of elements, each part requiring to be regarded as being the way it is in order to contribute to the pattern of the whole. With a beautiful object, the organized, purposive structure detectable by a human observer pervades every element and aspect. So there is an important analogy between the concerns of judgments of taste and teleological judgments.

The objects of these two types of judgment partly overlap; that is, often the same phenomenon can be regarded either teleologically (from a scientific standpoint) or aesthetically (from the standpoint of taste). Kant gives the example of a flower (*Crit. of Judg.*, 16). Botanists regard the parts of the flower as having been intelligently designed to be organs of reproduction; to advance their science, they make teleological judgments about the flower, which affords no aesthetic pleasure. Observers aesthetically appreciating the beauty of the flower contemplate the systematic interrelationships involved in its pattern of shape and color, and they too regard them as intelligently designed; but the features that concern them— how the color and shape of each part harmonize with every other part—do not seem to have anything to do with biological purposes such as reproduction, and they cannot say what intelligently designed purposes are served, if any (*Crit. of Judg.*, Introd., 16). So purposive organic structure is important in both cases, but in teleological judgments specific hypotheses about the purposes of the parts are formed, with no resulting aesthetic pleasure, while with judgments of taste no specific purposes are conjectured, although distinctively aesthetic pleasure does result.

Note that ordinary determinant judgments occur suddenly; one experiences a phenomenon and instantly one judges it to be a square or a mountain—the mental process of running through the schema and checking that the phenomenon conforms to it is nearly instantaneous. In contrast, the experiencing of a beautiful object is a continuing process that can take a long time. Kant says that the mind dwells on the beautiful object in some kind of prolonged process of reflection, tracing more and more of the interrelations within the object. "We linger" he declares, "over the contemplation of the beautiful because this contemplation strengthens and reproduces itself" (*Crit. of Judg.*, 12).

Kant further describes this process as involving play of the imagination in relation to the understanding. He wishes somehow to contrast the experiencing of beauty with the more work-a-day employment of the mind in determinant and even in teleological judgment. There is something playful, spontaneous, and free in the experiencing of beauty, in contrast to the more sober earnestness of determinant and teleological judgment. To speak of play suggests that there is some game that engages the mind, possibly with its faculties competing against one another. The more rewarding games are activities governed by rules of play that allow the participants scope to exercise ingenuity and self-expression in their pursuit of the game's goal. Kant seems to suppose that in appreciating beauty the mind plays a quite special sort of game, which affords disinterested pleasure.

But why does Kant think that this pleasure arises? One possible interpretation is that Kant regards this pleasure as simply resulting from the exercise of our cognitive faculties, especially the imagination. Using one's faculties in general gives the special kind of pleasure that comes from contemplation of beautiful things. He believes we do not derive this special pleasure even from imaginative reverie. In this connection, he mentions a fire on the hearth as a phenomenon that the imagination may take as a starting point for the free play of reverie; such a phenomenon has "charm" but need not be beautiful nor give disinterested pleasure (*Crit. of Judg.*, 22, Gen. Remark).

A more metaphysical suggestion to explain the special pleasure we take in contemplating beauty would be that beautiful objects make us think of suprasensible intelligence. The way these objects seem designed expressly to mesh with our cognitive faculties hints that human beings are not the only intelligent beings existing; there may be a divine intelligence in the suprasensible realm who controls the universe and adjusts it to our needs. The suggestion is that this thought pleases because it is comforting. However, this interpretation will not explain why Kant supposes pleasure is associated with beauty. Teleological judgment, such as when we regard a flower as designed to be an organ of reproduction, gives as strong a hint as beauty does that we are in some kind of touch with a suprasensible intelligence—thus providing an antidote for metaphysical loneliness. Yet, according to Kant, teleological judgment is not accompanied by the special pleasure associated with beauty.

Part of the answer here, I believe, is that we can expect to feel special pleasure when we have freely chosen to confront a difficult cognitive challenge and when we have handled that challenge with some degree of success. If the challenge is genuine and we are not certain ahead of time that we shall succeed in handling it, then success comes as a pleasant surprise. I believe Kant thinks that neither determinant nor teleological judgment presents this type of challenge. But in confronting objects one can decide freely whether or not to contemplate them with the aesthetic attitude, and then one's imagination may or may not succeed in meeting the intellectual challenges that they present. When success is achieved, a disinterested pleasure arises.

But what sort of challenge do we take up when we agree to contemplate objects with the aesthetic attitude? Cognitive faculties in general strive to find order in the phenomena confronted. The drive of the mind is to seek to comprehend phenomena in their every detail and interrelationship. Faced with a phenomenon, the faculty of understanding will subsume it under a definite concept or general law if it can. But suppose that the phenomenon is a scenic landscape or a sonata. If one has set oneself to contemplate these phenomena with the aesthetic attitude, then one is concerned only with the pattern of observable shape, color, sound, and so on; one is not seeking a scientific explanation of their physical causes. How is the drive to comprehend the detailed interrelationships of shape, sound, and color in these phenomena to be satisfied? One does have the concept of a landscape and the concept of a sonata, and the phenomena do conform to the respective schemata of these concepts (to judge that this is a landscape, or that a sonata is to make determinant judgments). But subsuming the phenomena under those concepts does not carry us very far at all. The general concept of a landscape provides no rule explaining why a particular Alpine view has its own distinctive pattern of shapes and colors; nor does the concept of the sonata tell us why the Moonlight Sonata contains the special interrelations of tones it does. Kant's position is that when we disinterestedly contemplate the patterns of shape, color, sound, and so on, in phenomena such as beauties of nature and great works of art, we are forced to view these phenomena as organic unities whose elements hang together systematically. But there is never a definite concept that adequately describes the structure of such a phenomenon. Determinant judgment is quickly defeated in its attempt to cognize the "why" of the detailed interrelations of the elements.[17] Also teleological judgment is defeated, for it cannot propose with plausibility any specific purposes served by the parts or their interrelations.

The mind's drive toward finding order in these phenomena persists, even though definite concepts fail to provide the understanding that is sought. What else can the mind do? It must now resort to indefinite concepts. The defeat of determinant and teleological judgment leaves imagination still undefeated and in the field. Imagination goes ahead, trying to build up some kind of grasp of the structure of these phenomena. That is, in considering each such phenomenon, it tries to develop a "feel" for how the organized elements of the phenomenon are interrelated, even though this "feel" cannot be conceptually articulated in any explicit way.

Earlier I noted how Kant supposes that in experiencing a concrete object one's imagination is continually forming images of parts of the object that have not yet been inspected. The same is true when one reflects upon the natural beauty of a work of art. There is always more to such a pattern of color, sound, and so on, than one can be aware of at one time. Moreover, the contemplated object always presents itself to the observer's attention in serial order, as an endless sequence of new perceptions. These are the experiences of attending first to one part of the pattern and then to another, and so on and on; and the series is indefinitely long because even after one has sensed every part of the phenomenon, one can go back and reexamine the parts anew, scrutinizing them and their interrelations in new ways. In imagining the further portions that have not yet been sensed, or not yet been sufficiently sensed, and in imagining how they are related to what has been sensed so far, the imagination has no firm guidance. There is no definite schema that it must obey. It is on its own, aided only by the indefinite conception of the purposiveness of an organized whole—the conception of thoroughgoing unity in diversity. The imagination must form images, hoping that they will turn out to be appropriate ones. The game it has to play is one of inductive projection: guessing from the character of what has been sensed what the character will be of that which is to be sensed later. Subsequent experience will settle whether the imagination has played its game well or badly; the understanding will preside over this testing. So if we wish to regard this game as a competitive one, we might think of imagination as competing against the understanding. But perhaps it is better to think of imagination and understanding as partners who compete against the mysterious object, and whose respective activities come into harmony when the mind is succeeding in the game.

Thus, if all goes well in the contemplation of the organized pattern of shapes, colors, and sounds, one will begin to develop a "feel" for how the pattern is organized. This "feel" will lead a mind to make many predictions (perhaps unconscious ones) about what is to be sensed later. The accuracy of this "feel" will be tested by the way the future part of the series of experiences unfolds. Do the similarities and differences that one has imagined to exist between the earlier and the later elements of the series actually turn out to be there? As the experience unfolds, it may happen that a majority of the conjectures are confirmed, and the inarticulate "feel" for the pattern in the unfolding sequence of elements shows itself to be largely reliable. In this case, a disinterested aesthetic pleasure results, for one is having unexpected success in meeting the cognitive challenge posed by the object being contemplated.

Both natural and artificial phenomena, living and nonliving phenomena can be suitable objects for this contemplative game. But of course not all phenomena are equally rewarding to contemplate in this way. Some phenomena are too crude in their structure; one quickly gets the "feel" of how their elements fit together, and it then becomes boring to continue with further contemplation because there is not enough cognitive challenge. Some other phenomena are too intricate in their structure of shapes, colors, and sounds; human observers cannot decipher or get the "feel" of their interrelationships and thus they are also aesthetically unsatisfactory. Still other phenomena exhibit a negative kind of purposiveness in their forms; through gross disproportions or clashing tonal contrasts, they are seemingly designed to defeat the mind's contemplative expectations when it surveys them. These phenomena are regarded as ugly.

The best and most aesthetically satisfying objects will be those having the kind of structure permitting a fairly ingenious human observer to make considerable headway toward getting the "feel" of how they are put together (in terms of their patterns of shape, color, sound), but where his or her efforts never totally succeed. An object of great beauty will pose a cognitive challenge that the human imagination is capable of making great progress toward solving. Yet, as one solves the initial stages of the puzzle, getting much of the "feel" of the pattern, additional puzzling aspects will challenge one further, and the object's challenge will never be finally exhausted.

In the aesthetic contemplation of beautiful things, the observer through the activity of his imagination engages in a process that is freely undertaken and that gives him scope for expressing his originality. We must classify this process as creative. Of course the creativity of the person who experiences beauty is different from that of the artist of genius; yet both do display creativity, each in his or her own distinctive way.

In review, according to Kant's philosophy several quite different forms of human mental process relate to creativity in different ways. Fundamental to Kant's philosophy is his view of determinant judgment, which involves the imagination operating under the concepts (or laws) of the understanding. Through this process, Kant holds, human consciousness of nature (the phenomenal world) is constructed. In this kind of process of creation, we "make" nature. But this process leaves no scope for originality or freedom for personal expression on the part of the individual human participants, since it must be carried out according to objective rules that necessarily are the same for all of us. Therefore, it is a cut-and-dried type of creation, without creativity.

In teleological judgment, the human mind finds itself less strictly constrained. In biology conjectures are made about how the parts function to contribute to the whole of specific organisms. In scientific thinking about empirical phenomena of any kind, competing hypotheses are evaluated in light of the guiding notion that a supreme designer has organized nature according to the goals of simplicity, continuity, and parsimony. These teleological conjectures cannot be confirmed by our experience, because of course we have no experience that can determine the existence and designs of a supernatural creator; but our experience can never disconfirm these conjectures, either. Therefore, they remain mere conjectures, unprovable and untestable, but indispensable in guiding and organizing the solid knowledge of phenomena. The mental process of framing such conjectures gives the imagination leeway to operate with inventive originality of a creative type.

In making judgments of taste the human imagination operates with a freedom like that exercised in teleological judgment. Not bound by definite rules that fully prescribe how it is to operate, the individual's imagination can organize creatively conjectures for itself in a fresh and original manner. However, there is an important difference between judgments of taste and teleological judgments in the interaction of imagination and understanding. In teleological judgments there is no way for the understanding to check the correctness of what imagination has conjectured since the imagination's conjectures remain untestable. But in judgments of taste there is a continual interplay between understanding and imagination, which I interpret as involving testing by the understanding of predictions made by the imagination. Having experienced a work of art to a certain extent, the imagination begins to get an inarticulate "feel" for the structure of the work, and on this basis projects how the work will unfold as it is experienced further. The understanding then establishes whether further experience of the work does in fact conform to the projection. Imagination and understanding are thus playing a cognitive game, where, if the work of art is a good one, they will win some innings and lose others as the dialectic of predictions and checking goes on. Here the creative activity of imagination is at a high level, with ample scope for ingenuity and originality.

Finally there is genius, in which creativity of the most powerful and mysterious kind is found. Genius is the power by which natural forces work through the unconscious mind of a human artist to produce great works of art. Kant surely supposes that these natural forces are themselves purposive, reflecting the design of a supreme creative intelligence; but human beings can never verify that this is so, nor can they predict or understand the detailed workings of genius. Its originality and uniquely individual modes of unconscious self-expression necessarily evade comprehension.

In Kant's philosophy these four forms of human mental process pertain to creativity in different ways. Just to become aware of Kant's views about these matters is worthwhile, for he thought deeply about them and influenced subsequent thought very strongly. But beyond this, are there any lessons about creativity that we should especially derive from him? I think there are, though I shall keep my claims quite modest. Even those who disagree with much of Kant's philosophy should, I think, be impressed by the following points.

For one thing, Kant's account of genius impressively emphasizes the essentially incomprehensible character of artistic creation. Against those who might profess to analyze and unravel the technique of creation in some comprehensive way, Kant insists that what can be fully analyzed and explained cannot be of aesthetic value and that great works of art must always defy any complete or final analysis or reduction to rules.

Another valuable point in Kant's account is his emphasis upon the creativity of the person who appreciates a work of art. It is not only the artist who must be creative; if great art is to play its role, there must also be cultivated observers who display a different but no less important type of creativity as they ingeniously engage in the dialectical play of appreciating beauty.

A third lesson that Kant's philosophy teaches is that there is an important kinship between artistic and scientific creativity. In his view, the scientific thinker must form hypotheses and choose among them; this is a mental operation requiring imaginative freedom and originality, akin to what artistic appreciation demands. The teleological judgment involved here operates differently from the judgment of taste, but with some of the same creative freedom. One might even carry Kant's thought further than he did and suggest that in science as well as in art there is a role for creative genius. This would be the genius of the great scientific theorizer, who invents original new hypotheses by an unconscious process that he himself does not fully understand, a process that cannot be reduced to rule.

Willing readers could certainly draw many further worthwhile lessons from Kant's treatment of these topics, but for present purposes I shall content myself with these points.

NOTES

1. In Kant's terminology, knowledge of what is the case is "theoretical" knowledge. Knowledge of what ought to be the case is "practical" knowledge. In the *Critique of Practical Reason* Kant holds that the faculty of reason can attain practical knowledge, despite its inability to attain theoretical knowledge.

2. Kant discusses this in "The Antinomy of Pure Reason" in the *Critique of Pure Reason.* He argues that contradictions inevitably result from supposing that things in themselves are spatial or temporal. The only way to avoid these contradictions, he says, is to recognize that space and time pertain merely to phenomena.

3. Kant does believe that we know there are things in themselves and that they are neither spatial nor temporal. What we humans cannot attain, in his view, is any knowledge of the positive nature of things in themselves.

4. Kant himself does not use this word in our sense, as having to do with beauty; instead, he gives it a special technical sense that he introduces in his theory of knowledge. See the "Transcendental Aesthetic" in the *Critique of Pure Reason.*

5. References to the *Critique of Judgment* are to section numbers in and translations are adapted from *Critique of Aesthetic Judgment,* trans. James Creed Meredith (Oxford: Clarendon Press, 1911).

6. What Kant calls "practical" knowledge—that is, knowledge of what ought to be the case—would also lead to determinant judgments. However, this belongs to ethics and is not of concern here.

7. *Critique of Pure Reason,* trans. Norman Kemp Smith (New York and London: Macmillan, 1929), A 51 (B 75).

8. Ibid., A 140 (B 179). A helpful discussion of Kant's doctrine of schematism is found in Robert Paul Wolff, *Kant's Theory of Mental Activity* (Cambridge, Mass.: Harvard University Press, 1963), 206–23.

9. The notion that all or most concepts are "open" concepts, so important in Wittgenstein's later philosophy, has certainly not occurred to Kant, who, I believe, regards ordinary schematized concepts as always completely definite.

10. *Prolegomena to Any Future Metaphysics,* section 36.

11. Kant's fullest discussion of these laws is given in his *Metaphysical Foundations of Natural Science.*

12. The most extreme expression of this idea is represented by Descartes' doctrine of the "automatism of brutes": the idea that even animals are merely machines.

13. For another treatment of these ideas, see the *Critique of Pure Reason,* A 650–663 (B 678–691). In my *Induction and Hypothesis* (Ithaca, N.Y., and London: Cornell University Press, 1957), I argued in more detail for the view that simplicity is an important criterion in scientific thinking; however, I tried to separate the idea of simplicity from the idea of design.

14. This idea of the character of an organic whole probably comes to Kant from Leibniz. A good discussion of this idea is found in Lewis White Beck's *Early German Philosophy* (Cambridge, Mass.: Harvard University Press, 1969), 226–27.

15. Kant emphasizes that objects can be found beautiful even though they are dangerous or evil; *Critique of Judgment,* 48.

16. Among the works in English dealing with Kant's third critique are: H. W. Cassirer, *A Commentary on Kant's Critique of Judgment* (London: Methuen, 1938); Theodore E. Uehling, Jr., *The Notion of Form in Kant's Critique of Aesthetic Judgment* (The Hague: Mouton, 1971); Donald W. Crawford, *Kant's Aesthetic Theory* (Madison: University of Wisconsin Press, 1974); Paul Guyer, *Kant and the Claims of Taste* (Cambridge, Mass.: Harvard University Press, 1979); Eva Schaper, *Studies in Kant's Aesthetics* (Edinburgh: Edinburgh University Press, 1979); Ted Cohen and Paul Guyer, *Essays in Kant's Aesthetics* (Chicago: University of Chicago Press, 1982).

17. Kant is of course committed to denying that there could ever be any complete reductive explanation of organic structures in terms of mechanical ones.

Schemata, Paradigms, and Prime Objects: The Role of the Imagination in Science and Art

W. H. BOSSART

University of California, Davis

Science and art are sometimes contrasted by the kind of thinking that dominates these apparently quite different activities. A fairly prevalent stereotype of scientific thinking is that the scientist proceeds conceptually, mastering the theories and rules governing his or her concrete procedures. The artist, on the other hand, is often pictured as creating intuitively, through flashes of immediate insight rather than according to definite rules. This is not to deny that intuition plays an important role in scientific thinking, but intuitions are soon integrated into the scientist's general conceptual framework. In contrast, art seems to be fundamentally intuitive, for even where the artist shows an interest in theory, for example, in pointillism or in the work of Kandinsky, theory is ultimately in the service of the intuitive creation of individual artifacts.

In what follows I should like to take issue with these somewhat overdrawn caricatures by examining the role played by the imagination in science and art. The imagination is also a logical point of departure for a discussion of creativity because of the connection that has frequently been made by the Romantics and others between imagination and creative intuition. However, I shall not draw any lessons directly from Romanticism. Instead I shall turn to Kant's epistemology for a suggestion as to how imagination functions in thought. Kant's views on knowledge are relevant to this discussion, for Kant denies that there can be any genuine knowledge without both intuition and conceptual thought, and he affirms that these apparently disparate modes of thought are brought together through the schema-producing function of the imagination. I shall then take up two examples of how schematic thinking functions: Thomas Kuhn's discussion of paradigms in science and George Kubler's examination of prime objects in art. Each, I shall argue, exemplifies certain aspects of schematic thinking that play a central role in the constitution and articulation of experience.

Schemata

We tend to think of perception as the primary mode of access to sensible reality and of the perceptual object as existing out there, independently of being perceived. The perceptual object is really present before us, but imaginary objects enjoy no such real presence. They are present in their absence, and this is why we sometimes refer to them as figments of the imagination. Kant describes the imagination as a faculty of producing images in the absence of the perceptual objects to which such images bear some reference. In this sense the imagination is free. Because of its freedom, Kant conceives of the imagination as the faculty of comparing, shaping, differentiating, and connecting in general.[1] Elsewhere, in some rather obscure passages of the *Critique of Pure Reason,* Kant distinguishes two different functions of the imagination, the reproductive and the productive.[2] Kant never makes this distinction perfectly clear, but I shall try to adapt what he may have had in mind to this discussion.

For Kant perception is a process of organizing sensations into recognizable objects that stand in certain determinate relations to one another.[3] Imagination is at work in this process whenever we encounter the phenomenon of presence in absentia. My immediate awareness of a house, for example, grasps only one of its sides. To perceive the house, I must walk around it, apprehending its other sides in turn. Since the perception of the house is a process that takes time, I must also keep before my mind what has been present when it is no longer present. Furthermore, each new view of the house does not come as a complete surprise; I anticipate what I am about to apprehend, once more in the mode of presence in absentia. Hence the imagination functions in anticipation as well as in recall. This, however, is the work of the reproductive imagination that does not create *ex nihilo* but merely reproduces, albeit sometimes in new combinations, images that originate in sense perception. But this does not exhaust the contribution of the imagination to perception. To perceive the house I must relate all these images together as images of different aspects of the same perceptual object. Thus the process of apprehension, anticipation, and recall also requires conception, for without the concept *house*, I would be unable to recognize that what I now apprehend and what I expect to apprehend are aspects of what I apprehended just a moment ago. But Kant holds that concepts and percepts are heterogeneous elements. Hence their union requires the mediation of some third term. This is the second contribution that imagination makes to perception.

Kant distinguishes sharply between concepts and intuitions. In intuition I am immediately related to an individual object. A concept, however, is a general representation that relates individuals given in intuition to one another by expressing something they have in common. Kant holds that the objects of intuition are, for man at least, all sensible. But this is not so for concepts. Although most of our concepts, like the concept *house*, are the result of empirical generalization, Kant maintains that there are also pure concepts that originate a priori in the understanding and independently of sense experience. It is by means of such concepts as *substance* and *causality* that the mind synthesizes sensible data into a coherent and structured world. Yet the application of these concepts to intuitions poses a problem, for the pure concepts of the understanding are intellectual and general and share no common ground with the sensible individuals of intuition. At this point Kant introduces the productive function of the imagination to bridge this gap. The imagination is able to mediate between intellect and sense because it is both intellectual and sensible. It is intellectual since its operations take place according to a rule. For example, when I imagine a house, I do not proceed haphazardly but form my image according to my concept *house*. The imagination is also sensible, since it deals primarily with images. The reproductive imagination works directly with images, while the productive imagination renders pure concepts sensible, thus facilitating their application to sense experience. It does this by producing what Kant calls "schemata." To carry out its task the schema must share in both the intellectual and general nature of the concept and the sensible individuality of intuited objects. Thus schemata cannot be derived directly either from understanding or sense. They must be genuinely novel products of the imagination.[4]

To avoid a long excursion into Kant's epistemology, I shall employ the somewhat inexact analogy of an architect's drawing to suggest how such schemata might function. The drawing is a sensible rendering of the architect's concept of the kind of house to be built. And when it is read by someone familiar with the conventions of architectural rendering, it may be identified as that individual house and no other. From another point of view, however, the drawing is also a general plan for building a number of similar houses. A schema, then, is the product of a creative act of the imagination that can be read as a general plan or as an individual exemplar.

Kant himself pays little attention to concepts other than the pure concepts of the understanding, but the analogy of the architect's drawing suggests that the productive imagination may not be limited to rendering pure concepts sensible. In his brief discussion of schematism Kant suggests that mathematics deals primarily with schemata. More important, his remarks concerning empirical concepts can be read as maintaining that, in the last analysis, there is no distinction between an empirical concept and its schema (A137/B176, A147, B187). Indeed it is difficult to understand in what this difference might consist. Empirical concepts like *house,* which function in our recognition of perceptual objects, already stand in an immediate relation to the sensible experience from which they are derived. And as the faculty of comparing, shaping, differentiating, and connecting in general, the imagination must also play a role in the formation of such concepts. Furthermore, despite the sharp distinction Kant makes between intuitions and concepts, there are a number of passages throughout the *Critique* that suggest that the pure concepts of the understanding are indefinable and meaningless apart from their reference to the sensible data of intuition (e.g., A240–41/B300, A242, A244–45, A248/B305). Thus the relation between concepts and intuitions remains basically ambiguous, and it is by virtue of this ambiguity that schemata fulfill their mediating function.

The schema exhibits an open texture. The architect's drawing, for example, is not exclusively sensible and individual or intellectual and general. It is in fact all of these, for it contains clues that enable a qualified reader to take it either way. Thus the schema appears as an individual that also discloses the general conceptual framework in which it takes on its meaning. How we come to read the schema, influenced by our interests and by our familiarity with the conventions according to which it was formed, decides under which of its guises it will appear. Thus it is tempting to conclude that the sharp distinction that Kant makes between concepts and intuitions is not fundamental—that the raw individuality of the intuited object and the generality of the concept are abstractions from their prior unity in the schema. For if the schema really does its job, the original distinction between concept and intuition appears to collapse into a more fundamental unity from which both are derived.

Paradigms

Observations and experience must restrict the range of admissible scientific belief if there is to be any science. But according to Thomas Kuhn these two factors alone are not sufficient to determine the body of such belief: "An apparently arbitrary element, compounded of personal and historical accident, is always a formative ingredient of the beliefs espoused by a given scientific community at a given time."[5] Normal scientific achievements that a particular scientific community acknowledges as supplying the foundations for its further practice, such as Aristotle's *Physica*, Ptolemy's *Almagest*, Newton's *Principia* and *Optiks*, Franklin's *Electricity*, and Lavoisier's *Chemistry*, served such a function. "They were also to do so," Kuhn observes, "because they shared two essential characteristics. Their achievement was sufficiently unprecedented to attract an enduring group of adherents away from competing modes of scientific activity. Simultaneously, it was sufficiently open-ended to leave all sorts of problems for the redefined group of practitioners to resolve" (Kuhn, 10). Such achievements Kuhn calls paradigms.

Paradigms are necessary because in their absence all the facts that might pertain to the development of a given science are likely to appear equally relevant. The paradigm also provides the motive for refusing to limit investigation to data that are all readily available. There are, Kuhn suggests, three principal foci for factual scientific investigations. Although they are not always distinguishable from one another, each is conditioned by its underlying paradigm. The first is the class of facts that the paradigm allows to stand out as revealing the nature of things. Next are facts that are of little interest in themselves but that become significant through their comparison with predictions from the paradigmatic theory: special telescopes confirm Copernicus's prediction of annual parallax; Atwood's machine demonstrates Newton's second law; and Foucault's apparatus shows that the speed of light is greater in air than in water. Finally, there is the empirical work undertaken to articulate the paradigm theory: experiments aimed at the determination of physical constants such as the universal gravitational constant; and the development of quantitative laws such as Boyle's law, which relates gas pressure to volume (25–28). Normal science, therefore, can be viewed as a problem-solving activity, and it is the paradigm that sets the problems to be solved (35ff.).

Kuhn argues for the priority of paradigms in the initiation of scientific inquiry by pointing out that scientists never learn concepts, laws, and theories in the abstract. "Instead, these intellectual tools are from the start encountered in a historically and pedagogically *prior unit* that *displays* them with and through their applications . . . to some concrete range of natural phenomena" (46, my emphasis). And when they discover the meaning of such abstract terms as *force* or *mass*, they do so less from the incomplete definitions in their texts than from applying these concepts to problems and their solutions. Thus scientific inquiry can and does proceed without formalized rules so long as the scientific community accepts the problem solutions or paradigms already achieved.

Kuhn maintains that the usual developmental pattern of a mature science can be read in the successive transformation of paradigms that he calls scientific revolutions:

> Discovery commences with the awareness of anomaly, i.e., with the recognition that nature has somehow violated the paradigm-induced expectations that govern normal science. It then continues with a more or less extended exploration of the area of anomaly. And it closes only when the paradigm theory has been adjusted so that the anomalous has become the expected. . . . Until he has learned to see nature in a different way—the new fact is not quite a scientific fact at all (52–53).

Scientists, however, do not renounce a paradigm until another candidate can take its place, for that would constitute a rejection of science. Indeed, the rules and theory that can be abstracted from an entrenched paradigm become increasingly important whenever that paradigm is called into question, for they provide the normal scientist with an articulated conceptual framework that sustains his practice. Thus the assimilation of Galilean and Newtonian mechanics gave rise to a series of confrontations with Aristotelians, Cartesians, and Leibnizians, and the transition from Newtonian to quantum mechanics provoked debates, some of which continue today (48).

The replacement of one paradigm by another must be understood as a change in world view. The world is determined jointly by the environment and by the normal-scientific tradition in which the scientific community has been trained. Hence when that tradition changes through revolution, "the scientist's perception of his environment must be re-educated—in some familiar situations he must learn to see a new gestalt. After he has done so the world of his research will seem, here and there, incommensurable with the one he had inhabited before" (112). The fact that the worlds established by conflicting paradigms are not wholly commensurable with one another leads Kuhn to a discussion of the truth of scientific paradigms and the manner in which a conversion to a new paradigm may be effected.

A survey of the experimental literature on perception confirms Kant's view that something like a schema or paradigm is prerequisite to perception itself; that what we see depends upon what we look at and upon what our previous visual and conceptual experience has taught us to expect. According to Kuhn, the history of astronomy provides many examples of paradigm-induced changes in scientific observation. Western astronomers, for example, first saw change in the previously immutable heavens during the half-century after Copernicus's new paradigm was first proposed, but the Chinese, whose cosmological beliefs did not rule out celestial change, had recorded the appearance of many new stars in the heavens at a much earlier date (116). The contrast between Galilean and Aristotelian physics provides a second example of perceptual shift in scientific observation:

> Since remote antiquity most people have seen one or another heavy body swinging back and forth on a string or a chain until it finally comes to rest. To the Aristotelians, who believed that a

heavy body is moved by its own nature from a higher position to a state of natural rest at a lower one, the swinging body was simply falling with difficulty. . . . Galileo, on the other hand, looking at the swinging body, saw a pendulum, a body that almost succeeded in repeating the same motion over and over again ad infinitum (118–119).

Are these examples really transformations of scientific vision or merely different interpretations of reality? The view that they are interpretations, Kuhn points out, suffers from a fatal flaw. Such a view is based upon a particular paradigm which maintains that there is a neutral reality behind sensible experience to which we can compare our various interpretations in order to test them for truth and adequacy. But this does not appear to be the case. Scientific revolutions are not merely a reinterpretation of data; rather the data themselves are different—the pendulum is a swinging stone, not a falling one, and oxygen is not dephlogisted air. Interpretation, Kuhn concludes, always presupposes a paradigm that it articulates but does not correct (122). Thus the testing of paradigms and theories always proceeds from within a particular paradigm-based tradition. Hence no testing procedures have access to all possible experiences or theories. The victory of a new paradigm over an old one, therefore, is a genuine revolution in scientific seeing and conceiving.

For the most part, however, these revolutions go unnoticed at the time of their occurrence since the textbooks and practice of normal science see their discipline as having developed cumulatively and continuously toward its present state. Textbooks, in fact, tend to rewrite history in just this way:

Newton wrote that Galileo had discovered that the constant force of gravity produces a motion proportional to the square of the time. In fact, Galileo's kinematic theorem does take that form when embedded in the matrix of Newton's own dynamical concepts. But Galileo said nothing of the sort. His discussion of falling bodies rarely alludes to forces, much less to a uniform gravitational force that causes bodies to fall. By crediting to Galileo the answer to a question that Galileo's paradigms did not permit to be asked, Newton's account hides the effect of a small but revolutionary reformulation in the questions that scientists asked about motion as well as in the answers they felt able to accept (139–40).

The result of such misconstructions is to render revolutions invisible. Their invisibility also makes itself felt in the resolution of revolutions. Practicing in different worlds, two groups of scientists see different things when they look from the same point in the same direction. How, then, are they brought to make the conversion from one paradigm to the other? Part of the answer, Kuhn observes, is that often they are not. As Planck remarked in his *Scientific Autobiography*, "a new scientific truth does not triumph by convincing its opponents and making them see the light, but rather because its opponents eventually die, and a new generation grows up that is familiar with it."[6] Where conversion is induced, a number of factors may be involved. The most important is the claim that the new paradigm enables its proponents to solve the problems that led the old paradigm to a crisis. This sort of claim is particularly convincing where the new paradigm exhibits greater quantitative precision (153–54). Finally, certain aesthetic considerations may also contribute to conversion—the new theory is said to be "neater," "more suitable," or "simpler" than its predecessor (155).

Prime Objects

Thought takes shape in the materials that provide it with a concrete expression. One often fails to notice this because we express thoughts in words and are accustomed to think of words as images of ideas. When thought is conceived exclusively in terms of one kind of material, the verbal sign, it is only natural to suppose that thinking plays a minor role in the procedures of the plastic artist. But verbal signs are not the only materials available to thinking. The mathematician and the logician employ abstract signs and the composer thinks in terms of signs that are neither verbal nor wholly abstract, for they refer to the sounds out of which his composition is to be constructed. The composer thinks musically, and while we might undertake to provide examples of such thought, we could not hope to frame an adequate verbal description of its nature without surrendering the very thing we want to describe.

Similarly, a distinguishing characteristic of artists' thought is that they think plastically, in the properties of their physical materials and their relations. For even where artists set out to give expression to an idea that has been formulated verbally, they must rethink that idea in terms of their materials if the transformation of idea into art work is to succeed. In plastic thinking, then, the properties of the wood or stone as materials for sculpture, the hue, value, and intensity of color, and the density, texture, and degree of opacity of pigment replace verbal signs. A verbal account of plastic thinking would also be incomplete. But I need not leave the matter here, for examples show how thinking plastically gives shape to these modes of thought.

Plastic thought is often taken to be characteristic of the so-called primitive artist for whom verbal expression and conceptual thinking do not interfere with what is sometimes referred to as the *immediacy of plastic expression.* But the thinking of such artists is not necessarily nonconceptual. Thus Ralph Linton observes:

> All the primitive artists of my acquaintance have regarded the European system of letting the design grow under the hand as nothing short of ridiculous. Before beginning to work they clearly picture to themselves not only how the object will look from every possible direction but also how it will look in the particular place or under the particular circumstances in which it will be used . . . Moreover, in making his design, the artist keeps constantly in mind the qualities of the material in which his work is to be executed. If it is to be in wood, he thinks in wood, with no intervention of pencil and paper.[7]

Linton's remarks make it clear that conceptual thought and thinking plastically do not exclude one another. The practice of letting the design grow under the hand, however, is certainly not characteristic of European Art in general. Its widespread acceptance as an artistic practice, in fact, is relatively recent. Nor do the intervention of pencil and paper and the gradual development of the form through the activity of the artist's hand conflict with the primitive artist's practice of thinking in his materials, as Linton implies. For that artist to sketch in advance in another medium the forms that he is going to employ is one way of becoming aware of the plastic vocabulary of art. And to permit the design to grow under the activity of the hand is to acknowledge that meaning, form, and medium participate in one another.

Thinking plastically, however, is not confined to artistic

praxis; it is present in the thought of the most reflective and conceptual of artists as well. That Delacroix was acutely aware of his methods of working as well as a master of words is confirmed in his *Journal.* Yet the following anecdote clearly demonstrates the dominance of the plastic over the verbal sign in his thought:

> Delacroix was in difficulties with the golden cloaks in "Marino Faliero" which still looked heavy after exhausting all his yellows. He decided to consult Rubens and called a cab to take him to the Louvre. A burst of sunshine turned the shadows on the gravel pure violet, and at once the canary yellow of the cab looked brighter and the blacks more mauve by contrast. Here was the key to his problem, the cab was dismissed and he returned to the studio.[8]

Delacroix's discovery of the relation of complementaries suggests another reason why the artist's thought is often identified with intuition—the form and meaning of his thought is sometimes discovered in the process of working or thinking in his materials.

My description of the artist's thought has not yet fully grasped what is peculiar to his thinking, for the artisan also thinks in terms of the materials in which she is working. But the artisan's materials are rarely permitted to exhibit their qualities for their own sake, since the intrinsic qualities of a utensil are subordinated to the function it has been produced to serve. The context in which artists work poses fewer restrictions, for despite the various social functions their work may fulfill, they also aim at the creation of a unique individual. In the work of the artisan, then, function determines in advance the form his or her work will take. In contrast, because it is a unique individual, the full conceptual framework of a work of art first comes into being with the creation of the work itself.[9]

George Kubler has suggested that structural linguistics can provide a model of artistic style that will enable us to integrate the uniqueness and individuality of a work of art with its social functions and its origin in history. Linguistics teaches that the structural elements of a language undergo fairly regular evolutions in time that are unrelated to meaning. There are, for example, certain phonetic shifts in the history of cognate languages that can be explained only by the hypothesis of regular change. "Thus phoneme *a* in an early stage of a language becomes phoneme *b* at a later stage, independently of meaning, and only under the rules governing the phonetic structure of the language. The regularity of these changes is such that the phonemic changes can even be used to measure durations between recorded but undated examples of speech."[10] Kubler holds that similar regularities can be observed to govern the formal infrastructure of every art, provided that we consider groups of artworks as comprising specific formal sequences. The key to any particular sequence lies in the fact that individual works of art can be regarded both as historical events and as the solutions to some problem. Just as every answer indicates its question, so every solution points to its problem. The phenomenon constituted by the problem and its solution is the "form-class." Historically, only those solutions that are related to one another by tradition and influence are linked together as a sequence. These linked solutions occupy time in diverse ways and are the subject of Kubler's study.

The boundaries of formal sequences are relative, since every major work of art forces upon us a reassessment of all previous work. But for the purposes of his inquiry Kubler takes the boundaries of a sequence as marked out by linked solutions that describe early and late stages of the attempt to solve a particular problem. He also distinguishes between open and closed sequences:

> When problems cease to command active attention as deserving of new solutions, the sequence of solutions is stable during the period of inaction. But any past problem is capable of reactivation under new conditions. Aboriginal Australian bark-painting is an open sequence in the twentieth century, because its possibilities are still being expanded by living artists, but Greek vase-painting is an arrested sequence . . . because the modern painter needed to renew his art at "primitive" sources rather than among the images of the Hellenic world. The transparent animals and humans of Australian painting, and the rhythmic figures of African tribal sculpture correspond more closely to contemporary theories of reality than to the opaque and unequivocal body forms of Greek art (35).

Thus Kubler's method of classification does justice to the influence of social-historical factors while maintaining that artistic style also exhibits a purely formal development that is to some extent independent of the course of other social-historical processes.

No formal series is ever really closed out by the exhaustion of all its possibilities in a connected series of solutions. Nevertheless, we can treat most classes as closed series. Whether we do so depends to some extent on whether we are inside or outside the events in question. From within, most classes look open, while from without they are likely to appear closed. Furthermore, taking a sequence as closed has a definite advantage in studying its formal structure. For any element of a formal sequence has its own systematic age, since we can, for any formal sequence, distinguish its beginnings, the middle period of its development, and its close. Finally, the analogy between the purely formal developments of a language and of an artistic style provides a model for interpreting the interaction between art and history. According to Kubler, the fundamental distinction between historical change and linguistic change is that in history the interferences that prevent the repetition of any pattern are, for the most part, beyond human control. In language, however, interference must be regulated or communication will fail. Thus the rate of linguistic change is regular because communication fails if language varies erratically. Linguistic structures, then, admit only these interferences that will not compromise communication.

> The history of things, in turn, admits more interferences than language, but fewer than institutional history, because things which serve functions and convey messages cannot be diverted from these finalities without loss of identity. . . . Within the history of things we find this history of art. More than tools, works of art resemble a system of symbolic communication which must be free from excessive "noise" in the many copies on which communication depends, in order to ensure some fidelity (61).

If Kubler is correct, it is their function as bearers of meaning which guarantees to works of art a certain formal independence from the caprice of history.

History, whether of institutions or of artifacts, is not something that merely happens to people, determining in advance the patterns of their activities. The presence of history requires not only consciousness but self-consciousness; it requires a being who lives through the present and reflects on what he has lived through. Only in this way are traditions established and passed on from one generation to the next. Hence to posit history as a force that exists independently of people and that directs their activities is to step into an inevitably vicious circle. Within the history of art the presence of great eccentrics like Bosch, Redon, Ryder, Fuseli, and Blake, whose innovations neither founded a lasting artistic tradition nor expressed the world of a particular historical people, prevents us from falling victim to this circularity. As Thomas Hess observes, the eccentric master "is, above all, the artist hostile to categories, outside the 'historical necessities' of tradition. Self-justified, he challenges all assumptions about what is possible and exposes our timidities concerning the infinite capacities of man."[11]

Kubler recognizes the fundamental openness of the concept of art with respect to the formal sequences that are his concern. This is one reason why he holds that no formal sequence is ever really closed, that a renewal of the problem or problems from which it springs is always possible. Furthermore, within any formal sequence in the history of things Kubler distinguishes prime objects from their replications:

> Prime objects and replications denote principal inventions and the entire system of replicas, reproductions, copies, reductions, transfers, and derivations, floating in the wake of an important work of art. The replica-mass resembles certain habits of popular speech, as when a phrase spoken upon the stage or in a film, and repeated in millions of utterances, becomes part of the language of a generation and finally a dated cliche. . . . Prime objects resemble the prime numbers of mathematics because no conclusive rule is known to govern the appearance of either, although such a rule may someday be found. The two phenomena now escape regulation. Prime numbers have no divisors other than themselves and unity; prime objects likewise resist decomposition in being original entities. Their character as primes is not explained by their antecedents, and their order in history is enigmatic (39).

To designate something as a prime points to its origin. The prime is first or original and replicas follow as its imitations, modifications, or articulations. We must, however, guard against identifying the original and the radically novel. The Parthenon, for example, is a fairly traditional temple. It is a prime, not because of the radical novelty of its general type, but because it exhibits many refinements that are lacking in other temples of its series. Prime objects are distinguished by the presence of artistic style, which transcends both time and place. Yet it cannot be the presence of style alone that marks an object as a prime, for style by itself is general while such objects are unique individuals. This is borne out by the fact that no work of art is ever adequate to the style predicated of it. As Kubler puts it:

> Strictly considered, a form-class exists only as an idea. It is incompletely manifested by prime objects, or things of great generating power, in the category of the Parthenon, or of the portal statues at Rheims, or of the frescoes by Raphael in the Vatican. Their physical presence is always dimmed by the accidents of time, but their prime status is unquestionable. It is guaranteed by direct comparisons with other things of lesser quality, and by a variety of testimonials from artists in many generations. Yet the Parthenon is built upon an archaic formula surviving into Periclean time. The portal statues of Rheims embrace the work of several generations, and all, including the frescoes by Raphael, have undergone damaging wear and diminution (41).

We are made aware of the individuality of a prime object by the impact that the work makes upon us when we read it within the context proper to it. It appears in what Kubler calls the phenomenon of "climactic entrance." Prime objects like the Parthenon, the frescoes of the Arena Chapel, and Cézanne's *Bathers* mark out against the broad background of history their striking originality. For although they point unmistakably to the social-historical context in which they originated, they also strike us as having come into being for the first time.

Despite their ties to what has preceded them, both paradigms and prime objects exhibit the phenomenon of entrance—they appear on the scene as genuine originals, as having come into being for the first time. Each forces us to reassess previous work, and each establishes a context of meaning, a scientific or artistic tradition, within which the subsequent work of the discipline is carried on. This quality of entrance, however, is not absolute. As Kuhn observes, "to answer the question 'normal or revolutionary?' one must first ask, 'for whom?' Sometimes the answer is easy: Copernican astronomy was a revolution for everyone; oxygen was a revolution for chemists but not for, say, mathematical astronomers unless, like Laplace, they were interested in chemical and thermal subjects too."[12] Similarly Giotto's painting initiated a formal series that was articulated throughout the Italian Renaissance, while the remarkable qualities of Cézanne's *Bathers* were apparent to only a few of his contemporaries. Hence the originality and fecundity of the paradigm and the prime object are relative to a particular social group that is in a position to recognize them for what they are.

Both the paradigm and the prime object present a general conceptual framework in and through the structure of a concrete individual. They can, therefore, be read in a number of ways and serve as exemplars for further articulation and specification within the conditions laid down by the conventions and traditions of which each is the bearer. Paradigms and prime objects also resemble one another in that the theories and styles that can be abstracted from them are never adequate to the individual exemplars from which they are derived. Finally, the primary motivation of the scientist and the artist is to bring a task to completion. Hence the activities of both resemble a kind of problem-solving in which a search for and articulation of meaning goes on in relative independence from the cares of daily life. In both cases the rules that govern these activities are not usually learned as abstract theories but in concrete application to the solution of particular problems. Their theoretical formulation becomes important only in moments of crisis, where art or science is in the process of transformation. Their responses to crisis are also similar. The tendency of normal science to place increasing emphasis upon rules finds its artistic parallel in the phenomenon of manner— an affected emulation of or adherence to a particular style for its own sake rather than for what it enables the artist to bring forth.

Kuhn uses the term *paradigm* in a number of ways.[13] In his "Postscript" he distinguishes two different senses of *paradigm:* "On the one hand, it stands for the entire constellation of beliefs, values, techniques, and so on shared by members of a given community. On the other, it denotes one sort of element in that constellation, the concrete puzzle-solutions that, employed as models or examples, can replace explicit rules as a basis for the solution of the remaining puzzles of normal science" (175). Kuhn himself remarks that the second sense is the deeper of the two. The structure of Kant's schema unites these two senses. As presentations of the general in and through the individual, paradigms and prime objects share the open-texture of schemata. It is this openness that makes possible the activity both of normal science as the ongoing interpretation and articulation of its underlying paradigm, and of replication that articulates and elaborates the prime objects in whose wake it occurs. The role played by schemata in both science and art also supports the contentions that (1) schemata provide the armature around which experience is built and (2) both raw individuality and the generality of theory and style are abstractions from them.[14] These schemata are not a priori in Kant's sense of the term. However, like the Kantian schemata, works of art and paradigms provide certain conditions of our experience since they constitute the situational a priori that structures our world. But they must do so in different ways or else one would be unable to distinguish between them.

Put crudely, the most obvious difference is that science unfolds as a continuous and progressive development of our knowledge about physical reality, while art changes styles but does not progress and is unfettered by any ties to the real. The question of why there is progress in science and not in art is, Kuhn suggests, at least in part a semantic question, for the term *science* is generally reserved for fields of inquiry that do progress (160). Furthermore, as a problem-solving activity and the articulation of its underlying paradigm, normal science is inherently progressive. Its progress is, however, somewhat in the eye of the beholder. "Scientific progress is not different in kind from progress in other fields, but the absence at most times of competing schools . . . makes the progress of a normal-scientific community far easier to see" (163). But why should continuity and progress also be ascribed to the succession of scientific revolutions that result from the overthrow of an old paradigm by a new one? First, Kuhn observes, revolutions close with the victory of one side over the other and the victor inevitably looks upon his victory as progress. Furthermore, "novelty for its own sake is not a desideratum in the sciences as it is in so many other creative fields. As a result, though new paradigms seldom or never possess all the capabilities of their predecessors, they usually preserve a great deal of the most concrete parts of the past achievement and they always permit additional concrete problem-solutions besides" (169). Given Kuhn's contention that there is no paradigmatic-neutral reality "out there" against which the adequacy of competing paradigms can be measured, it is clear that any progress attributed to scientific revolutions cannot be viewed as having a specific telos—e.g., the truth about physical reality per se. Hence his view of scientific development is evolutionary rather than teleological. The development of science is "a process of evolution *from* primitive beginnings—a process whose successive stages are characterized by an increasingly detailed and refined understanding of nature. But it is not a progress *toward* anything" (170–71). In the case of art, however, even this sense of progress seems to be lacking. We can, of course, speak of progress if we restrict ourselves to a particular artistic tradition. The history of the representation of the human figure from Giotto to Raphael, for example, exhibits a kind of progress similar to that found in normal science. But even in these restricted contexts progress is not inevitable in art as it is in normal science, for initial efforts may be just as effective as those which come at the end of a formal sequence. In its major schematic changes, art does not seem to progress. The images of Rembrandt do not render those of Raphael obsolete, and neither can be seen as a progressive improvement over the images of Lascaux or Altamira. This distinction between science and art can be articulated further if we consider the attitudes of these two enterprises toward novelty, diversity, their respective histories, and questions concerning reality and truth.

Novelty for its own sake, Kuhn has written, has no place in scientific investigation. Elsewhere he remarks that there is no scientific avant garde and that the existence of one would in fact threaten science.[15] Novelty in art, however, cannot be equated with the presence of an avant garde, for this is a relatively recent phenomenon that appears to be on its way out. James Ackerman has argued that the psychology of the avant garde artist was founded on public rejection:

> The fate of the significant innovation in art from the Romantic period to the Second World War followed the . . . pattern [of] [i]mediate massive rejection by an enraged middle-class and middle-brow audience, acceptance by a handful of fellow artists and a few of the intelligentsia and, long after, general, often posthumous, acceptance and apotheosis in the mass media . . . Rejection produced freedom along with suffering, and the artist of the avant garde in one sense depended on it in articulating toward his work.[16]

Public acceptance of the avant garde, however, made it redundant. Says Ackerman, "The avant garde is a phenomenon of the past, because the entire army, and a good part of the civilian population, has moved up to join it" (379).

A more fruitful comparison of the attitudes of science and art toward novelty might be made of their respective attitudes toward anomalies. According to Ackerman, Kuhn's thesis that a scientific revolution is stimulated by the discovery of an anomaly in normal science is not applicable to art "because an artist cannot encounter any evidence that upsets the prevailing paradigm. Because no mode of artistic representation can be shown to be right or wrong, there is no parallel to Copernicus' improvement of the Ptolemaic representation of the planetary system" (373). Ackerman, however, has misread Kuhn. Copernican astronomy is not an improvement over Ptolemaic astronomy in the sense that it is a more adequate representation of an independently existing planetary system to which each can be compared. The Copernican cosmology is a different cosmology from the Ptolemaic, one in which the earth becomes a planet and the moon its satellite. These two paradigms cannot, therefore, be measured against some independent standard of truth. Each can be evaluated only within itself and, insofar as they have certain elements in common, each in relation to the other, in terms of what they allow the astronomer to explain. Furthermore, if there were no anomalies in art, there would be no novelty, for novelty is always perceived against a background of the familiar and expected. The terms *gothic, baroque,* and *mannerist*, for example, were originally terms of derision, coined by individuals creating and viewing under different paradigms and unable, therefore, to read those works of art that have been grouped under these different rubrics. To such audiences, these works must have appeared anomalous indeed. Nor is the history of art devoid of encounters that lead artists to change the direction of their work. The phenomenon of climactic entrance testifies to such changes of direction. Despite these parallels, however, science and art still appear to differ in their attitudes toward novelty, but this difference is one of emphasis rather than one of kind. Although anomalies appear in both disciplines, the collective enterprise of art tolerates more diversity than does that of science.

This difference in tolerance toward diversity also manifests itself in the relation of science and art toward their respective histories. Science, Kuhn says, destroys its past. It rewrites its history in order to recast its development as a continual progression toward the present interests of normal science. In contrast, the history of art conserves and brings together divergent and often conflicting traditions. Furthermore, although certain formal sequences may fall into obscurity, no formal sequence is ever wholly closed. Hence there is always the possibility of a revival of past artistic traditions that have fallen into disfavor. The capacity of art to tolerate diversity also explains the retrieval in art of great exemplars that had previously been lost. Thoré-Bürger's discovery of Vermeer, the great Delft master whose work was nearly forgotten or confused with the work of lesser artists, has no close parallel in the history of science. Even where such a parallel suggests itself, in the case of Mendel, for example, it fails to hold up, for Mendel's brilliant work had no direct effect on the subsequent development of his field. Finally, the history of art also tolerates and respects the great eccentrics of whom I spoke earlier—artists whose work stands alone, neither founding nor continuing an ongoing formal tradition.

These last observations suggest one further distinction between the attitudes of science and art toward novelty—their stance toward individual exemplars. The doctrine of *l'art pour l'art* is of comparatively recent vintage, and despite its influence on much of the discussion of art in the twentieth century, we have been forced to recognize that throughout the greater part of history, works of art originated out of specific needs and to fulfill definite functions. Hence without some knowledge of the social-historical context in which they originated, many works of art are closed to us. And yet there remains an extraordinary range of art works that are at least partially accessible on the basis of their formal properties alone. Even more striking is the attitude people often take toward these exemplars—while they may stand in contemplative awe before Newton's *Principia* or the double-helix, they do not continue to contemplate them for their own sake, as is the case for the Crucifixion at Colmar.

The tolerance of diversity and the attitude of aesthetic contemplation both point to what appears to be the most significant difference between science and art—their attitudes toward truth and reality. For the scientist, and for the general public as well, scientific inquiry is usually understood as a progressive investigation into the nature of physical reality. Hence the adherents of each successive paradigm claim to be closer to the truth, to have a more adequate grasp of the reality they seek to comprehend, than do their predecessors. In contrast one often thinks of art as not being concerned with reality at all. Freed from the constraints of reality, art is able to explore the realm of the imagination. Or if it is concerned with truth and reality, its concern is with the more esoteric aspects of the real, with the inner life of the emotions or some other ineffable aspect of reality that is closed off to the more prosaic probings of science.

But this view of things does not hold up under even the most casual scrutiny. Kuhn has argued that science does not progress continuously toward its goal of complete physical knowledge. Rather, the progress of science is punctuated by a series of upheavals brought about by the overthrow of a dominant paradigm by a new paradigm. This paradigm does not interpret the world anew. It presents the scientist with a new world, populated, at least in part, by new kinds of things. In this respect the appearance of the primary exemplars of science is not unlike the appearance of prime objects in art. Art, on the other hand, exhibits no disdain for the real. The long tradition of representation in art, the inquiries of artists like Leonardo into the structure of the visible world, Rembrandt's and Turner's obsessions with light, and Mondrian's attempt to present the metaphysical reality underlying experience all testify to the contrary. Finally, because artists create out of their situation in the world, a work of art is immersed in time and illustrates history, humanity, and the world itself. But art also transcends this immersion, for it also creates history and the world. The space of Brunelleschi's S. Spirito, for example, was, without doubt, affected by the Florentine painters' discovery of the laws of perspective. And the portraits of van Dyke transformed an England still crude and violent by providing it with the image of the gentleman. Finally, works of art not only interact with history, they also rank among the principal means by which the historian reconstructs the past. Even today, when radio carbon tests often supplant stylistic analysis as a means of dating the remains of the past, it is not the carbon age of a culture but material objects that give insight into that culture's style of life. For the most part these are replications, but there can be no replicas without an original; and these originals lead back to the origins of human culture itself.

According to Kant, schemata provide the armature of experience. Schemata are not merely given to us, they are created by a productive act of the imagination working with raw data and conceptual constructs. If the analogy between schemata, paradigms, and prime objects holds up, one can conclude that it is through schemata that what one calls a "world" is first opened up. Hence there can be no question of determining the adequacy of various schemata by comparing them to some neutral reality of which they are the representations or interpretations. For representation and interpretation already presuppose schemata—that is, they presuppose a world and its objects. Thus the time-honored criterion of truth, the correspondence between subjective representations and the objects that they purport to represent, holds only within the world opened up by a particular schema. Prior to the opening-up of a world, no distinction between the real and the imaginary is made. Hence when we deal with schemata themselves the traditional epistemological model is, in Kuhn's words, "somehow askew" (121). The schemata governing one discipline *may* indeed be incomparable to those governing another. This incomparability would also exist within a discipline in which the worlds opened up by the schemata governing its history are wholly incommensurable with one another. Only where practitioners working under different schemata have something in common can there be a genuine dialogue and the possibility of a reasoned choice among competing paradigms. In science, with its commitment to an ideal of continual progress in its knowledge of physical reality, such a dialogue is indispensable. In art, while dialogues do take place across traditions and cross-traditional influences make themselves felt, there seems to be less need for communication between the participants in different formal sequences. In this sense science admits less interference in its activities than art, and this is why it is less tolerant of novelty and diversity. The history of art is the history of a relatively discontinuous opening up of diverse worlds. Science is the continuous articulation of what it takes to be *the* world. Its history is a history of rendering continuous what is sometimes discontinuous by rewriting its past so as to bring it into conformity with its present. Once again, however, this distinction between science and art is one of degree rather than kind, for both science and art are founded on the creative act of the imagination that originates schemata. In science the novelty of the creative act inherent in schematic thinking remains in the background for the sake of progress in normal science, which articulates and elaborates its paradigm. In art, with its emphasis upon the relative uniqueness and self-contained nature of its exemplars, the freedom of the imagination is stressed. Both remain, however, two aspects of a single process that is the origin, articulation, and comprehension of human experience.

NOTES

1. E.g., *Critique of Pure Reason*, B151–52. References to the first *Critique* will follow the standard practice of referring to the two editions as the *A* and *B* versions. Also see Martin Heidegger, *Kant und das Problem der Metaphysik* (1929; reprint, Frankfurt a.M.: Minerva, 1951), 177–84, for a provocative but controversial discussion of many of these points. Subsequent references to the *Critique* are incorporated parenthetically in the text.

2. There is no clear discussion of this distinction by Kant. He does, however, appeal to it in several places, e.g., A100, A118, A123, B152.

3. This is a modified version of Kant's discussion in A99–108.

4. I am not following Kant verbatim in this discussion. But Kant's own discussion is far from clear on a number of points, among them the relation between transcendental schemata and images. In any case, for our purposes his doctrine should be taken as primarily heuristic.

5. Thomas Kuhn, *The Structure of Scientific Revolutions*, rev. ed. (Chicago: University of Chicago Press, 1970), 4. Subsequent references to this work are incorporated parenthetically in the text.

6. Max Planck, *Scientific Autobiography and Other Papers*, trans. Frank Gaynor (New York: Philosophical Library, 1949), 33–34. Quoted in Kuhn, *Structure*, 151.

7. "Primitive Art," in Eliot Elisofon, *The Sculpture of Africa* (New York: Frederick A. Praeger, 1958), 15.

8. Related in the "Introduction" to *The Journal of Eugene Delacroix*, ed. Hubert Wellington and trans. Lucy Norton (New York: Phaidon, 1951), xx.

9. For a fuller discussion of this point, see my "Form and Meaning in the Visual Arts," *The British Journal of Aesthetics* 4 (1966): 259–71.

10. George Kubler, *The Shape of Time* (New Haven, Conn.: Yale University Press, 1962), viii. Because of the compactness of Kubler's argument, I will cite references only for direct quotations and not for my paraphrases. Subsequent references are incorporated parenthetically in the text.

11. Thomas Hess, "Eccentric Propositions," *Art News Annual* (special issue on "The Grand Eccentrics") 32 (1966): 9.

12. Thomas Kuhn, "Reflections on My Critics," *Criticism and the Growth of Knowledge*, ed. I. Lakatos and A. Musgrave (Cambridge: At the University Press, 1970), 252.

13. See, for example, Margaret Masterman, "The Nature of a Paradigm," in ibid., 59–89.

14. Unfortunately, limitations of space prevent any discussion of how schemata function in the interpretation and appreciation of scientific achievements and works of

art. That they do so is clear from Kuhn's discussion of the role played by paradigms in scientific education and from E. H. Gombrich's argument in *Art and Illusion* (Princeton, N.J.: Princeton University Press, 1960), which stresses the role of schemata in the creation and appreciation of art.

15. Thomas Kuhn, "Comment [on the Relations of Science and Art]," *Comparative Studies in Society and History* 11 (1969): 407.

16. James Ackerman, "The Demise of the Avant Garde," *Comparative Studies in Society and History* 11 (1969): 377–78. Subsequent references are incorporated parenthetically in the text.

Creativity and Contingency in the Light of Modern Science

MILIČ ČAPEK

Boston University

There is hardly any other term that is used more widely than *creation* or *creativity*. It is used indiscriminately not only by laymen, but also by professional philosophers of various persuasions, even by those whose views are altogether incompatible and who use it in entirely different senses. This indicates clearly that the term is highly ambiguous and that its ambiguity allows it to be used in very different contexts. This is why it is so important to define it; for only a definition, no matter how tentative it may be and even when it is negative, will assure the term's meaningful use in any philosophical discourse.

There are three main contexts in which the term *creation* appears: (a) theological, (b) cosmic, and (c) human. The traditional theological meaning is fairly definite: *creation* means the creation of the world by God in time, *creatio ex nihilo*. It is true that the original meaning was different, that *creation* meant the act by which the shapeless, chaotic material that had existed previously was ordered or fashioned into a definite form; such was the activity of Demiurge in Plato's *Timaeus* as well as the activity of Yahweh according to the modernized version of the first chapter of the Book of Genesis.[1] In truth, the notion of preexisting primeval chaos is common to all cosmological myths. The more sophisticated term *creation out of nothing* appeared considerably later and was gradually accepted by the three main theological systems—Christian, Jewish, and Moslem. Yet there were some dissenters, even among the earliest Christian thinkers; thus Origen, while retaining the notion of creation, rejected that of "creation in time." Even Saint Thomas conceded that while the existence of the First Cause can be proved, the temporal beginning of the world, creation in time, cannot be, and must be accepted as an article of faith.[2] It is obvious that the notion of eternal creation makes the expression *ex nihilo* meaningless since there was no time in which the universe was not in existence, even if its existence was eternally dependent on the sustaining activity of God. The majority of Christian thinkers retained the idea of creation in time while those who preferred *eternal creation* were moving, sometimes unconsciously, to the cosmic rather than theological meaning.

At the dawn of modern philosophy such philosophers as Bruno and Spinoza were still speaking of "divine creation," but this was understood by them in a pantheistic or even naturalistic sense; the divine creation became for them an immanent activity of the indwelling eternal principle, without beginning and without end. The visible universe thus became an eternal expression or an eternal effect of the Eternal Cause. Such a view became the central theme of all monistic philosophies from Bruno and Spinoza to the Neohegelianism of the present century. But what was even more important was that the allegedly creative activity of God-Nature or "Absolute" was regarded as a rigorously determined process. The physical nature, including its apparently most contingent and insignificant details, was viewed as a necessary unfolding of one single principle. This was consonant with the character of modern science, in particular physics; it was hardly accidental that Spinoza was a contemporary of Newton. Contingency was at first hesitatingly, but soon explicitly, relegated into the realm of fantasies that are due to a mere limitation of human knowledge; we call a certain thing "possible" or "contingent" only when our insight into its determining antecedent causes is limited.[3] In objective reality there is no middle ground between "necessity" and "impossibility": whatever is real is necessary, whatever does not happen is impossible.

This deterministic view of cosmic creation inevitably affected the view of what was called "human creation." The activity of humanity in all of its most diverse manifestations was as necessary as the activity of nature in its totality; human beings, being a necessary part of the necessary whole, cannot exhibit anything that would be intrinsically and irreducibly different. It is true that not only metaphysicians and poets but even scientists still continued to speak about human creativity, especially as it manifests itself in the works of poets, musicians, and artists in general; but the term itself was hardly taken literally. It was merely an elliptical and metaphorical way of speaking to call any human creation or action "unforeseeable" or "unpredictable." Even the most astonishing creations of a genius were programmed, so to speak, not only from birth, but from the beginningless eternity. Even Plato, Shakespeare, Newton, and Raphael were potentially present "in the fires of the sun," said John Tyndall in his Liverpool address (1870), to which he added significantly:

> I do not think that any holder of the Evolution hypothesis would say that I overstate or overstrain it in any way. I merely strip it of all vagueness, and bring before you, unclothed and unvarnished, the notions by which it must stand or fall.[4]

Tyndall merely stated in a more concrete form what Laplace said forcibly more than a half century before. It is far less known that the very same idea of assimilating the predictability of human actions to the predictability of the orbits of the celestial bodies was expressed with an equal clarity and vigor by Kant a quarter of a century before Laplace.[5] This shows that universal determinism was upheld not only by materialists and naturalists, but by idealists as well. Friedrich Paulsen, a Neokantian, was only consistent when he claimed that "the omniscient physiologist would explain the author of *Critique of Pure Reason* just as he would explain a clockwork."[6] This may appear disrespectful to Kant, but it was in complete agreement with Kant's own view. Human creation appears to us marvelous and astonishing only because we fail to see its very complex antecedent causes; there are simply too many variables that we are unable to detect and analyze and that nevertheless unambiguously determine that creation in all its specific and apparently contingent details. Taine and Lombroso in the last century and Freud in this century proposed deterministic theories of artistic creation that were different in their concrete forms, but based on the same metaphysical premises. In a completely determined world there is no place for genuine creation; there is a mere necessary unfolding of what preexisted virtually in antecedent conditions.

Yet are there other alternatives? To deny the view stated above would mean that there is a genuine novelty in human behavior and in the behavior of all living beings. But such a denial seems to run contrary to the instincts of a large portion of the scientific community, especially when we draw all consequences from it. To reserve the privilege of creation for man in a Cartesian fashion means to regard humanity as a separate realm within nature, not subject to the laws to which everything else is subjected. To restrict the privilege of creation to the realm of organic life in the way suggested by vitalism is to postulate an intellectually intolerable bifurcation of nature into two completely heterogeneous realms—"creative life" on one side and the mechanism of inorganic nature on the other side. Furthermore, even the vitalists could not deny that there is no difference between organic and inorganic matter except in complexity; in other words, the same elements occur and the same laws of physics and chemistry hold in the organic bodies as in the rest of nature. Thus no authentic creation can occur anywhere since any genuine novelty is excluded as long as we accept an all-embracing rigorous determinism. To affirm a real novelty means to reject determinism at least in its classical form.

Thus the position of anybody upholding the objective, i.e., nonmetaphorical, status of creation or creativity remained hopeless as long as the determinism of classical physics remained unchallenged. Yet, as we know today, the situation is significantly different since 1927. While the true meaning of Heisenberg's principle of indeterminacy is still a matter of controversy, there is no question that the classical determinism of Spinoza or Laplace is no longer a sacred and untouchable dogma. Consequently, the conditions are now present for a new discussion of the problem of determinism and of the related problems of causality, contingency, and freedom. In other words, creativity—which is just another term for novelty—may be a philosophically meaningful term after all.

This is what I am going to argue in the remaining part of this paper. Let me first state the essential points of my thesis and then answer the main objections that I anticipate.

1. Creation is a meaningful term only if reality in general, including the physical reality, is not impervious to a certain degree of contingency or novelty, no matter how small it may be. (See above.)

2. By contingency or novelty I mean that feature of an event that is irreducible—i.e., *not* logically contained in its past antecedents.

3. There is considerable circumstantial evidence that such contingency indeed exists in reality in general, including the physical world.

4. Furthermore, the denial of contingency led nearly always—at least in the philosophically minded and consistent determinists—to the denial of one of the most conspicuous and most pervasive features of our experience, succession.

5. Although there is an element of novelty in every event, there are different degrees of novelty ranging from its minimum at the inorganic level to its maximum at the human level. The term *creation* is usually restricted to the latter, but such restriction is probably unfair to the subhuman forms of life.

6. Finally, *creation* does not necessarily mean creation in a positive or moral sense. There are creations of disorder or "evil" that nevertheless share the trait of contingency or novelty with the creations of order. For this reason creation should not be equated with *freedom* as long as we regard *free* and *good* as synonymous terms. While I myself am tempted to identify contingency and freedom, I can see the correctness of John Dewey's claim that contingency is merely a necessary but not sufficient *condition* of freedom (if the latter is understood in a restricted sense, as mentioned above).

Now the possible objections:

1. I doubt that the first point can be disputed unless we agree that the term *creation* is a mere metaphor with an indefinite or ambiguous connotation; but then it would be pointless to have any discussion about it.

2. Neither do I think the definition of *novelty* can be disputed unless, again, the term is regarded as a mere *façon de parler;* but then such novelty is merely apparent. Professor Brand Blanshard's notion of novelty is of this kind; although in one of his letters he claimed that he does accept it, what status can genuine novelty have in his completely predetermined and virtually static universe? But I shall return to this point again in discussing the objections to Point Four.

3. The most obvious objection is that the meaning of the uncertainty principle is still being disputed; in other words, the opinion is still divided about whether microphysical indeterminacy is objective or whether it is due to the disturbing effect of the act of observation. This would require a rather lengthy digression and repetition of what I have said and written about it several times before.[7] But let me say at least this: So far the

search for the "hidden variables" that would restore physical determinism on the subquantum level has been fruitless. Furthermore, this search, as the cases of both Einstein and de Broglie show, is motivated mainly by philosophical assumptions of which the following two are the most important. The first is that any departure from classical determinism would mean a suicide of reason and the acceptance of a completely irrational and chaotic universe in which "anything can happen." This assumption is based on a too-narrow model of rationality according to which the only type of intelligible universe is that envisioned by Newton, Spinoza, and Laplace; in other words, that the only type of causal connection is of the necessitarian kind. As I shall point out, this is a simplistic view, no matter how historically understandable it is. The second assumption is often made unconsciously or semiconsciously: our instinctive belief in spatiotemporal continuity of all physical magnitudes as was codified in Kant's *Anticipations of Perception.* For only if energy is continuous—that is, divisible *in infinitum*—is it meaningful to speak of a subquantum level on which determinism of microphysical processes could be rediscovered. I am not the only one who regards this possibility as extremely implausible. Such implausibility is increased when we consider this point from an epistemological angle. What else is Kant's view that space and time are *quanta continua* but a mere extrapolation of our limited macroscopic experience? Finally, we must not forget that the tendency to interpret microphysical indeterminacy as an effect of the disturbing intervention of the observer is based on one particular example used by Heisenberg. But the presence of the observer is unessential since all physical interactions (not only that between the phenomenon observed and the instrument of observation) are dominated by the presence of Planck's constant h: from the indivisibility of the atom of action h, the indeterminacy of the microphysical events follows. I believe that the cumulative evidence—physical, epistemological, and historical—though still circumstantial, is against the recovery of classical determinism in microphysics.

4. There is an additional reason against classical determinism that is of a purely logical kind and that I am inclined to regard as decisive. If all consequences are explicitly drawn from it, it is incompatible with the reality of succession. This has been pointed out by a few daring thinkers in the second half of

the last century, hinted at first by Renouvier and Boutroux, then by James, and systematically stressed by Bergson and Whitehead, Hartshorne and Weiss; all these thinkers linked the reality of time with that of contingency. What is even more significant is that all consistent determinists linked their affirmation of causal necessity with an elimination of time or at least with its relegation into the realm of mere appearances; this is hardly an accident of history.[8] It is true that nothing is more familiar to common sense than the idea of necessary connection in time; but this is only because the very familiarity of this notion prevents its analysis in depth. For if future events are logically implied in their causal antecedents, their futurity is not authentic; they preexist logically in the same way as the conclusion preexists in the premises. So the very fact of succession becomes unintelligible. If the popular belief in the compatibility of succession and strict necessity still persists, it is because of the ambiguity of the words "it follows." We say that a conclusion follows necessarily and also that an effect follows from its cause. But while the latter type of sequence is genuinely temporal, the first type—the so-called "logical sequence"—is not a temporal sequence at all; it is more accurately referred to as a tenseless logical dependence. It would be even more accurate to say that the conclusion is logically contained in the premises; in truth, this is what we mean when we say the conclusion is *implied* or *inherent* in the premises. In other words, in logical implication there is neither novelty nor succession; the term *sequence* in logic is a mere metaphor based on the confusion of the psychological process of thought, which is successive, with the logical implication, which is not. On the other side, causal relation is inherently successive since *cause* is always before *effect*; the notion of simultaneity of cause and effect was always rather odd since it presupposed the possibility of instantaneous causal actions—i.e., of infinite velocities. Today, in the light of relativistic physics, it is more than odd; it is impossible.

5. The fifth thesis is really an answer to one popular and very frequent objection, that to admit any kind of novelty is incompatible with causality and destroys the very notion of an orderly and rational universe. I already dealt with this objection briefly before when I said that it is based on a too-narrow view of rationality as well as of causality. Let me now explain my point more fully. The objection above is based on the fol-

lowing false dilemma: Either the universe is orderly in the classical Laplacean fashion or it is completely disorderly and irrational. In other words, either there is the causality of the old *causa aequat effectum* type, according to which the future is completely deducible from the past (and vice versa), or there is no causality at all. This dilemma is avoided if we accept different degrees of causality, an assumption upheld by process philosophers in general and hinted at more recently by Norbert Wiener and Hans Reichenbach,[9] and, in truth, by those physicists who accept the objective character of microphysical indeterminacy. This view can be briefly described in the following way: The future, instead of being strictly implied in all its details by its past antecedents, is determined only in its general character;[10] instead of strict implication, there is only probable implication that can have all possible degrees between two equally unreal limits—one and zero. These limits are both equally unreal since they are both incompatible with temporality and with causation in a dynamic sense. Absolute certainty of all the features of future events would make them implicitly and in a sense even explicitly present while their absolute indeterminacy would completely destroy any causal efficacy of the past. Let me add that absolute indeterminism has rarely been held by any serious or even less serious thinkers. Even Buridan's ass is pushed by its hunger to choose freely between two equally distant and equally fragrant bundles of hay. In truth, one may ask whether the notion of *creatio ex nihilo* is a meaningful concept at all; for whenever it was upheld, some kind of causal efficacy of the past was tacitly assumed. Even the theological creation is not, strictly speaking, out of nothing, *ex nihilo*, since the world comes into being as an effect of the antecedent divine fiat.

A phenomenological analysis of temporal process points to the same conclusion: that the openness of the future and the causal efficacy of the past are two complementary aspects of every temporal process. In this respect the four most penetrating analyses of our introspective awareness of time—James's "stream of thought," Bergson's *durée réelle*, Husserl's *Zeitbewusstsein*, Whitehead's "creative advance"—are conspicuously similar despite some differences in details and terminology. It is true that Husserl remains because of his own method noncommittal about the nature of objective time, but the other three thinkers use the structure of psychological time as a clue to the nature of time in general. They believed (James, it is true, only in his last phase) that "the texture of observed experience, as illustrating the philosophic scheme, is such that all related experience must exhibit the same texture."[11]

The theory of different degrees of causation is far from being elaborated except in rather general terms; even Bergson's and Whitehead's writings are hardly more than general sketches. The essential idea is that the degree of freedom or novelty is correlated with the field of anticipated possibilities; the wider this field, the greater the freedom of choice and the degree of novelty. But the extent of "the field of possibilities" is, so to speak, measured by the span of the psychological ("specious") present or—what is the same—by the span of immediate memory. This is what is usually meant by the metaphorical term *intensity of consciousness.* The objective—i.e., neurophysiological—aspect of this fact is the presence of several motor mechanisms whose simultaneous functionings are incompatible so that they cannot be activated at the same time; hence the necessity of choice. Within the framework of classical science, still largely accepted by contemporary behaviorists, choice itself was only apparent since it was nothing but an incipient neural impulse—predetermined like any other physical event—that triggers one of the ready-made motor mechanisms leading to overt reaction. What is true in this view is the belief that the triggering impulse is very minute; it merely liberates, but does not create, the energy of the corresponding cerebral engrams. This is why organic life, including the human nervous system, presents such a mechanistic aspect. What is questionable in this view in the light of present physics is the predetermined character of the initiating impulse. In this context the prophetic words of C. S. Peirce acquire a new significance:

> On the other hand, by supposing the rigid necessity of causation to yield, I care not how little—be it by a strictly infinitesimal amount—we gain room to insert mind into our scheme and to put it into the place where it is needed, into the position which, as the sole self-intelligible thing, it is entitled to occupy, that of the fountain of existence; and in doing so we resolve the problem of the connection of soul and body.[12]

This is obviously a panpsychistic metaphysics that is not acceptable to everybody; but, in my opinion, it is the only metaphysics I know of that preserves the objective status of creativity and, more specifically, the causal efficacy of consciousness, without relapsing into the Cartesian bifurcation of nature. What is even more important is that it is far more in agreement with the new facts than any other metaphysics. It is rather interesting that the theory, proposed already before Peirce by Boutroux and after Peirce by Bergson, that the organisms are "the multiplicators" of the triggering indetermination that is itself too minute to be detected, was recently revived by physicists such as Neils Bohr, Pascual Jordan, and Walther Elsasser. Within the framework of temporalistic panpsychism, the duality of the mental and the physical is largely overcome, though not completely obliterated. In the light of what I said before about different degrees of novelty correlated with different degrees of temporal span, Whitehead's words—among the last ones he wrote—become intelligible: "The universe is material in proportion to the restriction of memory and anticipation."[13] This, obviously, is not Cartesian dualism, but it is not a neutral monism either. However, a more detailed discussion of it would transcend the limits of this paper.

6. I doubt that any serious objection can be raised against the sixth thesis distinguishing between creation or freedom in general and freedom in an ethical sense. To deny this distinction would mean to deny that a free act can be destructive and that the creation of evil is impossible. The authority of some outstanding process thinkers should not blind us to such a simplifying and unrealistic view. Unfortunately, the emergence of destructive novelties is a tragic fact of human experience, especially the experience of this century.

NOTES

1. The revised version of Genesis 1:1 reads: "In the beginning of God's creating the heaven and the earth . . ." (John Skinner, *A Critical and Exegetical Commentary on Genesis,* The International Critical Commentary, rev. ed. [New York: Charles Scribner's Sons, 1925]); or "When God began to form the universe, the world was void and vacant . . ." (James Moffatt, *A New Translation of the Bible* [New York: Harper, 1950]).

2. *Summa Theologica,* Q. 46, art. 2.

3. Spinoza, *Ethica,* pars 1, prop. 29 and 33.

4. John Tyndall, *Fragments of Science* (New York: A. L. Burt, n.d.), 440.

5. *Critique of Practical Reason and Other Works on the Theory of Ethics,* trans. T. K. Abbot (London: Longman, Green, 1909), 193: "It may therefore be admitted that if it were possible to have so profound an insight (*so tiefe Einsicht*) into a man's mental character as shown by internal as well as external actions, as to know all its motives,

even the smallest, and likewise all the external occasions that can influence them, we could calculate a man's conduct for the future with as great certainty as a lunar or a solar eclipse."

6. Friedrich Paulsen, *Introduction to Philosophy*, trans. Frank Thilly (New York: Holt, 1912), 88.

7. M. Čapek, *The Philosophical Impact of Contemporary Physics* (Princeton, N.J.: Van Nostrand, 1961), chap. 16; idem, *Bergson and Modern Physics*, Boston Studies in the Philosophy of Science, vol. 7 (Boston and Dordrecht: D. Reidel, 1971), pt. 3, chaps. 12–13.

8. The tradition to correlate rigorous determinism with an elimination of time goes back as far as Parmenides and has continued without interruption through the Middle Ages up to the present. Laplace's "omniscient mind," in whose timeless insight the distinction between the past, present, and future disappears, is merely a secularized version of the omniscient and predestinarian God of Augustine, Thomas Aquinas, and Calvin (see notes 3–6 above). On this point the difference between classical and modern physics was lucidly characterized by H. Bondi: "The flow of time has no significance in the logically fixed pattern demanded by deterministic theory, time being a mere coordinate. In a theory with indeterminacy, however, the passage of time transforms statistical expectations into real events" ("Relativity and Indeterminacy," *Nature* 169 [1952]: 660).

9. Norbert Weiner, *I am a Mathematician* (Cambridge, Mass.: M.I.T. Press, 1964), 323; Hans Reichenbach, "Les fondements logiques de la mécanique des quanta," *Annales de l'Institut Henri Poincaré* 13 (1952): 109–58.

10. On the general, unspecified, possible (i.e., nonnecessary) character of future events, see William James, "The Dilemma of Determinism," in *The Will to Believe and Other Essays in Popular Philosophy* (London: Longman, Green, 1897), 145–83; and C. S. Peirce, "Multitude and Number," in *Collected Papers of Charles Sanders Peirce*, ed. Charles Hartshorne and Paul Weiss, 8 vols. (Cambridge, Mass.: Harvard University Press, 1931–58), 4:172: "It is only actuality, the force of existence, which bursts the fluidity of the general and produces a discrete unit." See also Steven M. Cahn, *Fate, Logic and Time* (New Haven, Conn.: Yale University Press, 1967).

11. Alfred N. Whitehead, *Process and Reality* (New York: Macmillan, 1930), 5.

12. Peirce, "The Doctrine of Necessity Examined," in *Collected Papers*, 6:35. Cf. my extensive comment ("Microphysical Indeterminacy and Freedom") in *Bergson and Modern Physics*, 346–67.

13. Alfred N. Whitehead, "Immortality," in *The Philosophy of Alfred North Whitehead*, ed. Paul Arthur Schilpp (Evanston, Ill.: Northwestern University Press, 1941), 695.

Notes on Contributors

JOSEPH AGASSI is professor of philosophy at Boston University, Boston, Massachusetts, and holds joint appointments at Tel-Aviv University in Israel and at York University, Downsview, Ontario, Canada. His wide-ranging publications include *Towards an Historiography of Science* (1963), *Faraday as a Natural Philosopher* (1971), *Science in Flux: Collected Essays* (1975), *Towards a Rational Philosophical Anthropology* (1977), and *Science and Society: Essays in the Sociology of Science* (1981).

STEPHEN BARKER, professor of philosophy at Johns Hopkins University, Baltimore, Maryland, has published *Induction and Hypothesis* (1957), *Philosophy of Mathematics* (1964), and *The Elements of Logic* (3d ed., 1981).

W. H. BOSSART has written numerous essays on phenomenology, aesthetics, and the visual arts. He is professor of philosophy at the University of California at Davis.

MILIČ ČAPEK is professor emeritus of philosophy at Boston University, Boston, Massachusetts. He currently resides in Newark, Delaware. His many books and articles include *The Philosophical Impact of Contemporary Physics* (1961; rev. ed. 1969) and *Bergson and Modern Physics* (1971).

EDMUND DEHNERT is chair of the department of humanities and foreign languages at Truman College, Chicago, Illinois. He holds degrees in music history and theory and in philosophy. He has received numerous National Endowment for the Humanities awards for production work in urban culture and the visual arts. He has coauthored books on the humanities, Polish poster design, and Polish music, and has produced videotapes in humanities education. In addition to his writings on technology, painting, and popular culture, he has composed and performed original compositions for clarinet and piano, trombone, winds, and percussion, and for symphony orchestra.

JAMES WAYNE DYE has published articles on epistemology, Berdyaev, Plato, Hegel, and Kant. He has also coauthored *Religions of the World* (1967; reprint 1976). He is professor of philosophy at Northern Illinois University at DeKalb, Illinois.

MAURICE A. FINOCCHIARO is professor of philosophy at the University of Nevada, Las Vegas. His writings include *History of Science as Explanation* (1973) and *Galileo and the Art of Reasoning: Rhetorical Foundations of Logic and Scientific Method* (1980).

WILLIAM FRAWLEY, professor of linguistics at the University of Delaware, Newark, has published work in discourse and text theory, philosophy of science, and semantics. He is now writing a book entitled *Text and Epistemology*.

BRUCE H. WEBER is professor of chemistry at California State University, Fullerton. He has published numerous articles in biochemical research and recently has turned to writing about the history and philosophy of chemistry.

Index

205